Geek My Ride

Build the Ultimate Tech Rod

Auri Rahimzadeh

WILEY

Wiley Publishing, Inc.

Geek My Ride: Build the Ultimate Tech Rod

Published by
Wiley Publishing, Inc.
10475 Crosspoint Boulevard
Indianapolis, IN 46256
www.wiley.com

Copyright © 2005 by Wiley Publishing, Inc., Indianapolis, Indiana

Published simultaneously in Canada

ISBN-13 978-0-7645-7876-2
ISBN-10 0-7645-7876-6

Manufactured in the United States of America

10 9 8 7 6 5 4 3 2 1

1B/SQ/QU/QV/IN

For general information on our other products and services or to obtain technical support, please contact our Customer Care Department within the U.S. at (800) 762-2974, outside the U.S. at (317) 572-3993 or fax (317) 572-4002.

Wiley also publishes its books in a variety of electronic formats. Some content that appears in print may not be available in electronic books.

Library of Congress Cataloging-in-Publication Data Is Available from Publisher

About the Author

Auri Rahimzadeh has been tinkering with computers ever since he was six years old and loves all technology. Auri collects computers and has been involved with many computer projects, including teaching computers alongside Steve Wozniak, co-founder of Apple Computer. Auri has written hundreds of articles on various computer technologies, has contributed to many standards including HDTV, DVD, and interactive television. Auri has also contributed to computer education for students across the country and has promoted technology awareness through the Indianapolis Computer Society, where he has served as president for three years. Currently, Auri runs his own IT consulting firm, The Auri Group (TAG), and spends his free time programming, chatting in Starbucks, and going to Pacers games.

Credits

Executive Editor
Chris Webb

Development Editor
Gus A. Miklos

Production Editor
Gabrielle Nabi

Copy Editor
Alysia Cooley

Editorial Manager
Mary Beth Wakefield

Vice President & Executive Group Publisher
Richard Swadley

Vice President and Publisher
Joseph B. Wikert

Project Coordinator
Erin Smith

Quality Control Technicians
Dave Faust
Joe Niesen

Proofreading and Indexing
TECHBOOKS Production Services

Contents at a Glance

Contents

Part I: Laying the Groundwork

Part IV: Advanced Projects

Chapter 14: Adding Internet Access 235

Chapter 15: Networking and Sharing an Internet Connection 255

Foreword

Auri Rahimzadeh is one of those people you never forget. Not only is Auri capable with consumer electronics and computer technologies, but he is always excited by and about them. Auri relishes projects with computers and finds solutions that are deemed impossible or are very innovative and creative.

Auri also loves cars, particularly special, fast, and sporty ones. This passion for cars as technology traces back to Auri's father, who always liked to drive fast sports cars.

Not only is Auri passionate about technology, he thinks very fast. Auri is the fastest typist I have ever seen, and he talks at about the same speed. I have lots of friends who have instant answers for technology problems but they tend to answer quickly without thinking and are very often totally wrong and almost always partially wrong. On the other hand, Auri's lightning answers are almost always right—his answers could be about how to adjust text in a certain program or how to adjust a network setting for better performance, or what is causing a computer to act flaky.

In the 1990s I taught elementary through middle school students about computers. I forget how I met Auri, but I remember he indicated that he felt my teaching this was a good, worthy, and important thing to do. Auri not only savors learning, his greatest internal energy is directed to sharing technology knowledge with others, similar to my own ambition. Auri is like a giggling clown when he gets to show a student, young or old, new tech gadgets or procedures that few know about. Because Auri is good at finding and developing shortcuts, he always has better ways to show off and teach to others.

Auri always spoke about how important learning was and how so many schools missed the mark when it was so close and inexpensive. He dutifully maintained classes for our servers and helped prepare handouts for classes of young students and of district teachers. Auri helped instruct and assist students with problems and also diagnosed and fixed hardware problems. Auri, like me, loved bringing fun and pranks to the young students, the reward being their own smiles. Also like me, Auri saw that the brightest tech users are often a bit precocious and even irreverent. I could not have managed these classes without Auri's assistance.

Over the years that I have known Auri, I have seen him become a master at tying together technology devices, computers, and consumer electronics. He even finds ways to make disparate technologies work together. If I have a question about how to do something with a computer, particularly with a computer and accessories like wireless printers or routers, Auri is the best source for answers.

In the old days, you could pull out your car radio and install ones with more controls, better specs, fancier displays, and other features. You could install good speakers and amplifiers to make your car special, even in the driveway. But we are on the verge of a great technology shift in cars. I just attended the 2005 CES show, and about a third of the convention center floor space was devoted to telematics products. In just the last few years, it has become common to see rear LCD displays for DVD players in cars. We now have satellite radio for our cars. I tried it out in a car and wound up with 10 accounts for satellite radio in my cars, my kids' cars, my home, my office, and for travel. I can't remember the last time I listened to FM.

I like the choice of satellite TV channels at home. I like to drive instead of fly whenever possible, and I enjoy taking road trips. So I outfitted my Hummer with a satellite TV dish and have gotten great use out of it. I outfitted this Hummer with satellite Internet, along with servers and routers and even Wi-Fi within that car. It was like taking my home with me. A car is a much harsher environment for all this equipment than my home, I can tell you that. Just regulating the AC and getting enough power from cigarette lighters or from wires to the generator is a critical consideration.

A decade ago I'd go shopping for gadgets in Japan and I would see lots of mapping displays. When auto navigation systems came out it the United States I had to be among the first to install them. After my first car navigation system, I'd never go back. It was like moving to your first GUI in computers. Most of us go through that door and we know we'll never go back. Each of my cars has a navigation system to this day. I even have friends who can hack into the serial cables and install their own icons. One friend has a great idea to pick up the cop car GPS transmissions and display them in a car on your navigation system. He calls it Cop Finder.

Now I have friends with TiVo's in their cars and hard disk music servers. Heck, BMW even installs iPods, and so will other car manufacturers soon. Wi-Fi is the dominating wireless connection between your car music hard disk and your computers serving music in your home. It's a crazy world with hundreds of manufacturers now offering their own solutions. It's one of those exciting times in history when our concepts about a major facet of our lives are being shaken and rocked and there's no one clear answer. For those of us who like to live on the edge of the future and experiment with what works and what doesn't and why, the time is now for car technology. We work hard to set up systems that weren't designed by the manufacturer and have something more special than the next guy on our block or in our school. We always have the latest and greatest but are constantly adjusting things because one month later there's something new that is even greater. Without us, the end result of standards that humans can all live with and operate would take much longer to come about and would not be as good.

I've had cell phones since the beginning. I had other car phones before cell phones came along. I always opted for (expensive) in-car hands-free systems. Some early ones had their own phones but changed numbers when you plugged in your portable. Eventually, some law to prevent easy cell phone spoofing made Motorola get rid of that technology. They did come out with units that also let you speak names to dial, long before any other cell phones had this technology. I went through the stages of evolution of cell phone technology in cars, from the best-quality antennas mounted on my roof to ones built into the retractable FM antenna. It was always fun for me to keep up with the latest technology.

I chose to buy a car a year ago because it had lots of the modern technology built in. It's a Toyota Prius. This car comes with a touch-screen display for a navigation system and other car controls. It gets rid of the normal dashboard for the driver. The touch screen is a pleasure to use and shows informative displays of the fuel usage and consumption while driving. It has 300 voice commands. It has keyless entry. I always hated reaching in my pocket for keys. Extra steps bother a lot of us technology followers, in my encounters. I would keep keys in my cars and leave them unlocked. Now I carry the key in my pocket and the door opens for me and locks by pressing a button. I love this feature.

One major reason I wanted this car was that it was the first one I'd seen with hands-free Bluetooth operation. I've become a major Bluetooth fan and user in the last couple of years. I use Bluetooth for wireless headsets to my phone, to transfer address books from my computer to the phone, to control programs on my PowerBook, including iTunes, from my phone, to see caller ID on my computer screen when calls come in, to access the Internet from a park bench, hotel, or my car, and more. The 2004 Prius came with automatic hands-free phone operation if you had a Bluetooth phone. This was a big decision for me. I had stuck with analog phones all these years because of the better quality. I sound like Steve Wozniak over an analog phone, even if you don't know it's me at the start of the call. But I had to switch to a digital phone for Bluetooth. I had used digital phones with Bluetooth before, but not for my own personal voice phone. So I bought a car and switched phones mainly to try this new advanced technology that would simplify my life. I could get in my car and make calls from the touch screen and never touch my phone in my pocket.

Well, the first three Bluetooth phones I bought, first from Sony/Ericsson, then from Nokia, and finally from Motorola, all failed to implement what was needed for hands free operation in a car over Bluetooth. I finally went back to a slightly older phone, and it worked. Heck, we often make sacrifices to have the latest technologies; the bigger the sacrifice, the more impor- tant it must be to us.

Auri is one of these guys who knows a lot more about the brands and models of in-car and in- home technology than I can keep up with. He is one of a mass of people out there who are heroes of mine, representing where I came from. We are weird and hard to understand in our ways, but we are important to society. I was so glad to hear that Auri was writing a book because I know how good he is at sharing and explaining tech secrets and exposing a world of wonder to young inventive types of minds. It is an honor that Auri asked me to write this fore- word.

Steve Wozniak

Co-founder, Apple Computer

Acknowledgments

There are so many people that have helped me write this book that I am fearful I may miss some names. If I do, you know who you are, and I'll mention you on the Web site!

A thank you goes out to the following people: First and foremost, my parents, Karen and Fred, and stepparents, Richard and Julie—without their support, I would never have been able to finish, let alone have the aptitude to write this book. Next, my good friends Richard Doherty and Yan Volodarsky. Rick's inside knowledge into the industries covered in this book and his experience and insight in both designing performance cars and racing helped me tremendously. Yan was the one who finally convinced me to take a wrench and dremel to my car, and now I think about what I can change every day.

To Steve Wozniak, my good friend who has always believed that I can do whatever I put my mind to, even when I doubt myself, and for giving me the opportunity to learn so much from him and so many of his super-smart friends.

To the awesome folks at Wiley who have held my hand through my first book: Chris Webb, who got me hooked; Gus Miklos, my Development Editor, who kept me in line and even agreed with me (man, I like that!); Adaobi Obi Tulton; and the countless others involved in this project and working behind the scenes who I never got to meet!

To my siblings, Noah, Max, and Chloe, for really putting the stuff in my car to the test by playing with devices, pouncing on them, and getting mud on stuff. To the stores that helped me—CompUSA Castleton, H.H. Gregg's car install bay, Tom Rousch Mazda, and Ovation.

To my grandparents, Alvin and Irene Goodman and Devorah Rahimzadeh.

To my friends, the Smith Family (Geoff, Mary, Doug, Brad, Emily), my second family the Millers (Laurie, Phil, and Bryon) for giving me a place to stay and write, and my friend of over 20 years, Matt Banach. Oh, hey Mike Buschmann, you know you rock with cars.

Introduction

When I was approached to write this book, I had long been contemplating ideas about why it makes sense to add computers to cars. Being a software developer, I tend to take systems apart and think about the basics of what makes them tick. Besides the cool factor of having a computer in a car, it just makes sense. Consider Global Positioning Satellite (GPS) navigation systems: they're really just computers with an operating system and a single software application interfaced to an antenna. These GPS systems cost a thousand dollars or more if installed when you buy the car.

So, again, being the software developer, I asked myself: "Self, it's a computer that just runs one application. Why not install a full-blown computer and run as many applications as you want?"

Well, I guess I answered my own questions by writing this book. I didn't want to stop there, though. Throughout this production I've been learning a great many things, thanks to good friends and acquaintances who know more than I do about cars, technology, and more. I wasn't the consummate professional when it came to car technology. I'm a geek for sure, but even geeks specialize in certain areas. It helped a lot to have friends who are very into modding their cars. Those are the guys who look at a car and want to take it apart and add cool stuff. And those types of geeks have other geek friends who do the same thing. I used to be afraid to take my car apart, always paying a dealer or retail store to install stuff. Well, thanks to my fellow geeks, I'm a car mod geek now, too.

Let's Get It Started!

There are a lot of projects in this book that will let you do everything from adding a computer to your car to adding Internet access and game systems, videoconferencing between cars, and war driving (driving around in your car looking for free wireless Internet networks). In addition to the projects, which come later in the book, I have included a lot of introductory chapters to give you a lot of the background you will need before you start these projects. For example, you will learn about power considerations, how to mitigate extreme heat in the summer and freezing cold in the winter, and physics (without being boring) and how it applies to cars so you don't destroy all your peripherals that were never meant for cars in the first place. If you want to get started now, feel free to turn right to the projects, but I know you'll learn a lot reading the, ahem, educational chapters.

I realize that not all cars are alike. You may have a Honda Civic, while your friends have Mazda Protégés, and others may have Jeeps, other SUVs, or minivans. I have tried to address these differences the best I can in the project chapters, helping you to determine where to place many of these items in your respective car type. I've dealt with this issue first-hand. During the course of writing this book I was involved in an accident that totaled my concept car. I finally bought a new car, a Dodge SRT-4. To be sure, the car was much different to work on than my Mazda

Protégé 5, but I found that my steps worked well as I followed them to reinstall my projects in the new car. I also tried installations in my friends' trucks, and verified the OBD-II diagnostic tools by running them on my dad's Honda Odyssey minivan when he was having problems.

To further help you out, you can go to www.wiley.com/go/extremetech and then select the link for the companion site, which has a link to my own *Geek My Ride* Web site. You can post your experiences there, and share with others. I hope to build a wealth of information online so anyone can learn both with this book and the Web site and really geek their ride.

On another note, one complaint I always had about modding cars was that it actually *depreciates* your car's value if you're not careful. To this extent, I decided to make all of the projects in this car easily removable. This proved immensely worthwhile after my accident: I basically just unplugged everything and took the components off the carpet they were Velcroed to. How convenient!

I very much want to hear about your experiences both with the projects in this book and with anything else you've added to your car. I've had a great time writing this tome, and I have learned so much, but it's the conversations with other geeks sparked by seeing my car that have really taught me how much can be done. Please drop me a line with your projects, or just post them to my forums. Thanks for buying this book, and have fun geekin' your ride!

Who Should Read This Book

This book is for anybody who wants to add more entertainment and cool tech gadgets to their car. From first time modders to seasoned pros, you'll all find something in this book. I've written it so that even families with minivans who want to add a game or GPS system but aren't sure how to actually do it. The steps are very straightforward. Being an Extreme Tech series book, however, I have left out certain things geeks already know, such as how to build a PC or how to use a Dremel tool. In places where I assume certain knowledge I will clearly let you know, and what professionals (or your geek friends) should do for you. I went through a number of learning experiences building the project chapters for this book, so I want to make everything as easy for you to install as possible by pointing out pitfalls along the way.

Please Don't Play and Drive!

Many of the projects in this book require use of a screen. This screen is meant to be enjoyed by your passengers, not the driver. Of course, while parked, you can do whatever you want. Taking your eyes off the road is dangerous at any time, so please put driver and passenger safety ahead of entertainment. I don't want you to get hurt! Furthermore, keep in mind that there are many laws that cover "distracted driving," so pay attention to the laws in your state and the states to which you plan to travel so you don't get in trouble.

How to Read This Book

I've written this book so you can turn directly to a project and get started. However, I recommend reading Parts 1 and 2 before you start on the projects so you can prime yourself to modifying cars and implementing higher tech solutions in mobile environments. There's a lot of information in there I know you will find interesting and educational, and it will save you a lot of trouble, and money, in the end. The projects will then be much more self-explanatory as well.

How This Book Is Organized

Here's a breakdown of how this book is organized. If you're *really* comfortable installing stuff like computers and game systems into cars, feel free to jump directly to the projects. I still recommend reading the educational chapters, though.

In addition to the project chapters, I have included fun, and oftentimes useful, side projects throughout this book. The side projects didn't need an entire chapter to themselves, but look out for them to geek your car even more!

Part I: Laying the Groundwork

In this section you will learn how to plan these projects so you can get them done more quickly and with less hassle. You'll also learn how to save money, plan power requirements for your devices, choose the right components for a mobile environment, mitigate heat concerns, and to route cables properly.

Part II: The User Interface

In this section you will learn how to choose the right input devices for your car and determine the ideal display type(s) to install.

Part III: Foundation Projects

Foundation projects are projects that all future projects will likely require. The projects here include installing a PC in your car (which I will often call a *Car PC*), installing a game console in your car, and adding a DVD player or other audio/video device in your car.

Part IV: Advanced Projects

Building on the projects in *Part III: Foundation Projects*, these projects are the real nitty-gritty cool stuff you want. From adding Internet access and television reception to war driving and video conferencing, controlling your car's computer and diagnosing your car's maintenance troubles yourself, you'll be busy for a while adding all this cool stuff to your car. There are also a number of side projects in these chapters that I feel make each project even better.

Appendixes

Following the project chapters are the appendixes, which are there for your reference. Information there includes summaries of the laws covering use of all this stuff in different states, a handy guide to OBD-II interfaces, and how to choose the right one for your car, neat projects I have come across and want to share with you, and additional resources.

Conventions Used in This Book

As you read through the book, you'll see various icons to alert you to notes of interest, cautions, warnings, tips, and other helpful recommendations. The following are some examples of the various icons used throughout the book.

These icons pertain to items of interest related to the subject at hand. Although you can safely skip these, I recommend that you read them at your leisure. They may help you build a better-modified ride!

These give you valuable information to help you avoid making serious mistakes in performing various steps. Although Cautions are not as serious as Warnings (see below), you should pay heed to these, so that you don't experience equipment malfunctions or other related frustrations.

These icons pertain to bits of information you may find interesting, such as the history involved with a technology I'm discussing or a brand-name change so you know both the old and new manufacturers of a single product.

These are recommendations of best-practice methods, ways to save time or money, and information on the best products or tools to use as you work through the projects.

Warnings contain important information you should read. The information in warnings will help keep you out of trouble with the law, help you stay away from potentially dangerous activities, save you from expensive warranty repairs, and much more.

You'll see this icon for terms in a chapter that may be unfamiliar to you, that need to be defined, or that you'll need to know in order to better understand some of the project steps.

The Difficulty Meter appears at the top of every chapter in Parts 3 and 4 to tell you how difficult the chapter is likely to be for the average geek. There are three difficulty levels: easy, intermediate, and advanced. Easy projects should be fine for people who haven't even built a computer before but are good with a screwdriver, plugging things in and installing software. Intermediate projects require you to be comfortable with changing operating-system settings and using a Dremel tool. Advanced projects are for those geeks who are cool working with power cables and making modifications to their cars and possibly voiding the warranty, as well as building computers and removing parts from their cars without a second thought. All of these projects can still be done by non-geeks or people only comfortable with a certain level—just be sure to have professional installers do the stuff you're not comfortable with.

The Budget Meter appears at the top of every chapter in Parts 3 and 4 to tell you how much the project will likely cost you. There are three cost levels in addition to the approximate cost so you can tell at a glance how the project will affect your pocketbook—*cheap*, *not bad*, and *credit card*. If there are multiple approaches to a project, such as when you have to buy a screen, or if you already have one installed, I will list both with-screen and sans-screen costs.

The photos in the icons were provided courtesy of Corbis Digital Stock and PhotoDisk/Getty Images.

Laying the Groundwork

part

Planning Your Projects

L et's face it, geeks don't like to plan—we get into the thick of it quickly. If you don't plan these projects, you may go broke before you start. Know what you're getting into before you do this, and know where you want to go with it when you're done.

In this chapter you will learn how to:

➤ Plan out your projects

➤ Save money on equipment by keeping things in scope

➤ Learn how to mitigate extreme heat and cold concerns

➤ Protect your investment and learn about security

➤ Address warranty and legal concerns

➤ Buy your equipment before starting a project

Some of the projects in this book require a fair amount of equipment and processes. It will help tremendously if you read through a project's entire chapter first and make your decisions on what to purchase beforehand. In many cases, once you start installing items in your car, you'll end up having to finish the project, too, unless you want a big mess. If your dash is torn apart and you have a red cord in your hand, it's a bad time to decide which operating system to install on the computer. To help you through this, each project lists all of the equipment you should need before starting each project, as well as all preinstallation steps. Don't worry, I won't ask you to build a computer outside!

Keep Things in Scope and Save Money

For many of the projects in this book, there are a lot of choices when it comes to equipment. However, a lot of that equipment may do a lot more than what you may actually need. For example, a gaming console and audio/video (A/V) system setup only requires a low-resolution, low-power, analog screen. The computer projects, on the other hand, could get by with that same low-cost screen and analog output if you're just using them for playing music and video. Buying a high-resolution digital extended graphics array/adapter (XGA) screen with touch-screen abilities may sound cool, but it's overkill and could easily be three or more times the price of a regular screen!

Keeping projects in scope doesn't mean you can't expand later. Many of the projects I've included have interchangeable parts. If you build a computer with an analog screen, you can always swap that screen out with a higher-resolution digital one later and sell the old one on eBay®. I will try to not lock you into any particular technology. Like any good chef, you can (and are encouraged to!) improvise and make these projects truly your own.

Watch Out for Heat!

Computer and electronic equipment are obviously very sensitive to heat. In your own home, a poorly ventilated computer can overheat and shut down, possibly damaging components and losing data. Cars are an order of magnitude more complex in this case because they aren't continuously environmentally controlled like your home. For example, on a sweltering summer day, you may run the air conditioning to keep yourself a cool 70 degrees. Once you've parked your car, however, the inside temperature of your car could soar to hundreds of degrees and damage all of that equipment you've bought!

To help mitigate the heat threat, there are a few things to keep in mind:

- Keep the computers, game consoles, CDs, catridges, tapes, and other components in the shade, and preferably in a much cooler area, like the trunk. Only particular portions of the PC really need to be exposed, such as the optical drive, USB ports, and so forth. Those ports can be extended to areas of the car using longer cables.

- Consider tinting your windows if you are keeping electronics out in the open, like an LCD display on your dashboard. Make sure you purchase LCD displays made for cars. Do not place a home computer LCD display in your car because direct sunlight can easily damage it.

- A black or dark color car will absorb heat much more quickly than a white or lighter color car.

- Metal computer cases can heat up very quickly, and black cases can be even worse, especially in direct sunlight. See Chapter 4, "It's So Hot in Here: Dealing with Heat" for additional information to consider when choosing computer cases.

- Before starting your electronics in a hot car, allow the equipment to cool for a few minutes. Remember, that hot air circulating through your vehicle will run over the processor, across disk drives, and so forth and could possibly damage them! Speaking of heat, let's discuss how to provide power to our creations.

Make Sure You Have Enough Power

Unless you have an AC jack in your car, you are going to need to purchase some sort of adapter to make home equipment work in your vehicle. In many cases this will be through an AC inverter, but in some cases there will be special boards you can buy to control power (such as in the case of the car computer projects). If you have a car with a small engine, the drain on your vehicle's generator and your fuel may be higher, so be prepared. This is all explained in detail in Chapter 3, "Giving Your Creation Life: Power Considerations."

 Make sure to verify that the power sources you are using have a high enough amperage or current rating to handle the tens to hundreds of watts of additional electornics you are installing. When in doubt, check with your car dealer or a professional service manual to make sure you do not overextend a crucial car circuit—such as brake lights or engine computers.

Keep Security in Mind

If you're going to put all of this equipment in your car, don't forget there are people out there who may want to steal it! I know it sounds paranoid, but just as much as someone will steal a radio out of your car, an LCD display on your dashboard and game controllers all over your car scream "TAKE ME!" (hey, there's an LED display chapter in this book, you could use that to flash the words). Either way, keep in mind where you put things. The keyboard and mouse can easily be tucked away in door side panels as shown in Figure 1-1.

FIGURE 1-1: Keep the wireless keyboard neatly tucked away in the door's pocket where it's harder for thieves to see but still very accessible.

The LCD display, shown in Figure 1-2, should be dismountable so you can hide it in your glovebox. The easily disconnected cables can be placed on the floor, under the seat.

FIGURE 1-2: The display is mountable and can be removed just by turning a knob and is also small enough to fit in the glove compartment.

Having a security system in your car is a good idea as well. If your car does not already have an alarm, look for one that disables the engine and makes lots of noise. It's not a bad idea to park in a public, well-lit place, either. A dark alley where few people pass by is surely a better place to break into a car than a well-lit shopping mall parking lot. Furthermore, the crime you want to avoid is "Smash 'n Grab," where a thief breaks your window and quickly grabs whatever he or she can. If everything is mounted exceptionally well, a thief is less likely to take the time to remove equipment, so make sure everything is very well mounted or out of site in a locked compartment. Regarding car insurance, an alarm system often may lower your premiums. Taking the steps given here may prevent your car from getting broken into in the first place, which will save you the hassle of dealing with your insurance company.

Warning

Don't keep sensitive or irreplaceable documents and files on your car computer. Not only can thieves take your computer and files; heat, water, accidents, and extremely cold weather can damage them, too!

Don't Void Your Warranty

If you are installing this equipment in a new car, I would like to suggest that you check with your dealer beforehand to determine whether any projects would void your warranty. If you have to make any modifications to your car's power system, for example, it's not only potentially dangerous; it could damage some equipment in your car if you're not careful. Such damage could void your warranty and may even create a dangerous situation under the hood, endangering both you and your passengers.

Tip Many of the car projects can have portions installed by dealers, with you doing the rest. So, if you do not feel comfortable modifying your power system or installing a new head unit (a.k.a. stereo), you can have that done by qualified professionals and still connect the other necessary equipment to make your project work. Nobody has to know that you didn't do it all!

Learn the Law

Another very important subject to take into consideration is the rule of law. Some communities may not allow a display to be mounted on your dashboard. Others may have regulations over the use of LED message displays or flashing lights on vehicles. The last thing I want to have happen is for you to get a ticket or get hurt, so please be aware of the law when choosing projects to build. I've tried to compile a nonexhaustive list of laws for you in Appendix A, "Legal Concerns," to give you an idea of what to expect.

Tip When it comes to LED displays and flashing lights on your car, use common sense. You're going to make our friends in blue angry if you put expletives on display boards. Flashing blue and red lights to make your car seem like a police car may not only get you pulled over; it could get you arrested.

Safety First!

Many of these projects have displays and interfaces that may distract you while driving. Although they are cool to look at, I don't want you to get in an accident or violate any "distracted driving" laws.

Warning When working with the projects in this book, please be aware that some projects are meant to be controlled by a passenger—not by the driver! Some displays and controls may distract you while you drive.

The National Highway Traffic Safety Administration (NHTSA) did a survey on distractions and how they relate to accidents. I suggest you read it—just go to www.nhtsa.gov and go to the "Driver Distraction" area. More details of the NHTSA report can be found in Appendix A, "Legal Concerns."

Furthermore, some of these projects may require you to work with power systems in your vehicle and other live wires. Be careful in working with these projects. Wear gloves and protective gear when necessary. If you do not feel comfortable working with power connectors and so forth, fear not! Many of these projects can be built outside of the car and then installed by various dealers for, most likely, reasonable fees. I want you to get the most you can out of this book, but I don't want you to get hurt!

Summary

This chapter discussed planning your project, mitigating heat, and protecting your investment via security. It also discussed saftey and legal concerns over projects you may build.

For more details, you can turn to the following sections. If this is your first time tackling projects such as those in this book, I suggest you read all of the chapters in order to familiarize yourself with the issues you will most likely deal with and to learn a lot of stuff you can amaze your friends with!

- For money-saving hints and tips, turn to Chapter 2, "Saving Money"
- For power considerations, turn to Chapter 3, "Giving Your Creation Life: Power Considerations"
- For heat considerations, turn to Chapter 4, "It's So Hot in Here: Dealing with Heat"
- For cabling considerations, turn to Chapter 5, "Working with Cables"
- For shock, vibration, and G-force considerations, turn to Chapter 6, "Physics Man, Physics: Preparing Home Electronics for the Road"
- For legal considerations, turn to Appendix A, "Legal Concerns"

Saving Money

You don't need to spend a lot of money to build the projects in this book. In this chapter I present many options for saving money. From asking your friends for stuff they no longer use to taking advantage of user groups and enthusiast clubs, and even tips for buying things off eBay®, I want you to get the best deals possible so you can affordably do these projects!

Use eBay to Find Cheap Stuff

When it comes to finding affordable equipment, it's pretty hard to beat eBay. I was able to get my Xenarc high-resolution widescreen digital touch-screen display for under $400, or about $200 less than it was selling direct from the manufacturer. You can also find good deals on used laptop hard drives and laptop-style optical drives that you normally wouldn't find in stores. Heck, you can even buy complete car computers that you can slide into your dash (but where's the fun in that?). I can't vouch for every eBayer, but I've rarely had a bad experience, as long as the seller has had good feedback.

In the same light, when you are deciding to upgrade equipment in your car, you can sell it on eBay, in your local newspaper, or to your friends to get funding for more advanced projects. If you're upgrading your car's stock stereo to one that accepts auxiliary inputs, for example, you can sell that stereo to someone on eBay who needs it.

Another great use for eBay is to look for other items you want for your car and get a good idea of what you will end up spending. For example, with a gaming console project, you may want to look for a used Nintendo® 64 and Mario Kart®, a used power inverter, and a used LCD panel. The rest of the cables and other such equipment you can buy locally, but the actual electronics could come for cheap from eBay.

in this chapter

- ☑ Saving money on parts
- ☑ Taking advantage of user groups and enthusiast club discounts
- ☑ Building for expansion
- ☑ Considering monthly fees
- ☑ Using eBay to find cheap stuff
- ☑ Upgrading a hard drive

Here are a few pointers for buying on eBay:

- Make sure a seller has good feedback. A feedback rating of 98–100% should be preferred if they have 50–200 individual feedback ratings; 97% or greater for larger feedback rating quantities. Your own standards on what to accept may, of course, vary.

- Even if a seller has a very positive feedback rating, check their recent feedback history to make sure they are not starting to slip.

- Watch for other auctions selling the same thing. Many times you will see the same item for vastly different prices. Go for lower-priced items if they all appear to be the same and come from reputable sellers.

- Don't be the first to bid on an item. Wait until similar auctions have a few minutes left and you will see that many of the prices usually vary, even for the same item! Now that you can see the cheaper ones to bid on, you can try *sniping* them to get the lowest price.

- *Sniping* is the art of bidding on an item in the last few seconds to try to get it for a low price but without revealing your maximum price beforehand. When you see the price at 30 seconds, try to time it so you can set your price with 10 seconds to go, and submit with 5 seconds to go. For the 10 seconds before you submit your final offer, keep refreshing so you can watch the price and see if other people are trying to snipe you! Note that sniping only tends to work well if you are on a fast broadband connection, not dial-up, because it takes too long to reload the page. Although some people may frown on this practice (such as the people who lose the auction), it is effective in getting what you want for a cheap price.

- Make sure you read descriptions carefully, especially the condition of the item, the return policy, and the dollar amount for shipping. If you can't return a defective item, think twice about buying from that seller.

- Always pay with a credit card or with a reputable payment service such as PayPal® (www.paypal.com). If you get a bum seller, those services can help you get your money back. Also, if you're buying something and the seller is outside the United States, *never pay cash or money order*, because if they rip you off, it's pretty hard to get your money back. If a seller in the United States takes money (for example, check, cash, or money order) you sent through the mail and never sends you the product and doesn't give you your money back, it can be considered mail fraud, which is a federal offense!

There are many books out there on how to use eBay. A good one (shameless plug) is *eBay For Dummies* (ISBN 0764556541), also published by Wiley.

Check What You Already Have

The first place to find cost savings may actually be your very own car's manual! I know, it's that evil *manual* word again, but I'm telling you—it helps! For example, if you have a minivan with a video system, there are probably jacks for auxillary audio and video inputs. Look at that, no need to buy any seriously new equipment! Even if you don't have a minivan, your car stereo may already have auxillary audio input jacks built-in, as in the case of the 2004 BMWs and Saabs. This negates the need to acquire a new *head unit* (car stereo system). When it comes to powering various devices, your car may already have an AC jack, such as the Pontiac Vibe, saving you the cost of a power inverter.

Tip
If you need to transmit audio but don't have an auxilliary audio input jack and don't want to purchase a new head unit, consider purchasing an *FM Radio Sound Transmitter*. These devices take audio signals from, say, a portable MP3 player or similar device and retransmit that audio over shortband radio frequencies that you can tune on your car's stereo. The sound is pretty good for what it's worth, and the devices are usually around $30. Ask your local retailer, such as Best Buy, Circuit City, CompUSA, Wal-Mart, Good Guys, and so forth. I'm sure they carry them!

User Groups and Enthusiast Clubs Are Your Friends

Many folks seem to have forgotten about computer user groups, and it seems few people seek the help of enthusiast groups when it comes to, first, finding out more about something they're interested in and, second, saving money. Many of these groups offer discounts to their members. In the case of the Indianapolis Computer Society, a large user group I run in Indiana, members get discounts at CompUSA, PC Club, and a host of other places. These group discounts can save hundreds of dollars on computer and A/V equipment and supplies. And now, CompUSA is in the home theater biz too!

Tip
To find a computer user group in your area, your best bet is to first check the Association of Personal Computer User Groups (APCUG) at www.apcug.net. Your next best bet is to use some of the popular Internet search engines.

Obviously, there are car-specific groups as well, such as Ford Probe and Mazda 626 enthusiast groups, racing clubs, car modification clubs, and more. A search on the Internet is sure to give you a host of choices, with many of them offering discounts at places in your local area on parts you need for your particular fancy.

Check out the Sports Car Club of America (SCCA), a very large auto enthusiast group, for a sampling of what you can expect from one of these types of club meetings. At last check they offered discounts on car audio equipment, car magazine subscriptions, car rentals, and more. The SCCA can be reached at www.scca.com.

Both user groups and enthusiast groups often offer discounts on products at their meetings. Many times there are vendor presentations on software, equipment, service providers, and limited-time offers that are many times too good to pass up! For example, my user group offered Trend Micro Internet Security 2004 for $20 instead of $50! Many sponsors and manufacturers also give away software, hardware, and more at clubs, too, so who knows what you might win!

So You Think You're Getting a Deal at Retail?

Be careful when you purchase items at retail, or even on a Web site. Just because the price on a Web site is cheaper than retail, that doesn't mean it's at the lowest cost. This is especially true with accessories (cables, toner, speakers, keyboards, mice, and so on), which have margins often in excess of 40%. A wireless keyboard and mouse combo may cost $99 at retail, but with my user group discount it goes down to about $68. Online retailers sometimes can knock it down to $89 or $80, but rarely as low as my user group discounts (which are really volume-purchasing discounts). Many consumers are wrongly under the impression that because something is sold online that it's already at the lowest price. Always consider all of your options, and take advantage of entusiast and user group benefits.

Did You Know

Have you ever noticed that an item sells for the same price at many stores, both online and retail (sometimes called "brick & mortar")? This is because these items are sold at *minimum advertised price* (MAP). This price is set by the manufacturer as the lowest price retailers should sell the product to continue getting various credits from that manufacturer. This is different than *manufacturer's suggested retail price* (MSRP). This is why many deals say you're saving a fortune over MSRP (terms like "valued at" and "usually retails for"), but they're really telling you the MSRP and not giving you a better deal than anyone else.

Saving Money with Business Accounts

Another way to save money is to open a business purchasing account. Some stores may allow to you create a *credit card–only* business account, which means you must pay up front (like you normally do anyway). If your business is larger, you may be able to set up a Net 30-day account, but that's all out of the scope of this book. Business accounts usually give you so-so to excellent discounts on products you would normally pay retail for, and it shouldn't cost you anything to open one. Many retail stores and online stores have business account options, and you can even get a dedicated salesperson who can negotiate prices with you. Some examples of stores that offer this are CompUSA and Computer Discount Warehouse (CDW).

If you can't open up a business account, see if one of your friends has access to a business account they can use (with permission, of course). Apart from joining user groups and enthusiast groups, or hoping you find a good deal on eBay, this can save you a ton of cash. I buy a lot of computer equipment from CompUSA, and my personal business account saves me well over $1,000 every year!

Reuse Old or Broken Components

When finding the parts for a car computer or an A/V system in your car, don't forget about using stuff you have lying around your home. Spare cables that you never use, game controllers that aren't always in use, computer peripherals that you've replaced or upgraded—these can all be candidates for systems you build into your vehicle.

Another note: If you need to purchase equipment such as laptop CD-ROM drives and hard drives, try to find broken laptops and use them for parts. It may be cheaper sometimes to buy a broken system and take parts out of it than it is to buy a part by itself. Try your local Salvation Army for stuff they want to throw away, or ask your neighbors if there are any cables or other such equipment that they aren't using anymore. Local, individually owned computer shops and places like Computer Rennaissance (a chain in the Midwest and East Coast, www.computer renaissance.com) may have all the parts you need at very low prices.

Another place to try for parts is a local business. Ask if there's any equipment they want to get rid of—items such as broken laptops that you can take the hard drives and optical drives out of and place into your creation. Many of these organizations may just give items to you because they don't have any time to sell it themselves.

Build for Expansion

I realize that many of the projects in this book may require more than your pocketbook is willing to part with. I feel your pain and thus have tried my best to build all of these projects so you can piecemeal them with different parts and expand them later. As I pointed out in Chapter 1, "Planning Your Projects," you don't have to buy a high-end LCD screen right away. You can start with the more affordable, and more readily available, analog screens made for vehicle game consoles and graduate to a digital VGA model later. It generally shouldn't affect a project, except maybe for running a few new cables.

A couple of things are certainly true about the consumer electronics industry that weigh in your favor: Costs go down over time, and competition lowers prices. This has been true with cell phones, computers, DVDs, VCRs, answering machines, and most mass-market consumer electronics (CE) devices that have survived the *early adopter* (people who buy technology when it first comes out, before mass market adoption) phase. Taking this into account, you can plan out your purchases and may actually save money by doing so.

Tip In many cases you can use the devices in these projects in your car *and* at home. For example, the game console in your car can be kept at home and used until you go on a trip where you'd want to use it. Why buy two consoles if you don't have to? The same goes for some computers, although I strongly recommend against keeping any irreplaceable or sensitive data on a computer you leave in your vehicle.

Keep in mind, however, that when you install parts you should install them for expansion. Permanently mounting items to your car's dashboard, or supergluing panels over cables will seriously hinder your ability to expand later and could damage your car in the process. Note also that if you add new parts, you will need to reevaluate power and heat concerns—you can't *just* swap stuff out.

Compromising on Parts

I mentioned earlier that you can buy lower-resolution screens, cheaper cables, and so forth to help defray your initial project costs. Keep in mind, however, that not all solutions are compatible with my suggestion. For example, if you are going to add an analog gaming screen for a computer project, you need to make sure the computer you are installing supports analog (composite or S-Video) video output. Furthermore, make sure you test that the screen is readable and works *before* you install it into your vehicle.

Here are some of the items on which you can easily compromise:

- **Memory**—You don't have to buy the fastest memory money can buy. Many types of memory are backwards compatible, and thus you can use a slower and less expensive memory. PC3200 is backwards compatible with PC2700 and PC2100 memory speeds, and each higher speed tends to be compatible with its predecessor. Check with your memory vendor for details (for example, PC2700 is *not* compatible with PC-133). For the most part, you shouldn't need super-fast memory in a car computer anyway, since media playback worked fine well before many of today's higher-speed solutions became available.

- **Optical Drives**—Most are upgradeable. You may not need a DVD burner now, but you can easily upgrade in the future.

- **Hard Drives**—There's no reason to buy more space than you need initially. For example, 20 gigabytes may be plenty for your music and some apps and games. If you need more down the road, you can always upgrade. Software utilities that come with the hard drives and programs like Norton Ghost™, NTI Backup Now!™, and many others can migrate all of your data from the old hard drive to a new one. Hard drives are getting bigger and cheaper all the time, so buying a smaller drive now can actually benefit you as you wait for larger drives to come down in price.

- **USB Devices**—Any USB device can be swapped out for a different device at practically any time. Keep in mind your power usage, however. You don't want to run out of power for your USB devices. Try to keep the number of devices you use that require computer bus power (i.e., they don't have an external power adapter) to a minimum. A GPS unit *or* an external hard drive is better than both running at the same time, since a car PC may not have enough power in its small power supply for both.

- **Wired versus Wireless Keyboards, Mice, and Game Controllers**—Ideally, you will want wireless everywhere. However, if only passengers will tend to use the systems you put in, wired solutions can be much cheaper and can be changed out for wireless versions down the road.

- **Don't Just Buy for Your Car**—You can use many of the items you purchase for your car at home as well, so your investment can bring returns even if you decide not to use the item in the car anymore!

Caution Keep in mind that some equipment compromises require different cabling and power needs. For example, an analog screen may require a composite RCA-type cable or S-Video cable, but if you switch it out for a digital display you may need a VGA cable. Some displays *do* support both. Determine beforehand what you want to upgrade and the cables you will need to perform such an upgrade.

Upgrading to a Larger-Capacity Hard Drive

When the time comes to upgrade your hard drive, there are many utilities to choose from to seamlessly move all your data (including the operating system, all files, applications, and preferences) to the new media with minimal effort.

Many drives actually come with utilities for migrating from an old drive. Maxtor drives usually come with the MaxBlast® disk utility. Seagate units are bundled with the "Seagate Hard Drive Utilities." In case your drive does not come with free transfer software, you still have many commercial options to choose from, such as Symantec's Norton Ghost (www.symantec.com), Future Systems Solutions' (www.fssdev.com) Drive2Drive and Casper XP, and NTI Software's BackUp Now! Suite's DriveImage, which makes a backup copy of your hard drive to CD or DVD, which you can copy to the new drive.

In this sidebar I won't go over how to do the transfer, because the details come with those software packages.

Before you transfer your hard drive, there are some steps you should follow to ensure everything goes as smoothly as possible:

1. Run Scandisk or a similar disk utility before the transfer. This will make sure that problems don't follow to your new hard drive. Scandisk isn't hard to find on Windows machines. On Windows 9x machines, go to the Start menu and click Run, then type **scandisk** and hit Enter, and it should appear. On Windows 2000 and XP, open up My Computer, right-click the hard drive you will be upgrading and select Properties, then Tools, then click Check Now . . . in the *Error Checking* box. (See sidebar Figure 2-1.)

2. Optimize your hard drive to make sure all of the data is contiguous. This may also speed up the transfer. On Windows 9x machines, go to the Start menu and click Run; then type **defrag**. On Windows 2000 and XP machines, open up My Computer, right-click the hard drive you will be upgrading and select Properties, then Tools, then click Defragment Now . . . in the *Defragmentation* box. (See sidebar Figure 2-1.)

3. Back up the hard drive just in case something goes wrong! Copying all of your files to an external hard drive is a good idea (and something you should do often). In addition to copying all of your files, making an image backup of your hard drive to CD or DVD using programs like Symantec's Norton Ghost or NTI Backup Now! Suite's DriveImage can be a life saver, since you can basically just copy that image back to any hard drive.

Continued

Continued

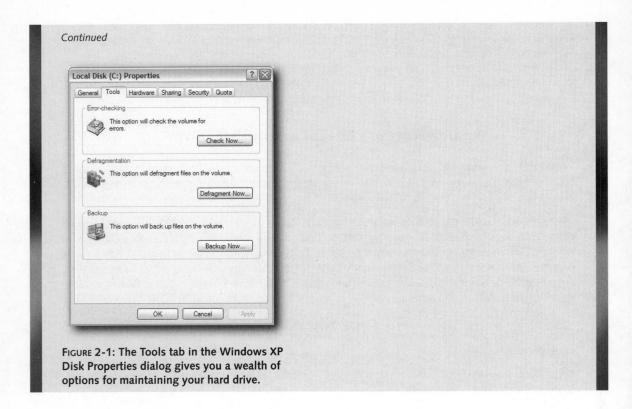

FIGURE 2-1: The Tools tab in the Windows XP
Disk Properties dialog gives you a wealth of
options for maintaining your hard drive.

Considering Monthly Fees

When you build your computer or add devices, such as GPS navigation systems, you may have
to pay monthly fees for services such as wireless Internet access, mobile traffic reports, and so
forth. Keep these fees in mind before you start a project that may require them. I will often
point these fees out before you start a project, but sometimes it depends on whether you go
with a free or paid service provider (a decision often made between basic and premium service
offerings). Remember that $10/month is $120/year, and having just a few services in your car
can add up to hundreds of additional dollars spent annually.

Summary

In this chapter we discussed many ways to save money when building projects. From taking
advantage of local groups to using what you already have, the object of this chapter is to help
you keep the costs down so you can build many of the projects in this book—and improvise
some on your own!

Giving Your Creation Life: Power Considerations

As Tim Allen said in the television series *Home Improvement,* "We need more power!" All of the projects in this book require some sort of power, usually provided by your car. In this chapter, I will show you a number of different options you have, from cigarette lighter adapters to AC (alternating-current) inverters, to connecting directly to your car's power system and upgrading your electrical system.

Does My Car Provide Enough Power?

Unless you intend to add a lot of equipment to your vehicle, such as a high-end amplifier, high-end head unit (another word for a stereo or audio system in an automobile), lots of speakers and subwoofers, GPS navigation system, high-end car alarm, a computer, two gaming systems, and so on, all at once, your car's electrical system should be fine. Just having a high-quality head unit, a computer, and a gaming console shouldn't overload most cars, as long as the computer uses a low-power processor and you only have either the computer or the game console on at once. My Mazda Protégé 5 handled all of those with ease.

Let's start out with a run down of how power is distributed in your car between the alternator and the battery. You use your battery to start your car, which, in turn, turns the engine and starts the alternator rotating (a.k.a., gas-powered power generator). Your alternator should have enough power for most of the projects in this car, possibly to have them all run at once. Normally your battery won't drain while you drive because your alternator should provide plenty of power. Excpetions include when window defrosters, headlamps, and fog lamps are all running or, if you have them, when heated seats or steering wheel warmers are running. At those times, many alternators can *barely* keep up the battery charge, so running your computer is not recommended. However, if your alternator cannot provide enough power, your car may start draining power from the battery. In this case, you could run down your battery, possibly very quickly. Note that although your alternator does charge the car battery while it's running, this assumes it has enough power left over to do so. If you're overloading your alternator, it may not recharge your battery, and thus you still have the potential dead battery issue to deal with.

Know Your Car's Output

I recommend that before you start the projects in this book you talk to your car dealer's service department, or at least check with an auto enthusiast group, a car parts store, or the many forums available on the Internet, to find out how much power your alternator provides and how much it is already providing to the rest of the systems in your car. Be sure of your *exact* car model, because often, larger alternators and batteries are installed when heavy-draw electrical power system options are installed, so your car dealer needs to know to give you the exact specs for your model. What's left over is gravy for the projects in this book. If you don't have enough, you may need a new, more powerful alternator or a second battery (also known as *teaming* batteries), or you may need to revamp your electrical system (see the sidebar "Amps, Alternators, and Batteries: Upgrading Your Electrical System," later in this chapter).

How Much Power Is Enough?

So how do you determine how much power you will be using? It's fairly easy. Give yourself a good magic number of watts you want to be the maximum. I chose 550 watts (written as 550 W), since 350 W is the size of a good AC inverter that claims to work in most cars, and my head unit (the Kenwood) advertises that it's capable of supporting four 50 W speakers. Most devices you will put in the car don't pull too many amps, so unless you're doing something way out of the ordinary I wouldn't worry much about the amperage—the worst you will do is blow a fuse. If you are planning on installing a 1,000 W sound system, which will draw well over the 60 or so amps a stock alternator provides, you will either want to upgrade your electrical system or scale back the number of components you're installing, as discussed in the sidebar later in this chapter, "Amps, Alternators, and Batteries: Upgrading Your Electrical System." Regardless, it's a good idea to keep spare fuses at the ready, especially when running the system for the first few weeks while you're getting the kinks out.

Note A good rule of thumb is if your system will draw X number of watts, use an inverter with about 30–40% extra reserve so that the inverter is not straining or running too hot.

Know Your Device Requirements

The device you are going to use should have information in its manual regarding how many watts it uses. In my car I connected a personal computer (with the well-performing but low-power Via C3 x86-based processor), a Nintendo® Game Cube®, a few screens, and a medium-range Kenwood MP-922 head unit. Table 3-1 outlines how much power (in watts) is used by various devices.

Table 3-1   Power Used by Various Devices

Device	Power Used
Computer power supply	~120 W
Kenwood head unit	~200 W
Nintendo Game Cube	~35 W
Touch-screen VGA display	~40 W
Seat-back displays	~80 W

Building a Power Requirements Worksheet

Prior to installing devices into your vehicle, you should build a worksheet to help you plan how much power you will need, how many outlets you may need to install, whether you need a more powerful alternator, and so forth. Table 3-2 shows a template for planning your power needs.

Table 3-2   Power Requirements Worksheet

Device Name	Total Watts	Total Amps	Powered By	# of AC Sockets Required
Computer	120	12	Barrier strip	n/a
Game Cube	35	2	Inverter	1
Head unit	350	10	Battery	n/a
Amplifier	1000	60	Battery	n/a
Screen 1	???	???	Inverter	1
Screen 2	???	???	Inverter	1
Additional devices...	...	...	...	...

Using an AC Inverter

Most of us are used to plugging computer and game power cords into walls. The connector is usually the same (plus or minus a ground prong), and you can just assume it will work when you plug it in. At home you plug into AC, or alternating current, power outlets. In the car, however, not only do you lack the convenient power sockets (although some new cars are coming with them), but you have DC, or direct current, power. To address providing AC power to devices from your car's DC power system, you need the sockets and an AC-DC power converter, which is provided via a device called an *AC inverter*, or just an *inverter* for short.

AC inverters are notoriously inefficient—whenever possible you want to power your devices without using an inverter. Every time you convert AC to DC or DC to AC there is a loss of energy, so an inverter needs to use more wattage to provide an equivalent effective wattage (consider this overhead or an energy penalty). Keep this in mind when deciding how to power your solutions.

You can pick up an inverter at almost any electronics store. I purchased mine at CompUSA. More specifically, it's a 350 W inverter made by APC, as shown in Figure 3-1. It comes with two grounded AC power sockets and a set of cables to connect the inverter directly to the car battery (this is the direct-connect port on the inverter) if more power is needed than is available through the cigarette lighter port, which is often located on your center console or in an ash tray. In some newer cars the cigarette lighter is now called the *power outlet* port (although it still looks just like a cigarette lighter port). Note that you can connect these extra cables to the barrier terminal strip described in the next section, "Getting Power Directly from the Battery." Again, having a 30–40% higher-rated inverter than your needs require can help assure both that your battery has a cool, long life, and that you have some reserve should you add other accessories later on. The 350 W inverters are around $60, and you may be able to get them for much less online. Figure 3-1 shows a typical AC inverter.

Note that AC inverters can get *very* hot, so getting one with a fan is ideal.

FRONT   BACK

FIGURE 3-1: Front and back views of a 350 W APC AC inverter with fan, cigarette-lighter adapter, and battery direct-connect ports.

Note that although connecting directly to the battery, which will be explained in the next section, is a great solution, there are some instances in which you should opt to use an AC inverter for devices you place in your car. For example, if you install a gaming system such as a Nintendo Game Cube into your vehicle, the power for that device is handled via a standard AC plug. Unless you want to pay more money for an additional AC plug from Nintendo and modify it to work with the 12 V DC power supply from your vehicle (which may not work), it's best just to plug the system into an inverter. That way you can transfer it from car to home and back by just unplugging the unit from each location and transferring it with minimal effort and hassle (and you have to buy only one Game Cube for home and for the car).

Warning Make sure when shopping around for inverters that the one you choose has a feature where it will stop drawing power when it detects the battery is running low. This is especially true if your car leaves the cigarette lighter adapter on, or "hot," when the car is off (many German cars do this). If you leave the inverter plugged in and switched on, it could drain your battery, and you might come back to a dead car!

Also, should your battery die, be sure to *disconnect* the inverter before you either cable or jump-start your car. Otherwise, power surges may irreparably harm the inverter and/or your computers, games, and other devices!

In the following section you will learn how to wire your car so you can power your devices directly from your battery. The end game is to have an internal central access point where you can connect all your power cabling—streamlining your power solution and making it easy for you to expand your power capabilities as you implement more gadgets and gizmos in your car.

Getting Power Directly from the Battery

This section describes how to feed power directly from the battery for devices when the ignition switch is turned on. Specifically, this section will walk you through the steps to add a central internal location for power delivery to all your devices in your vehicle. Some car computer power supplies can support this (that's what you're hooking up here, although building the computer is covered in more detail later in the book). You can also use the battery direct-connect port on an AC inverter to draw more power when connected directly to the battery (instead of the power from the cigarette-lighter port), and other devices may also have direct power connections. Specifically, you will feed the power to a battery *barrier terminal strip*, which will let you make internal connectors in the vehicle for any devices that need access to power (and so you don't have to keep working under the hood) You will also need to attach a cable from a car PC power supply that allows it to be powered when the ignition switch is turned on, all to the barrier terminal strip so you know where all of your power is coming from and can easily manage your power connections.

Amps, Alternators, and Batteries: Upgrading Your Electrical System

The following article, by Wayne Harris, originally appeared in the July/August 1988 issue of Car Stereo Review *magazine:*

One of the most overlooked aspects of a high-powered auto sound installation is its effect on a car's electrical system. No amplifier, no matter how sophisticated it is, can change the laws of physics. Energy can neither be created nor destroyed; it can only be changed from one form to another. This is exactly what an auto sound amplifier does: It takes power from the electrical system in your vehicle—the battery and alternator, primarily—and converts it into usable power to drive your speakers. When installing an amplifier into your system, remember that it cannot produce more power than you make available for it to convert—so you need to know what your electrical system is capable of, and how to upgrade it.

Say you have a 1,000 W audio system and you want to know whether your car's electrical system can drive it. At full output, the system will produce 1,000 W of power to your speakers at about 62% efficiency. This means that the input power to the amplifiers is 1,000/0.62 or 1,612 W. The standard equation for power is:

$$P = V \times I$$

Where P is input power in watts, V is input voltage, and I is input current in amps. If we assume that the battery's voltage is the typical 13 VDC (volts DC), then the input current, or alternator power, required by your system can be calculated from the given equation. Rearranging the equation, we get:

$$I = P / V$$

By plugging in the numbers and solving the equation, we get I = 1,612/13—or 124 amps.

Most stock alternators produce only about 60 amps maximum. Of this, about half is used to run the car itself. So this leaves you with about 30 amps for your system, 94 amps less than the 124 you need. Where will the other 94 amps come from? The battery will try to supply it, but it will be able to do so only for short periods before the voltage drops to an insufficient level. Your system will not be able to play at its full potential for any significant length of time.

There are several things you can do to increase the performance of your electrical system. First, you can replace the stock alternator with a high-output alternator, the single most important modification you can make. There are many high-output alternators on the market, with outputs ranging from 105 to 190 amps at full load.

When comparing these alternators, there are several important questions you should ask, the first probably being, Will it fit? Some high-output alternators replace Original Equipment Manufacturer (OEM) equipment bolt for bolt. If this isn't the case, you'll have to construct custom brackets; this is a very involved and time-consuming task.

The most important specification to query is the alternator's *current rating*. Make sure all ratings are for a hot alternator; output current usually drops as the unit heats up to its normal working temperature. Find out what the output current is at both *idle RPM* and *highway RPM*. When comparing alternators in this manner, make sure both units have pulleys of the same size and thus the same rotor speed.

The last question you will have to ask concerns *regulation*. Some alternators have *internal* regulation, while others have *external* regulation. I recommend using external regulation, if possible, since this type makes it easier to adjust the electrical system's voltage.

Using multiple batteries will also improve the performance of your electrical system. The extra battery or batteries will supply additional power to the system when the current demands of the amplifiers exceed the full output capability of the alternator. Multiple batteries also allow you to play your sound system longer when you're parked and the engine is shut off.

Ideally, you should opt for a high-output alternator and additional batteries. A good rule of thumb is to use the largest alternator you can fit on the engine and an additional battery for every 500 W of amplification.

There are many types of batteries available, of course—which one is right for you? For audio installations, experience has shown that the best results will be obtained using deep-cycle marine batteries. These batteries can be obtained from almost any dealer for approximately $60. *Lead-acid batteries* are preferred over calcium-based (*maintenance-free*) batteries because of their superior internal characteristics. Maintenance-free batteries are usually designed to provide a large amount of current for a short period of time. This is great for starting your car but not so great for running a high-powered system.

Deep-cycle marine batteries, on the other hand, are designed to provide a moderate-to-large amount of current over a long period of time. The plates in each cell are thicker, and they are made for deep, cyclic use. This is important because you can severely drain this type of battery without damaging it, which is ideal for car audio installations.

There are three ratings you should check out when selecting a battery. The first is the cold-cranking amps (CCA) rating. This indicates a battery's ability to provide a large amount of current for a short period of time at cold temperatures. (If you're looking for a battery that will be used just to start your car, this is the rating you would be most interested in.)

The second rating, and the one that is most important in terms of your system, is the amp/hour (AH) rating. This rating simply states how much current the battery is capable of delivering for a period of time. The greater the rating, the better. Typical deep-cycle marine batteries have AH ratings of 85 to 105.

Continued

Continued

The third rating you should look at is *reserve time*. Deep-cycle marine batteries really shine here. Reserve time represents the battery's ability to recover and produce electrical energy after a discharge cycle—without recharging. The longer the reserve time, the better.

Installing the extra battery (or batteries) in parallel will result in the most efficient use of its (their) power. When using this method of connection, your total AH rating is the sum of the AH ratings of all of your batteries. Note that batteries installed in this manner should be identical (the same make and model). If they're not the same, their internal impedances will differ and, eventually, one battery will discharge the other.

When wiring the electrical system, don't skimp on large-gauge wire. Welding cable is preferable because of its tough outer jacket, fine wire strands, and good flexibility. The bottom line is that you should never use less than No. 4 wire. Also, don't forget to install 150-amp circuit breakers at each end of the power cable running from the front to the rear of the car. The circuit breakers will protect the vehicle in case of a short somewhere along the length of the cable.

It's important to take the time to plan out your electrical system. A properly designed and installed system will provide a good foundation for your auto sound components while maintaining reliability and safety. The audibly superior performance will be well worth the added time and expense.

What You Will Need

Most of these items you can pick up at a local Radio Shack or hardware store, and may come in handy on any number of other projects (like ingredients for recipes).

- **Two People**—Although you could do this yourself, it's much easier to work as a team for running the wires, holding the flashlight, and so forth.

- **Street Wires® Power Delivery Kit™ Battery Cable**—You need at least 8 gauge or similar for running under the hood (but their package comes with a lot of good stuff and high-quality cable) and 10 feet or longer depending on your vehicle and where your battery is located. This kit (shown in Figure 3-2) comes with the ring terminals you need for connecting power to the battery. You can pick this up for about $35 from Circuit City.

Note   Some stores will have the full Street Wires display that helps you decide which wiring kit is right for your car. It will be obvious when you see it, so use it. You can also check the Street Wires Web site at www.streetwires.com for research and information.

FIGURE 3-2: The Street Wires® Power Delivery Kit for connecting the battery to the barrier terminal strip. Note that it comes with ring connectors.

- **Battery Barrier Terminal Strip**—Find the strip that will work for up to four devices (has eight ring screw connectors; approximately $2.29 from Radio Shack), as shown in Figure 3-3.

- **Twenty-Two (22) Gauge Wire, Stranded**—For connecting device on the inside of your vehicle (see Figure 3-4). If you're just running the battery terminal strip and not connecting any devices as part of this project, you can ignore this piece (about $5.49 from Radio Shack).

FIGURE 3-3: The battery barrier terminal strip to which
everything is ultimately connected.

Warning You can't just use any type of wire under your hood! Make sure you have wiring made specifically for car environments, and for under the hood. The intense heat could cause your sheathing and wires to melt and create a very dangerous situation! This is especially true if a live wire ignites any fluids or gasses. The Street Wires cable recommended in this project should work very well. However, you may want to verify this with your car dealer based on your particular vehicle's specifications.

- **Coat Hanger**—To feed power wire through your car's firewall (free!).

- **Shrink Tubing**—For connecting car computer power outputs to extended wire connections. If you're just running the battery terminal strip for use later, you can ignore this piece (about $3).

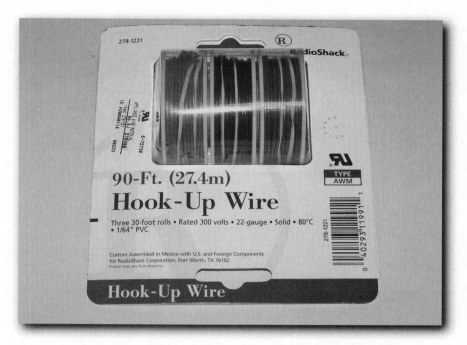

FIGURE 3-4: Hookup wire used for connection to the battery barrier terminal strip.

- **Soldering Iron**—For soldering car computer power cables to extended wires. If you're just running the battery terminal strip for use later, you can ignore this piece (borrow a friend's for free or pay around $8 for your own).

- **Soldering Wire**—For use with the soldering iron to link the cables together. If you're just running the battery terminal strip for use later, you can ignore this piece (about $2)

- **Heating Element**—For shrinking the shrink tubing to the wires. If you're just running the battery terminal strip for use later, you can ignore this piece (about $5). You can also just use a hair dryer on "High" setting.

- **Wire Crimper or Crimping Tool**—For crimping ring connectors and fork connectors to cable ends (about $10).

- **Crimpers**—For crimping wires together. Figure 3-5 shows some of the basic tools used for this project.

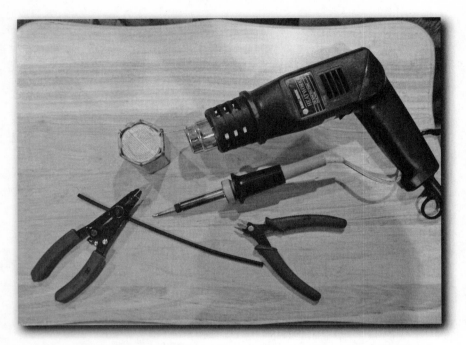

FIGURE 3-5: Tools used include a soldering iron, needle-nose pliers, wire cutter, shrink tubing, and soldering wire.

- **Ring Connectors**—For the ends of wires so you can connect them to the barrier terminal strip shown in Figure 3-6.

- **Six (or more) Appropriately Sized Screws to Connect the Barrier Terminal Strip**—About $6 if you buy a complete set of different screws; less if you just buy a few—check your hardware store. The screw size will vary on what barrier terminal strip you purchase. Having a set of different screw sizes is helpful for many of the projects in this book.

- **Rubber Washers**—To seal the holes under the screws you use (about $1).

- **Electrical Tape**—For wrapping cables and wires (about $2).

- **Socket Wrench Set and Screwdriver Set**—Every car is different, so it's always best to have a full socket wrench and screwdriver set to handle many different projects (about $20–$50).

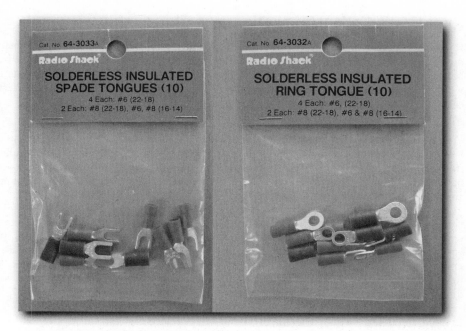

FIGURE 3-6: Ring and spade connectors.

Note

This project requires a small amount of soldering work because you will need to extend some wires.

If you decide not to let the ignition switch decide whether power can be supplied, you may run into some issues with draining your battery. For example, if you continuously provide power to your devices and you forget to turn them off when you leave your car, you could come back to a dead battery. An AC inverter usually gets around this problem because many inverters can sense when a battery is close to being fully drained and stop drawing power. When connected directly to the battery, you don't have such a luxury and may not be able to start your car.

Warning

It is *imperative* that you keep the battery disconnected the entire time you do this project. I don't want you getting shocked or injured from playing with live wires. The only time your battery should be connected is when you go to test that power is successfully running to the battery terminal, computer, or device. If you are not comfortable working with power systems and cabling, you should ask a professional installer to do this part for you. Once you have disconnected the main (usually red) positive battery cable, it is best to keep it in a plastic bag well away from the battery terminal until you need to reconnect it.

Know Your Car's Wiring Diagrams Thoroughly

It pays to be prepared, both in terms of safety and in saving time spent fixing things (hopefully, none is necessary). Before you connect any device directly to your car's power system, you had better know what you're connecting to. By far the easiest way to do this is by studying your car's wiring diagram. Wiring diagrams show you every electrical system in your car, how the electrical system is connected to other systems (such as the car's battery and alternator), as well as all wire colors, fuses, and other important wiring details.

Wiring diagrams are often available in book or loose-leaf form from your car dealer if your car isn't too old (the service department can likely get manuals from at least 10 years ago), online from manufacturers and auction sites, third-party suppliers, and auto enthusiast clubs for your particular vehicle. My Mazda dealer was kind enough to let me go to a local store and photocopy theirs (at my expense, of course).

Note

If your own dealer won't help you, ask another one or ask an enthusiast group for the diagrams online. Auto manufacturers are trying to get away from printed maintenance publications, so your dealer may be able to get you an electronic version (often times a PDF) of the wiring diagram—just check with them for details. You can also check with your auto manufacturer directly. Refer to Appendix C, "Additional Resources" for the online service technician Web sites for many auto manufacturers.

Looking through the wiring diagram, my friend and I decided the best course of action was to hook into the windshield wiper system's power. This is a noncritical system (at least where I live), so if we blew the fuse while testing power or running the computer, it's not a big deal. Other options may be fuses for your radio or dome lights. You don't want to connect to any critical systems, such as SRS (airbag) or turn signals—this should all be well defined in your car's wiring diagram.

Prewiring the Device

Before you even step near the car, you must decide where you are going to tap into the car's power system. As mentioned in the preceding section, for this project, I chose the windshield wiper system.

You should also prepare the computer power supply for connection to the battery terminal strip you are about to install. It is obviously best to do this indoors or in a workshop area since a car is not an ideal location for soldering. You can skip to "Preparing the Car" if you're not installing a device similar to what my friend and I did.

This step is very easy, especially if you know how to solder! Simply solder the ends of the 18 guage wire to the ends of the computer power supply wires so you can run any length of wire needed to the battery terminal strip once it is installed.

The following steps cover how to prepare the wiring for your devices:

1. Give yourself some slack and strip the wires so you can solder the connectors together, as shown in Figure 3-7.

FIGURE 3-7: The wiring and the ends of the computer power cables you are about to connect it to.

2. Wrap the shrink tubing around the wires after you solder them, as shown in Figure 3-8.

FIGURE 3-8: Put the shrink tubing over the wires.

3. Solder the wires together. In this case (even though this book is black and white) use red for ignition, green for power, and black for ground. Never fear, for those Kodachrome® lovers out there, I will make these images available in color on the *Geek My Ride* Web site! First straighten out the stranded wire and then twist the wires together helically (one around the other) and then solder them together as illustrated in Figure 3-9. This is called *splaying* the wire.

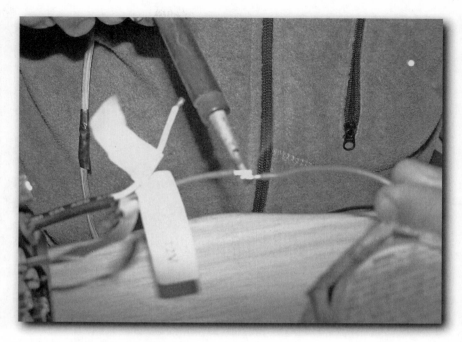

FIGURE 3-9: Solder the wires together.

Note

Make sure you heat the wire with the soldering iron and apply the solder to the wire, not to the soldering iron. When the wire takes the solder, you know it's hot enough to take; otherwise, you get what's called a *cold solder joint*. Cold solder joints will fail under high current because only a few strands of copper are actually carrying the current, not all the strands (which is your goal).

4. Now that the wires are soldered together, you can shrink the shrink tubing as illustrated in Figure 3-10, and you're done preparing the device!

Note

If you can't find what you need for the shrink tubing, you could use tightly wound electrical tape, but I recommend shrink tubing both for its effectiveness and good looks.

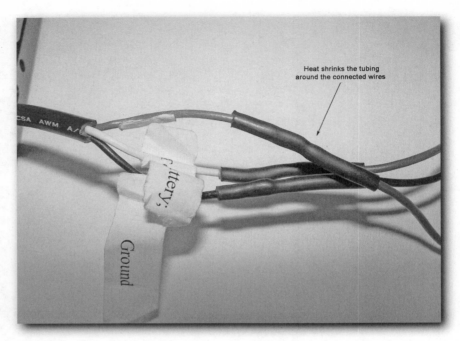

FIGURE 3-10: Use a heater to shrink the tubing around the wires so it doesn't come loose.

Now you can see the finished product, ready for installation to the battery terminal strip (see Figure 3-11).

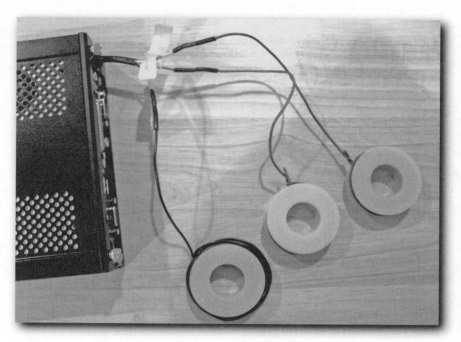

FIGURE 3-11: The finished product, with shrink tubing in place and ready for extending wires as long as you need them.

Tip

To make removing your computer from your car easier, you may want to use quick-disconnect connectors on the end of your power connectors instead of the more permanent shrink-tubing solution. This way, you can easily disconnect your computer from your car and bring it upstairs to work on. To get power to a computer with a DC power supply, you can either purchase a DC power inverter or temporarily swap out the DC power supply in the computer with an AC solution. Make sure you buy connectors that are both *fully insulated* and appropriate for the gauge of wire you are connecting (this will be clearly marked on the connector packaging), as shown in Figure 3-12. Quick-disconnect connectors can be picked up for under $10, and DC power supplies can be picked up for under $200 at any electronics store, such as Radio Shack.

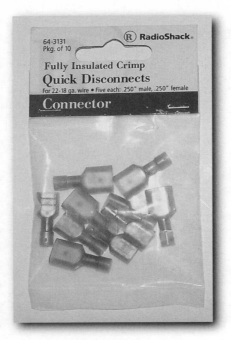

FIGURE **3-12: Fully insulated quick-disconnect connectors.**

Preparing the Car

Now that you have the device ready, you need to prepare the car for installing the battery barrier terminal strip (refer to Figure 3-3). The first thing you need to do is plan the following:

- Where the battery is (under the hood, stored in the trunk, located under a car seat)
- Where the power cable needs to be run
- Where the barrier terminator strip will be placed

Locate Your Battery

Since you're going to connect to the car's battery for power, it's obviously best to know where the battery is. You shouldn't have any trouble finding it, of course. Pay attention to how far away the battery is from the car's firewall and which side of the car it's on. Also pay attention to whether there are fans or belts nearby and to how close the battery is to the engine and hot surfaces. You don't want the power cable you run to get caught in the fans or melt because it's on a super-hot surface.

Luckily for me, in my Mazda Protégé 5 the battery is on the driver's side and near the car's firewall. This made the wire easy to run (around the side, and for a very short distance). If the battery is far from the car's firewall, you just need to run more cable, which will run along the side of the car (again, away from any belts or fans), and then can cross over to the battery.

Determine Where to Run the Power Cable

Once you know where your battery is, you need to find where you can safely run the power cable from your battery and through the *firewall* in your car. The firewall is the portion separating the passenger compartment from the engine compartment. Don't worry, you're not going to need to drill through your car's metal frame. Instead, you'll be running through holes already poked through your firewall for your car's other power wires.

When batteries are located inside the car, such as under a seat or in the trunk, the firewall routing problem lessens. That is, *if* the main fuse block is also near the battery. Sometimes the fuses are in the trunk, under the dash, behind a glove box, under a protective air-inlet cowling, and so on. Make sure you know before you start!

Look toward the back of the engine compartment to see where other power cables are running. The easiest way to do this is to start from the fuse box and follow those cables, because they should lead to the fuse box in your passenger compartment. If you install everything in the fuse box areas, it will probably be easier to gain access to power cabling and keep all of your power centralized in your vehicle. Your car's owners manual should tell you where the fuse boxes are located under the hood and inside your car.

When you determine where the fuse box is inside the car, you can decide how to run the power cable through the area in the firewall where the cables leading to it are running. In Figure 3-13 you can see where the battery is in my car, and in Figure 3-14 you can see where the wires leading from the fuse box run through the firewall into the passenger compartment.

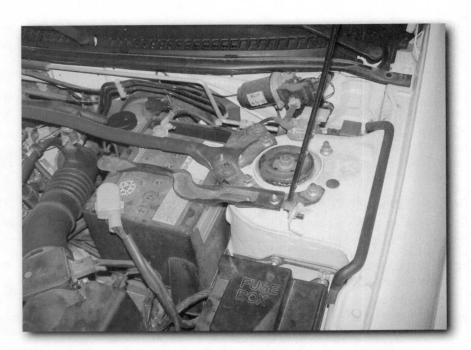

FIGURE 3-13: The battery (center) and the firewall (back, white, under the windshield).

Determine Where You Will Install the Battery Terminal

Now that you know where you are going to connect the power cable and run through the firewall, you need to determine where to place the battery barrier terminal strip in the passenger compartment. As I mentioned earlier, if you can put it in the fuse box, you'll keep your power centralized. In this project, you will do exactly that. If the barrier terminal strip doesn't fit in the fuse box or on the inside of its casing (although it usually will fit just fine), attach the barrier terminal strip to nearby plastic, away from legs or other wires. If the strip is exposed to the open air of your vehicle, find a piece of plastic and a latch from a hardware store and make a drop-down cover to protect it from exposure to other wires in its proximity.

FIGURE 3-14: The area where the flashlight points is where the wires pass through the firewall into the passenger compartment.

Running the Power Cable

Now that you know where everything is, it's time to get started!

1. First: *Disconnect the battery cable from the positive terminal on the battery* (see Figure 3-15). Like I said earlier, protect the removed cable in a plastic bag.

Warning

While you do this, do not touch any metal on the car with your bare skin, and *never* bridge the positive and negative terminals or you could be seriously injured or even killed. I don't want you to get hurt! Second thing: *make sure the engine compartment is cool*. There is no reason to get burned. While you do this you should also have plenty of light, but that should be a given.

FIGURE 3-15: Disconnect the power cable from the positive terminal on the battery.

2. Once the battery is disconnected, you need to feed the power wire through the firewall from the passenger compartment to the engine compartment.

Find the place where the wires are coming through the firewall first. To do this, unwind the coat hanger so it's straightened out and run one end of it through until you can see it in the rubber seal. You can poke through the rubber seal, *but be careful not to poke through any wires!* Once you can see the coat hanger in the engine compartment (this is where having a friend comes in very handy), pull it up a bit and take the long blue Street Wires main power cable (it tends to be thick and blue, refer to Figure 3-2) and tape the wire end to the other end of the coat hanger as shown in Figure 3-16.

Tip

If you can't poke through the seal, you can go around it, but you may invite water and other elements into your vehicle. I suggest you reseal after you've run the right length of wire to keep your vehicle (and the exposed wires) protected. Silicone rubber will ensure a good water-proof and heat resistant seal. However, once used, your wires will no longer slip through easily—the silicone rubber bead contact area would need to be sliced away first.

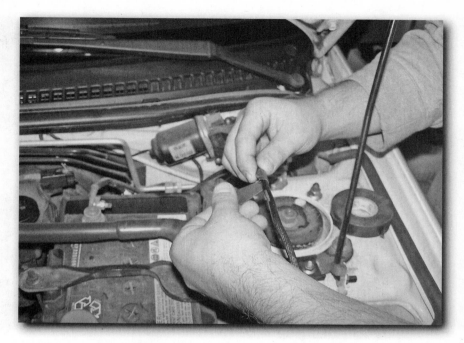

FIGURE 3-16: Wrap electrical tape around the power wire and coat hanger.

Warning Only use quality electrical tape when running these wires. Do not use masking tape, duct tape, scotch tape, or similar, because they are not made for electrical applications!

3. Now pull the coat hanger with the wire attached through the hole in the seal into the passenger compartment, as shown in Figures 3-17 through 3-19. Don't use the short Street Wires cable; it will be used to connect from the fuse to the battery!

FIGURE 3-17: Run the attached power cable through the firewall.

Note the wire you're running here is near the fuel line, which shouldn't get hot. Also, you're running *very* well-insulated wire, so you should be safe from heat and sparks. The pipes near where you run the cable in your car may, of course, vary.

FIGURE 3-18: The power cable (center) runs through the firewall.

Warning

If your wiring needs to run near or across any fuel lines or pollution-control plumbing or wiring, you may want to increase the wire's insulation thickness at those points using fiberglass electrical tape, ribbed tubing, or insulating spacer. Although there was little choice here, it is best to stay away from fuel lines and other combustible lines if a wire shorts and melts.

Tip

Whenever and wherever possible, *label your wires* with either slip-on writable tags or markers. You, your service center, and the next car owner will appreciate these wires being labeled.

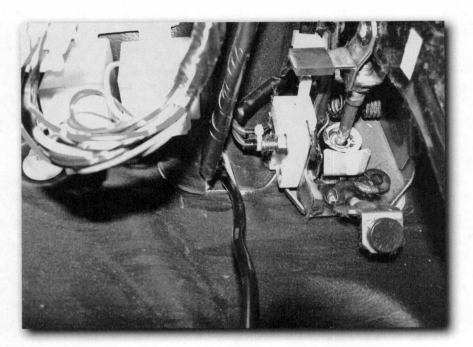

FIGURE 3-19: The power cable connected to the hanger passing into the engine compartment.

Connecting the External Fuse

Now that you've run the power cable, you need to connect it to its fuse and mount it so it doesn't move while the car is moving.

1. When my friend and I worked on my car, we decided to mount the fuse on the fuse box cover because it was close to the battery and was a plastic surface we could easily screw it on to. The Street Wires set came with a mountable fuse, but we had to get our own screws. The type of screw you use may vary, depending on what product you use, of course.

Note The fuse rating should be *no more* than the maximum current needed to run your equipment plus an additional 20%. So, if your system draws 10 amps, using a 12-amp fuse is fine; however, using a 15-amp fuse may be too much.

2. In Figure 3-20, you can see where we ran the power cable along the side of the engine compartment and over to the battery. Then, as shown in Figure 3-21, we mounted the fuse to the fuse box by screwing it to the plastic case. Make sure you use the rubber washers under the screws so you can keep water out! As stated earlier, a thin bead of silicone rubber can help ensure a good water-tight seal.

FIGURE 3-20: The power cable runs along the side of the vehicle (right).

FIGURE 3-21: The mounted fuse on the side of the fuse box.

3. Now take the car's battery cable and unscrew it and attach the ring terminal from the Street Wires short blue power cable to the battery connector, as shown in Figure 3-22.

4. This allows you to run the power from the battery—how easy! Use the cable ties that come with the Street Wires kit to bind the battery power cable and the Street Wires cable together so they don't move around (this also helps keep everything organized). After you disconnect the battery and strip-tie it to the Street Wires cable, protect the end of the battery cable by placing it in a plastic bag so it doesn't touch anything else in the engine compartment, and especially keep it away from the positive battery terminal so you don't shock yourself while working on this project.

FIGURE 3-22: Unscrew the battery cable and attach the Street Wires ring connector.

Warning

Make sure the wires do *not* run near moving surfaces (throttle or choke cables, hood release, etc.) and do not come too close to hot surfaces.

Figure 3-23 shows how the product will look when you finally reconnect the battery. (*Don't connect the battery yet*—this is just an example!)

FIGURE 3-23: The battery cable and the power cable run to the battery.

Preparing the Barrier Terminal Strip

Now that the power cable has been run, you need to prepare the barrier terminal strip for expansion. Doing this enables you to add as many as four devices to your new power source from the inside of the car (or more, if you purchased a barrier terminal strip with more than eight connectors).

Take the strip and bridge the four screws on one end with wire, as shown in Figure 3-24.

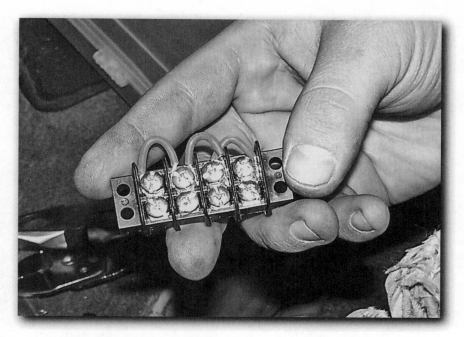

FIGURE 3-24: The bridged barrier strip terminals.

Connecting the Battery Barrier Terminal Strip

Now that the strip is bridged, you are ready to finally attach the power cable to it.

1. Determine how much of the Street Wires power cable you still need and give yourself about an extra foot of slack.

2. Cut and strip the wire to expose the stranded wire. Connect a ring connector to the exposed wire.

3. Now, insert the wire into a ring connector and crimp the two together when it's in there good and tight, so it won't budge. Test the connection by trying to pull the wire out. It should not budge.

4. Once the ring connector is attached, connect it to the bridged side of the terminal strip, as shown in Figures 3-25 and 3-26. This enables power to flow across the strip and leaves all four terminals open to easily connect device power cables.

This barrier strip vibrates quite a bit, so make sure the screws are tight, and check them for tightness in the first days and weeks after your installation. Very high vibration may necessitate using serrated lock-washers under the terminals, which resist vibration better than bare screws and terminals alone. You may also want to use thick rubber washers to absorb some of the vibration.

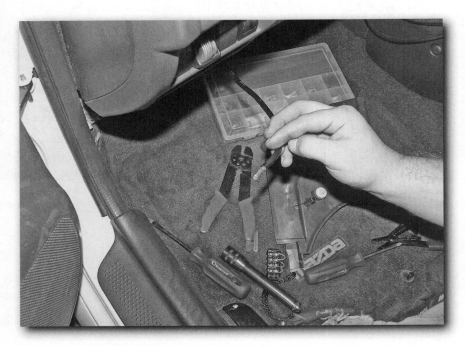

FIGURE 3-25: The exposed, stripped end of the power cable.

FIGURE 3-26: The power cable with attached ring connector and the bridged barrier terminal strip it connects to.

Mounting the Barrier Terminal Strip

Now that we have the cables connected, it's time to mount the terminal strip. Earlier I mentioned that my friend and I decided to mount the strip inside the passenger compartment fuse box cover. Using a razor blade, we sliced off some of the plastic to make room for the strip and mounted the strip in the same way we did the fuse in the engine compartment as shown in Figure 3-27.

FIGURE 3-27: The barrier terminal strip connected to the fuse box cover.

Connecting the Computer Power Cables

Now that you have the battery power prepared, you need to tie the computer power to a ground, the new barrier strip, and the ignition switch. The power-stepping module in the installed computer's power supply keeps the computer on for a few moments after the switch has been turned off to give the computer time to properly shut down (computer power-stepping units are discussed in Chapter 11, "Adding a General-Purpose PC"). It gets this power from the barrier strip. However, it only knows when to turn on and off when the ignition switch is turned, so we must connect to that as well. The ground is obvious—you need to ground the power supply in the computer. Always connect the ground first. This protects you and your equipment, especially from the perspective of static electricity.

Warning

It is very dangerous to have the barrier terminal strip exposed. Keep it mounted and hidden—do *not* let it float around in the open, which is very dangerous. (After all, it's like a live power socket!)

Note

If you are not going to use the computer for a long time, such as when you go on vacation, it is a good idea to temporarily disconnect it from the barrier terminal strip. Even when the car and computer are off, the PSU (power-stepping unit) still uses a nominal amount of power. For day-to-day use, however, you need not worry. Earlier, I mentioned quick-disconnect wire connectors—this is one situation where those come in handy.

Connecting Computer Power to the Ignition

Based on the wiring diagram, my friend and I found that the ignition wire was a black and red wire behind the fuse box. You need to connect our computer's ignition-monitoring wire to this cable, and for that you simply use a special crimp. Consider using a 12 V lamp (available from almost any hardware store, possibly even Walmart) between ground and the suspected ignition wire to ensure you have located the right connection. In my case, I had to connect the Street Wires ignition cable (in this case it was red) to the black and red cable and crimp them together. The color of your car's cables will likely vary, so make sure you read and understand your wiring diagram well *before you crimp.*

Grounding the Computer Power

Connecting the ground for the computer's power supply is as easy as finding a screw mounted to the car's frame. If you are installing a ground screw for the first time, ensure it is a good ground by testing it with a lamp or voltmeter to the ignition switch "hot" side. In my car's case, there was already a "grounding" screw in the fuse box. To connect to it we added a ring connector to the end of our computer power supply's ground wire, unscrewed the grounding screw, put our ring connector under it, and screwed it back in. See Figure 3-28 for what the finished product looks like. Look at that, another easy step!

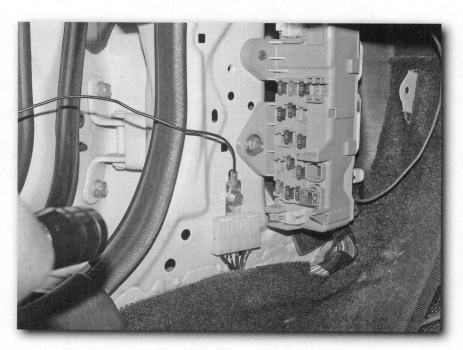

FIGURE 3-28: Connect the ground to the grounding screw next to the fuse box.

Attaching the Computer Power Supply

Now that you have the fuse box connected, you can connect the power to the computer.

1. Make sure you know where you want to locate the computer. Ideally you should place your computer in a location away from heat sources and solar exposure and where your normal luggage movements will not be impeded or blocked.

2. Also, make sure the computer's media slots are not blocked (such as the CD or DVD drives, USB ports, and so on) or you won't be able to plug things in or change media.

3. Once you know where you want it, run the power cables to where the barrier strip is, giving yourself about 2 or 3 feet of slack, just in case you need to move the computer later. See Figure 3-29 for what the finished product looks like. That's it!

FIGURE 3-29: The power cable from the computer connecting to the barrier terminal strip. Note the ring connector is used to keep the connection clean and easy to both disconnect and reconnect.

Reconnecting the Battery

Now that you've hooked up the computer, you need to test to make sure the computer powers on. Reconnect the battery carefully, making sure the Street Wires cable is snugly connected before you screw it back onto the battery terminal. Don't touch the metal of the car while reconnecting the battery or you may get shocked.

Warning

Use a single hand to connect the wire wherever possible—try not to touch ground and hot wires at any time. Also, never let the same piece of metal touch both the positive and negative terminals of the battery or you could be seriously injured or even killed!

Figure 3-29 shows what the terminal will look like if properly connected. Note you should keep the positive battery terminal covered at all times, such as with a plastic bag as suggested earlier.

Testing

This part is simple. Once the battery is reconnected, turn the ignition switch and see whether the computer comes up. If all was done right, it should! Ours worked on the first try, and if you followed the instructions here, and your computer was built properly, yours should, too!

Troubleshooting

If the computer isn't powering up, make sure all of your connections are solid. Also, make sure no wires have come loose with all of the wiring you have been working with. If you are going to work with the power cables again, make sure to disconnect the battery first (as described earlier in this chapter). If you still can't get power, check your fuses, verify the power supply on the computer is still good, and revisit your vehicle wiring diagram to make sure you plugged into the right wires. A voltmeter, 12 V test lamp, and wiring harness diagram or schematic will be of tremendous help in finding the problem.

Summary

This chapter went over the various ways to power the projects proposed in later chapters (and for other projects you may create on your own). You can usually switch between the options in this chapter as you choose, such as moving from an AC inverter to the direct power solution, and possibly back if you share your equipment across more than one car. Try to stick to your decision once you've made it when it comes to power, as switching how you will power a device mid-project can cause complications such as starting the whole project over or leaving a bunch of wires lying around while you replan, which is bad if you have only one vehicle!

It's So Hot in Here: Dealing with Heat

This is a hot topic (sorry). Whether in the searing heat of summer or the chilling cold of winter, temperature *will* affect your car electronics. As I stated in Chapter 1, "Planning Your Projects," the electronics that you keep at home are in a climate-controlled environment, whereas your car is subjected not only to the harshest elements on the outside, it experiences vast differences in temperatures on the inside. In the winter, your car can easily experience temperatures of –22°F (–30°C), and over 212°F (100°C) in summer. This is especially true if you have a black or dark-colored car, because the "color" black (yeah, I know it's not really a color) absorbs all light energy, transforming kilowatts of solar light energy to kilowatts of heat.

Did You Know

Car windows tend to let all types of light in, but don't let infrared light out. Infrared accompanies heat, making cars perfect solar ovens and thus making it very hot in your car during summer and even warm on a winter day. Technically speaking, the heat energy is from *black body radiation*. This is called the *greenhouse effect,* named for windows being used in greenhouses to keep such converted infrared light energy in to keep plants warm. Placing a tint on your vehicle that halves visible solar rays can considerably lower the heat buildup in your vehicle.

Colorado Ain't Florida Ain't Alaska

Where you intend to drive your vehicle after you've added the various projects in this book (or elsewhere) has a great deal of influence on what items you must take into consideration for or during placement in your vehicle. For example, if you live in Palm Springs, where it's 80°F (27°C) to 110°F (42°C) most of the year, you will have to deal with heat issues more often. In Alaska, where the temperatures can get to more than 50°F degrees below zero (–45°C), many computer components may not even start up, and can even be permanently damaged by extreme cold weather. If you thought weather was your only problem, consider Colorado, with some areas sporting altitudes of over 10,000 feet above sea level. Some computer hard drive air seals may not work well above 6,000 feet (although for the most part, there's very little you can do about that).

Cooling fans have only half the effectiveness at mountain altitudes as they do at sea level.

Your own experiences in your own climate will surely affect how you deploy the various projects you build. For example, you will most likely know the coolest place to keep your equipment in your car (or the warmer areas, if you're in extreme cold). Determine where these locations are before you build, and your creation will definitely last longer!

Pay Attention to Heat Specifications

When purchasing equipment for your car computer, pay close attention to the heat specifications, or what's usually called *operating specifications*, in the owner's manual. If the equipment cannot take extreme cold or heat, depending on your climate, you may need to take measures to mitigate the heat concerns. When adding a computer to your vehicle, you have many options to buy *hardened* equipment, which is equipment that has been specially treated for severe conditions of heat or cold, high shock, and other abnormal environments and extremes. However, with devices such as gaming consoles you may not have the luxury, and those systems' manuals generally do not list operating specifications. As a guide, most popular modern gaming systems can tolerate a minimum of 50°F–86°F (10°C–30°C) and a maximum of 122°F–212°F (50°C–100°C) maximum.

As you can see, you need to protect the electronics built for home environments that are placed into your vehicle. However, besides those, you can buy equipment made specifically for vehicles. For example, there are many LCD displays that work great in a vehicle and can easily withstand the temperature and glaring sunlight. The same is true for *vehicle hardened* VCRs and DVD players. When you go out shopping for equipment to place in your car, most devices will have operating specifications right on the box—pay attention to those and make sure they work with the climates you will experience when the car is *off* (unless you have no air conditioning, in which case you need to consider heat inside your car when attempting to cool it off).

Be careful with batteries! Many devices you place in your vehicle will require batteries. For example, wireless keyboards and mice, wireless game controllers, and remote controls all tend to require AA or AAA batteries. Some portable devices may use lithium-ion batteries, which are not friendly to high-temperature environments. Batteries leak or explode in high temperatures, and almost surely lose capacity when subjected to temperature extremes outside of traditional indoor temperatures, so keep battery-powered devices out of the sunlight. Refer to Figure 1-1 in Chapter 1 for a picture of a keyboard stowed away in a door side panel, keeping the keyboard easily accessible *and* away from direct sunlight.

Beating the Heat

The next few sections give you some ideas on how you can effectively deal with the heat.

So What's Your Case?

Most computer and console cases were never meant for the extreme heat a vehicle can experience. Choose your case wisely, following these tips:

- Metal computer cases can heat up very quickly. Aluminum cases are preferred because they dissipate heat evenly and quickly.

- Try to have a white or light-colored case; black cases absorb more heat.

- Be wary of using plastic cases unless they are tempered for 180°F (82°C) or above. To test this at your own risk, heat your home oven to 200°F (93°C) and see how your case handles it on aluminum foil for several minutes.

- Note that the plastic upholstery in your car is tested for temperatures above about 392°F (200°C), and about –58°F (–50°C) below.

Is the Heat in a Small Car Higher Than in a Large Car?

From MadSci.org (www.madsci.org/posts/archives/dec2000/975942563.Ph.r.html)

If you parked a large and a small car side-by-side on an asphalt parking lot in Phoenix, Arizona, I don't think you would be able to perceive that one was hotter than the other. If there were a difference, it might be due to one of the following:

- In a larger car, the hotter air may rise farther—so that the temperature difference noted may be partly due to the position of the thermometer relative to the top of the vehicle. For instance, if you were to glue a thermometer to the top and the bottom of the large and the small cars (both thermometers inside the compartment), you *might* note the temperature differences between cars were larger for the thermometers glued to the floors. Most of that difference would be due to air circulation inside the vehicle.

- In a larger car, usually also a more expensive car, there is "more car" to be heated (the car can absorb more heat—greater thermal capacity). Though the larger car could eventually be heated to comparable interior temperatures, the amount of time needed (except in Phoenix) would exceed the amount of time a car would generally be parked in full sun. So, with the same thermometers used before, if you recorded temperatures at regular time intervals, you should note that the smaller car heats faster initially but the larger car interior tends to reach comparable temperatures if the experiment is allowed to continue long enough.

- If the temperature difference is based upon perception rather than a thermometer reading, then the difference may also be due to the occupant being closer to the thermal radiating surfaces of the smaller vehicle.

The best reference for this sort of dialog—more a practical engineering guesstimate—is a university-level heat transfer textbook. But, to be certain, you might want to try experimenting with thermometers in the manner described in this section.

Placement Matters

When deciding where to place system components in your vehicle, you must take heat into consideration. Most computer projects in this book do not require the computer to be fully exposed to the user, let alone the sun. Keep your equipment in cooler, shady places in your vehicle, such as the trunk or under the seat. If you are purchasing a DVD player or VCR, keep in mind that heat of any kind can easily warp discs and melt tapes. If a device is used once before you drive (for example, loading a DVD video to watch), keep it in the trunk (preferably) or if that's not feasible or it needs to be accessed often, under a seat and away from kicking feet.

Tip An ideal place for a car computer to mitigate temperature concerns is in the spare tire compartment, where there is appropriate airflow and the computer can be bolted to the car frame. This of course assumes your tire is not underneath the car and facing the road, or mounted adjacent to the fuel tank (be careful where you drill!). Many vehicles have their spare tire compartment in the trunk under a mat.

Indeed, some projects may require their slots to be exposed. For example, a computer's CD or DVD drive, USB ports, and so on may need to be used by passengers. Try to place these items in accessible but shady areas, such as the center console. Keep in mind that, if you do put a device in the center console *and* you have a sunroof, be sure the sun shining on any devices you add won't damage them (such as heat-sensitive devices plugged into a console-mounted USB hub). The fundamental general computer project in this book will cover building a computer and placing it directly into your dash, under your seat, or in the trunk.

Adding an iPod® or Digital Media Player to Your Car

If you plan on keeping a digital music player in your car, you need to keep it in the shade as well. The screens on iPods, and most digital media players, were never made to be exposed to direct sunlight for long periods of time. They were made to be in a home or on a hip with a breeze running over them. Just because they're "portable" doesn't mean they enjoy a sun tan (or getting burnt)! A friend of mine mitigated this issue by adding RCA jacks to the center console of his Acura, so he can leave his iPod in the console and use his car stereo's Auxiliary Input feature to hear his music. See Chapter 9, "Building a Single-Source A/V System" for a side project to show you how to add the same to your car.

If your stereo doesn't have an auxiliary audio input feature (some support auxiliary video sources as well), you can use radio transmission substitutes that transmit your digital media device's audio over short-range FM radio to your car's stereo and you can just tune in your music. Cool! For iPods, a popular product is the Griffin iTrip (www.griffintechnology.com), while other products include the Belkin TuneCast, NewerTech RoadTrip, and many more (check your local Best Buy, Circuit City, CompUSA, or similar stores and you're sure to find many to choose from).

Keep It Flowing: Window Louvers

You obviously don't want to keep your car running the entire time you're in the store shopping. But since you have to worry about your car getting too hot, there's a solution: window louvers. These devices embed between the window and the frame (roll the window down, stick them in, roll the window up) and many use solar-powered fans to remove heat from your vehicle without using any batteries! There are also nonpowered louvers, but your chances of getting your car broken into may be higher (there aren't any fans to get in the way of the theive's coat hanger and hands).

Note The most popular method of cooling processors and other equipment in your computer and other components you add to your car is via fans. The primary function of fans is to circulate air around the device in an attempt to equalize temperatures between the surrounding air and the cooler air. Fans are not a panacea, however! If the surrounding air is hot, you're just circulating hot air over all your components, so you can't rely only on fans to keep your devices cool! Shade helps mitigate this problem to some extent. Some additional systems you may want to implement are the window louvers (discussed earlier) or possibly a liquid cooling system (for the computer). Liquid cooling systems can be expensive, and you need to make sure everything is incredibly well-fastened, so make sure if you go the liquid cooling route you fully test your computer on bumpy roads and with sudden stops (with nobody near your car, of course).

So What Can You Do about Sunlight?

Of all the enemies your equipment will have, sunlight, vibration, and shock will be the worst ones. Chapter 5, "Working with Cables," covers vibration and shock to a higher extent, but in this chapter I want to focus on that bright light bulb in the sky—the sun. The sun warms up our cars in winter and turns them into ovens in the summer. This is mainly due to infrared light energy passing through the vehicle and then not escaping, turning into that scathing heat you may feel when you open your car door in July, and why your car doesn't always get freezing cold in December (ever notice how much warmer it is in your car in winter?). Figure 4-1 shows a diagram of how this process works. When all wavelengths of light pass through vehicle windows and then hit any light-absorbing material, it converts into heat, and this heat cannot escape back through the window. This is also known as the *greenhouse effect*.

But sunlight doesn't just heat up your car. It also makes it hard for you to read existing gauges and status displays on your dashboard and, conversely, much of the instrumentation (such as an LCD screen) you may add to your car. If you can't see your computer display in the daylight, what's the point?

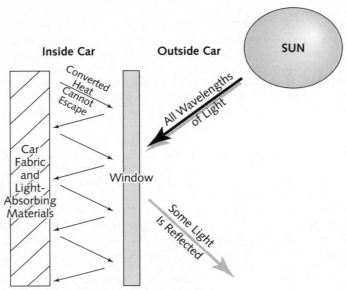

FIGURE 4-1: The greenhouse effect inside a car.

Here are some tips to help mitigate sunlight heat and vision issues:

- Consider tinting your vehicle. It's not unnecessarily expensive (on the order of a couple hundred dollars), and it usually looks pretty cool. It will also keep your car cooler and darker in one fell swoop, allowing you to use your devices sooner, cool your car more quickly, and see your instrumentation both in the day and at night.

- If tinting is not an option and you cannot read your devices' screens, consider placing a light control film (3M sells these as its Vikuiti™ line of products) to increase contrast and diminish glare.

Warning

If you tint your vehicle, check with the installer to make sure your tint level doesn't break the law. Many states have regulations over what percentage of tint you can have on your front windshield, and possibly other window surfaces. For example, in Indiana the highest amount of tint is a 30 (and the front windshield cannot be tinted past the rear-view mirror), which means 70% of light is blocked by the tinting film. It can be very dangerous if you get pulled over by the police and they can't see what you're doing. (A couple reasons those spotlights are so bright when the police officer pulls up behind you is so you can't see what the officer is doing and so they can see what's going on in your vehicle.) It is also important to consider that tint doesn't let any more light in at night, so tints that are too dark can actually impair your driving by infringing on your ability to see the road ahead.

Black Cars Gain and Lose Heat Faster Than White Cars

From MadSci.org (www.madsci.org/posts/archives/oct98/904941057.Ph.r.html)

For this discussion, we don't really care about the subatomic causes of heat or why black bodies are the best absorbers and emitters of electromagnetic radiation (EMR). We only care about three things:

1. Which parts of each car are sunlit?

- The majority of the direct sunlight will build up on the exposed surfaces of each car—the roof, the hood, the trunk. As a rough estimate, let's say that 20% of the light hits the interior directly. So 80% of the light is hitting the painted outer surfaces of each car.

- Now, about half of the EMR given off by the sun is in the infrared (IR) range. This is light with a wavelength longer than red light and that can't be seen by humans, but that still causes heating effects. Sunlight also includes a small portion of invisible ultraviolet (UV) light, which has wavelengths shorter than visible light. Keep this in mind as we move on to . . .

2. What materials are in the sunlit portions of each car, and which of those materials are better at absorbing and emitting heat?

- Basically, there are only two types of material here: metals and nonmetals. In any case, we've decided that most of the sunlight is falling on the body of the car, which is metal and paint.

- We know that sunlight includes IR and UV as well as visible light. Certain types of paint may reflect more or less IR and UV light than others. You may have heard of Light Reflectance Value (LRV), which is used to measure how much *visible light* a certain *color* reflects, but there's also a Solar Reflectance Index (SRI), which measures how much *solar heat* (i.e., infrared light) a given *material* reflects.

- For this discussion, we're only concerned with visible color, so we'll assume that all materials in the two cars reflect UV and IR equally well. Note that this may not be the case in real life.

- So what's reflecting the visible portion of sunlight? Metals are much better conductors, but, being naturally shiny, they don't absorb a lot of light. But—and this is important—it's the *paint* on the car that is *absorbing* the heat, and the metal *underneath* that is *conducting* and emitting heat through the entire car. The sheen (shininess) of the paint will affect its LRV, but we'll ignore that for the time being. Only the color matters.

Continued

Continued

3. Which of those materials has the most impact on the temperature inside the car?

- No contest. A car is mostly metal, and that metal surrounds all the interior areas. If the metal gets hot, the car gets hot.

If we look up the LRVs for the colors white and black, we find that white reflects 80% of visible sunlight, and black reflects only 5%. So we can conclude that, regardless of the color of the interior, the car with the darker paint job will have the higher temperature.

Of course, leaving any car out in the sun for many hours will make driving it later an unpleasant experience. My advice? Install air conditioning.

Summary

This chapter discussed the heat concerns for your vehicle. Knowing your climate conditions, planning the placement of your components related to heat, and making sure sunlight is controlled will help you enjoy and safely use the projects you build throughout this book. Tackling these issues before you start your projects will help you keep your equipment safe from possible damage, helping it last as long as it can.

Working with Cables

I f there's one thing you're definitely going to deal with a lot, it's cables. From running them to cutting them to hiding and "compromising," cables will make or break the appearance of what you've done—turning it from "man, that's just a mess" to "wow, where's all the stuff?" For all the occasions where you will be running cables in your car, this chapter will help you choose the right ones and make sure you put them in the right places. We will also cover cable placement on a project-by-project basis because sometimes you will have to tweak the tips found here based on the project you're working on.

Watch Those Cable Lengths!

The distance between computer devices in our home is usually much less than it is, or has to be, between devices in our car. For example, a USB hub may only be 2 feet away from the computer, while in a car it may need to be 8 feet away. Considering USB 1.1 cables are only intended to be up to 10 feet long, it becomes an issue if you're putting your computer in the trunk and want to have USB ports in the front of the car, especially if it's a mini-van or SUV. Extension cables don't solve the problem, and power adapters for the hub or other devices may be unwieldy as you require more of them due to the distance constraints.

Keep this in mind when deciding where to position the computer in your car! I ended up putting mine under the front passenger seat so the cable lengths could be shorter (no more than 10 feet, and usually only 6 to 8), and so I could power the USB off the computer's bus and avoid overpopulating (not necessarily overpowering) the AC (alternating-current) inverter.

Table 5-1 shows the maximum cable lengths for various technologies.

Table 5-1   Maximum Cable Lengths by Type

Technology	Max Cable Length
USB 1.0/1.1	~16.4 feet, max ~80 with repeaters
USB 2.0 (high-speed)	~16.4 feet, max ~64 with repeaters
Firewire® / IEEE-1394 / i.Link®	~72 meters
VGA	5 meters, depending on wire guage (many consumer VGA cables are 28 guage)
PS/2 Keyboard / Mouse	~500 feet

Measure Your Car before Buying Cables

The cables you install for your computer should only be as long as they need to be. Remember the old carpenter's rule—"Measure once, cut twice." This goes for cutting cables, but more especially *buying* cables, because returning the wrong ones could result in restocking fees, especially if the cables are out of the box. My own corollary is "Measure twice, buy once." (grin)

Measure the distance between where the cable will start to where it will end and add 3 feet and then buy a cable to that specification, plus or minus 1 foot. This will give you enough slack "just in case" and will prevent you from having too much cable. Too much cable can be difficult to hide and just ends up getting in the way.

True, it can be hard to find prebuilt computer cables that are exactly what you demand. Usually there is something very close to what you need. However, you can always build your own cable by finding specifications online and going to a local cabling supply store to find the right sheaths, wiring, and connectors.

Other Cable Considerations

There are some important factors to consider when you're talking about installing cables in your car for new devices. The next few sections cover some of these considerations—before you actually start installing and running the cables.

Always Have Proper Shielding

Your car is susceptible to much more noise, hum, static, and other electrical issues that you generally don't have to deal with at home. Your home computer and gaming systems don't have an alternator a few feet away from them, or static build-up from rubber tires spinning at 50 miles per hour. This electrical noise can be heard through poorly shielded audio cables, slow down USB data transmissions, short your computer, or produce so much noise on the input line that the computer may act erratic or even halt.

When shopping for cables, audio cables should be of a high quality, such as Monster® cable. Monster also makes high-quality video cables.

Keep Those Cable Connections Tight

When connecting cables to your computer or video devices, make sure that they are screwed in tightly (if they have screw connectors). This is especially important when the computer is near passengers, because their feet may bump a connector loose. With audio connectors, you will usually notice quickly whether a connection is loose because there will be a lot of hum and noise in the car due to the loose connector, or no audio at all if it comes disconnected entirely. It is better to use a USB keyboard/mouse combination instead of PS/2 connectors because PS/2 connectors come loose very easily, and the pins have a tendency to break.

Furthermore, you should physically try to shield any removable connectors that might be impacted by passengers or cargo in your vehicle. Plastic conduit can work wonders here and is available from any hardware store.

Always Match Gauge

Whenever you are going to splice wires or solder them together, make sure you use the same guage of wire from the original to the extension. Different gauges can affect conductivity, and there is usually a very good reason the original cable manufacturer decided to use the cable design they did.

Don't Run Wires over the Engine Block, High-Heat Areas, Fans, and Other High-Risk Areas

Be careful where you run your cables when running cables under the hood. Keep cables away from extremely hot areas and high-risk areas. An electrical cable melting near a combustion system could cause an explosion or other dangerous condition. The same goes for fans—a cable getting into a fan could cause serious (and expensive) damage to your car *and to you*. Other high-risk areas include cables running near the gas pedal, clutch, or brakes (you don't want a cable preventing you from hitting any of those pedals), gear shifter, or emergency brake. It is imperative that you keep cables secured via appropriately heat-tempered conduit, cable fasteners, and by other appropriate means you may conjure, because driving your car is sure to loosen up cable placement, move cables, and so forth.

Always Secure Extension Cables

If you have to use an extension cable, say, for extending your USB cable or VGA cable, make sure the connection between the two cords is secure and that the elctrical ground is maintained across the connection. The best way to prevent disconnections of the extension cord is to use electrical tape after connecting the two cables. Wrap it tightly around the cables so a passenger's foot tap doesn't cause them to come loose, and to prevent water and other elements from causing a short or damage to your equipment. In Figure 5-1 you can see where I wrapped the USB extension cord connected to my in-dash USB hub (which you can learn how to build in Chapter 18, "Syncing Portable Music Players").

FIGURE 5-1: Electrical tape keeps extension cables from coming unplugged.

If you use a cigarette-lighter extender, you should also plug up the unused extender ports or cover them entirely with electrical tape to protect them from the elements. The last thing you want is wet shoes or snow bringing water into the adapter and shorting your equipment or shocking someone in the car.

Choose the Right Connectors

When choosing a cable, make sure it's one that will not come loose, and make sure it comes with very rigid connectors. For example, a USB keyboard or mouse cable will most likely not come loose from a USB port and likely will not snap under slight pressure. However, PS/2 type connectors can easily come unplugged because they were not built to be rigid connections, nor were they made for mobile environments. Note also that PS/2 connector pins are very thin and tend to be pretty cheap, so they can break easily. If a PS/2 cable pin breaks off in your computer's PS/2, port it will be almost impossible to get out, and then the port is unsuable! Keep this in mind when deciding which types of cables to use. Note that wireless input devices are not necessarily the solution to the connector problem—they can help you get around the issue only to the extent that their connectors, too, are rigid as stated previously.

Of course, Bluetooth-enabled input devices running in tandem with a Bluetooth-enabled computer (such as a feature of the motherboard or as a PC card), are a good solution as long as the PC's BIOS supports using them as a keyboard or mouse when no drivers have been loaded for them.

Keep It Clean—Dressing and Hiding Cables

The majority of cables you use with home and business computers are made for indoor scenarios. Although your car computer will be indoors in one perspective, those same indoor cables were never meant to be exposed to elements such as rain, snow, extreme heat and cold, or constant bumping or stepping on by passengers. These issues can lead to fraying wires, cables coming loose, getting shocked or electricuted, tripping, and dangerous driving scenarios, such as cables preventing you from hitting the brakes (as discussed earlier in the section on high-risk areas). If you look around your car, you will notice that you can't see any of your car's wiring in the passenger area. You need to keep that motif with your computer's cabling, combining loose cables where possible in readily available plastic sheathing and neatly hiding them away to keep things clean and safe.

In Figure 5-2 you can see how messy my car cabling was before I started putting things away. You can see the AC inverter just sitting in the middle of the carpet near the passenger seat. The cables aren't put away, and it's easy for water to damage the inverter and for passengers to step on all the equipment.

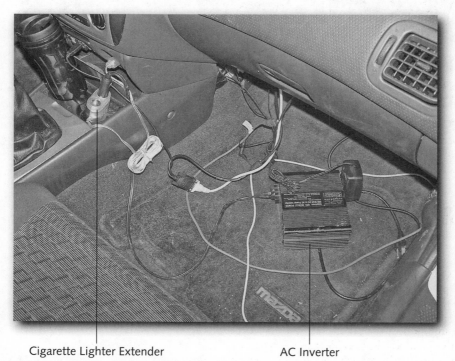

Cigarette Lighter Extender   AC Inverter

FIGURE 5-2: Not a good place for the AC inverter.

In Figure 5-3 you can see the power cables from my barrier switch hanging from under my steering column, potentially dropping down and preventing me from hitting the brakes while driving.

FIGURE 5-3: The hanging power cables from the barrier switch are a safety hazard.

In Figure 5-4 you see where my computer, conveniently placed under the seat, has cables surrounding it, making it difficult for a rear seat passenger to sit in my car without stepping on its cables.

FIGURE 5-4: A poor way to place cables surrounding my car PC.

Planning Your Cable Runs

The most obvious first step is to find a place to hide the cables. Luckily, many cars have removable moldings you can tuck the cables into. This will come in handy for hiding the computer cables and the AC inverter cables. These are usually very easy to find—just look for the screws; many times, things easily come loose.

Tip Having a battery-powered electric screwdriver will save you countless minutes and frustration when working in your car. You can find them for under $20 at any hardware store or Walmart. If you can, make sure you get magnetized heads (which end up magnetizing the bits as well, so don't worry), so you don't drop screws under seats or in other hard-to-reach places.

Tip One good place to get "take apart" advice is from radio installers at the various shops in your area, or even online in forums specifically for your model of vehicle. The guys in the shops take apart so many different cars that they can usually say "oh, yeah, you're going to have one heck of a time with that" or "wow, that's easy stuff—let me tell you what to do." You may also find the same attitude online, but before you start screwing around (or, in this case, unscrewing), make sure you know what you're doing.

When running cables from a device in your dash to a computer under a seat or in the back, keep in mind that the area behind the dash usually has some open space. Although it could be cramped, it shouldn't be too hard to run at least a few extra cables. In this case we'll run the cables from the back of my computer display to the computer by running behind the glove compartment, into the side molding of the car, and finally to the computer.

The first thing to do is *make sure the car is off*. Better yet, disconnect the main positive battery lead to lessen the chance of shorting out some circuit—or blowing a fuse—behind the dashboard. You don't want any power going to anything. If you need to work near an AC inverter, disconnect it from the car first and move it and anything else in the glove compartment and related areas out of the way so you can work without being inhibited by obstacles.

When running cables, make sure they don't get in the way of any mechanical devices in your car. You don't want a cable preventing your emergency brake from working or getting in the way of the mechanical gears connected to the climate control knobs in your console. Always, always be aware of where you're running cables, and secure them well against the vibrations and movement in your car to prevent dangerous situations.

To gain access to the back of my center console I removed the glove compartment door (see Figure 5-5). Your car may be different, so you may have to remove your center console panels. Check with your car dealer or a local enthusiast group on how to gain access to the back of your center console without damaging anything.

FIGURE 5-5: Behind the glove compartment.

Note You don't want to try pulling plastic or removing panels that may be expensive to replace. Some car manufacturers even have panels that are purposefully made to be replaced if removed, so watch out! See the tip where I said to make sure you know what you're tearing out *before* you start tearing things apart.

Now that I have the access I need, I can place my cables behind the console with some plastic conduit that I can Velcro to the fabric behind the console or glue or screw to some component surfaces.

Caution Make sure that if you decide to screw anything into your car, you cover any screw tips that are popping out; otherwise, passengers (including you) could be injured.

Using a Cable Organizer or Conduit

The conduit I ran was about 2 feet wide and flat, with cable guides—yours will vary based on the size of the area in which you are placing it. You can buy my kind of conduit, sometimes called a *cable organizer*, from any computer store, such as CompUSA or Radio Shack. Regular plastic wiring conduit that looks like a plastic tube can also be used and can be purchased at any hardware store.

The main benefit of the conduit (see Figure 5-6) is that it separates your cables from those already in your car; also, it's very easy to work with to keep things organized. If you don't have fabric such as carpet to place it on (say, in a Hummer or Honda Element, where there's a lot of metal instead of carpeting in many areas), you can glue or screw the plastic conduit in place. Before affixing the conduit, make sure you can still close or put down your glovebox, doors, and seats with it securely in place. I strongly advise against screwing the conduit into your car because it may invite rust, cause moisture or leaking issues, and affect wires on the other side of the metal. If you decide to glue or screw make sure you don't place the conduit on anything that gets extraordinarily hot or cold because it could melt and damage equipment, expose you to a dangerous situation (a system could stop working), or cause injury. Also try to avoid any loops that might trap moisture or condensation in the area of the conduit.

In this case I decided to glue the Velcro to a cable organizer under the carpet behind the glove box. The carpet goes high enough that I can keep the organizer high up and away from the pasenger's feet, and I can put the floot mat over it when I'm done to keep things hidden and protected.

Before Velcroing, I placed all of the cables I needed into the conduit, as shown in Figure 5-6. I then ran the cables toward the side of my car, near the molding, so I could tuck them under the molding with minimal, if any, visibility by passengers.

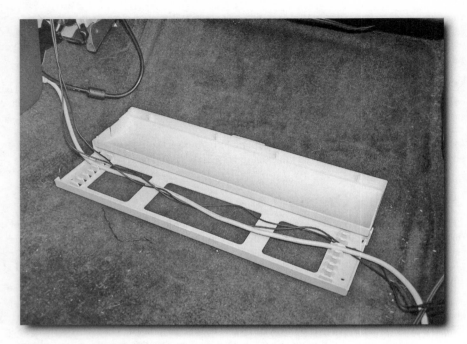

FIGURE 5-6: The cables placed in the wiring conduit.

Keeping the open end up also lets me stack cables on top of each other without always having to be neat about it (of course I'll clean it up later, I swear).

Taking Advantage of the Car's Molding

Once the cables have been run toward the molding, I lifted up the molding enough to move the cables under it. Your car should be very similar because most car molding is meant to be removed. Although you *can* pull the molding up and off entirely, in most cases, you don't need to do so, and probably shouldn't—it could break some plastic or be hard to put back on, which is way too much trouble (and can be expensive to replace). Just neatly tuck the cables under there, one by one, horizontal to the molding as shown in Figure 5-7.

Tuck the exposed cable under the molding for the length it takes to get to your computer. You may have to expose some cable if you're passing some door panels. You can choose to cut a small hole and run under the carpet, under other molding, or just keep the cables exposed for a few inches. Once you reach your computer, pull the cable a little bit to make sure it's straightened out under the molding and so you have all your excess cable available to you.

FIGURE 5-7: Tuck the cables under the molding.

Now, if you've chosen the right cable lengths, you should have only a couple of feet or less of cable left so you can run it to the computer without a cabling mess. If you have a lot more left, you have a couple of options. One option is to get a shorter cable and run that one instead. If that is not an option, then try to go behind your glove box again and pull back a bit on the long cable, coiling the cable behind the glovebox and tying it with a plastic tie. Alternatively, you can pull the remaining cable into the trunk or under the seat, if your computer is located in the trunk or under the seat. This should let you cleanly hide the cable from passenger view, and there should be plenty of space for you to coil the cable a bit behind the glove box without inhibiting its operation, or in the cable organizer itself if there's room.

Now you should be able to connect all of the cables and all of your wires are out of sight and out of danger, as shown in Figures 5-8 and 5-9.

FIGURE 5-8: Look ma, no wires!

Protecting from Power Cable Exposure

The power cables in your car can be dangerous if they become tangled up or frayed and exposed. As with all other cables, power cables especially need to be hidden and kept secured. The easiest way to do this is to use plastic ties to tie multiple power cables together and then use electrical tape and conduits to keep them organized behind the dash or under molding. Do not put power cables under the carpet, because foot traffic may kink (that is, bend or pinch, causing a poor connection or disrupting it entirely), fray, or in other words damage the wire and could cause systems not to work, damage equipment, or potentially create a shock or fire hazard.

Back in Figure 5-3, you can see where my power cables were dangling after I ran power cables from my barrier terminal switch to my computer's power supply. There were only three wires, so I tucked the power cables under my dash and used electrical tape to keep them running along the inside plastic. Note that my power cables are pretty thin, so I didn't have to run conduit or use a stronger tape. Your mileage may vary depending on what you decide to use for power and what cables you end up running.

FIGURE 5-9: The cleaned up computer area.

Caution Make sure when taping that the surface you will be applying the tape to is clean—free of oils and dust. You don't want the tape to come loose because of grime that prevents it from sticking. A good way to get rid of this is to use a cotton swab and some 90%+ rubbing alcohol. Put some rubbing alcohol on the swab and wipe the area clean, and then use a paper towel (not one with lotion or moisturizers, of course), and make sure the surface is clear. You can also score the surface in a criss-cross pattern to help the tape stick better.

After taping the power cables to the bottom of the dash, I ran them down to the molding and carefully tucked the cables under the molding so I wouldn't kink the wire. I then ran the cable to the computer under the seat so foot traffic would not affect my cables. That was it—neat and clean and safely out of the way!

Keeping the Inverter Available and Hidden

If you have to use an AC inverter to power devices, it is best to keep it out of sight yet still accessible. The problem with passengers is that they can kick the adapter, turn it on or off, or get shocked if they get the adapter wet.

The other problem is that many AC inverters may only plug into the cigarette lighter adapter (sometimes called the Power Plug in newer, more politically correct cars) and have a short cable. This appears to limit you to placing it out of the way of the passenger, but it's still there in the passenger area.

To mitigate this threat, you need to find a way to position the adapter in an accessible location but out of the way of feet and where it can enjoy as much free-air circulation as possible, to minimize heat buildup. The easiest and most convenient place to put it in most cars is under the seat on the side of the center console the cigarette lighter is on. This lets you route the cable down and back without getting in the way of the shifter or passengers' feet. You should also be able to run the inverter's cable under the molding or under the center console without any issues and keep everything looking clean.

In many cases the center console is removed simply by removing the cupholders and then pulling up the console, or first unscrewing a few screws and then pulling up the console. Check with your dealer or an enthusiast group or mechanics guide on the specifics pertaining to your vehicle. In Figure 5-10 you can see where the center console has been removed.

FIGURE 5-10: The center console is removed.

Another option to keep the inverter cable cleanly out of the way is to route its cigarette-lighter adapter cable entirely under the center console, meaning that, instead of keeping the plug running in the open, you would run it entirely under the center console and leave just enough out to plug it into the cigarette lighter socket. In this case you would have to remove the top of your center console area, where the shifter, parking brake, and so forth are, so you can run the cable. Check with your dealer or an enthusiast group regarding how to do this, because the routine will vary based on vehicle.

Figure 5-11 shows where I ran the power cable under the center console molding to keep it cleanly out of the way. I had to cut a very small square groove with a razor blade so the cable could come through without blocking the cup holder's covering flap. You may have to do something similar so that the original units all snap in place properly. Keep in mind, when modifying cars you have to be creative to get around certain obstacles when they come up!

FIGURE 5-11: Running the power cable under the center console.

You should be able to easily pull power cables through the center console plastic molding and down under the seat, as illustrated in Figure 5-12 (but your experience may again vary depending on the type of vehicle you have—like I said before, be creative, every car is different).

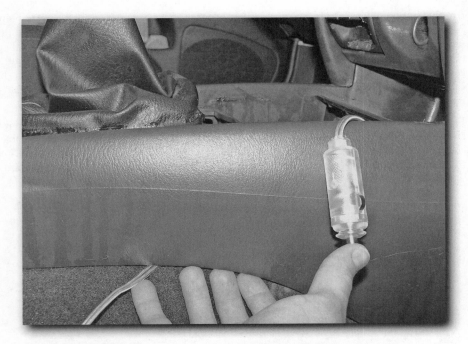

FIGURE 5-12: Tucking the power cables under the center console molding.

In Figure 5-13 you can see where the cable comes from under the center console and to the inverter.

The reason you keep the inverter accessible is to have access to its power switch. If your car keeps providing power to the cigarette lighter adapter when the key is out of the ignition, then your AC inverter could keep drawing power and powering your devices, potentially draining your battery while you're away. Many AC inverters will automatically stop drawing power when they sense the battery power is too low, but you shouldn't take the risk of trusting the inverter's sensor and end up not being able to start your car.

If you can't move the inverter under the seat, see if you can Velcro it under the glove compartment, or on carpet to the side of the passenger. The position in your car will vary, but you want to find the best position for the device, where feet will not touch it.

Figure 5-13: The AC inverter cable is barely seen under the passenger seat.

Tip

If you need more than one cigarette lighter socket, there are products you can buy that give you more than one socket. I purchased the StreetLights adapter, which provided me four sockets *and* it lights up red when power is flowing! Too cool!

If your inverter has battery terminals for connecting directly to the battery, you can run the power directly to your battery by following the instructions in Chapter 3, "Giving Your Creation Life: Power Considerations." However, this doesn't negate the fact that you could keep drawing power when the car is turned off. Keep in mind that you could connect the inverter's positive terminal to the barrier terminal switch installed in Chapter 3 and connect the ground cable to the ground connector illustrated therein as well.

Summary

This chapter discussed how you can hide the cables in your car and protect your equipment from getting trampled on by passengers. It also discussed how to run cables under molding and under your center console as well as how to take advantage of plastic conduit to keep cables organized and safe. Because wires are so delicate yet so important, you must always keep them out of the way of your passengers and yourself. Cables that get in the way while you drive can cause accidents, and power cables stepped on by passengers could cause shocks or fires. This is why your car's wiring systems are hidden from you!

Physics Man, Physics: Preparing Home Electronics for the Road

Adding computer technology to your car has a number of gotchas. You may not have liked physics in high school, but it definitely comes into play here. Don't worry, we're not going to go over gravitational formulas and differential equations. However, I do want to give you a heads up on what equipment you should select to accommodate an automobile environment and give you some information on what all of those gizmos in your car have to go through while they run.

After reading this chapter, you should understand:

➤ How to choose a storage device for a computer in your car.

➤ How to mount electronics in your car to accommodate for shock and vibration.

➤ What G-force ratings are and how they affect hard drives and optical drives.

➤ Why optical discs skip and how to mitigate that problem in game consoles, computer optical disc drives (CD-ROMs, DVD-ROMs, etc.), and other disc-audio/video (A/V) equipment (DVD players and VCRs).

Home Equipment Was Never Meant for Cars

Let's face it, your home computer leads a pretty boring life. It sits there, on or under a desk, churning away without a care in the world. Game consoles are the same way, sitting on top of the TV or on the floor, with the most strenuous part of their day being you yanking a cord out of the front when you made the wrong move. You don't worry much about cables, since you can hide them through convenient holes in the desk and they generally don't get in the way other than cosmetically.

A car is an entirely different beast. The electronics in cars have to deal with potholes, speed bumps, high-speed maneuvers, accidents, and even just regular roadway shocks. Most stationary systems you would use in your home (or office) were never designed to deal with such harsh environments, and you can go through a lot of replacement equipment (and money!) if you choose the wrong equipment or implement it without taking the environment into careful consideration. Heck, imagine that hard drive in your computer having its head crash into the platters at 2 Gs (G-forces). Say goodbye to your data! (To see the sheer amount of force dealt to equipment in a car, take a look at Table 6-1.) Keyboards, mice, and so forth *are* a problem. They can drop down and interfere with the driver's operation of the vehicle, causing accidents. There are no readily flat surfaces to use a mouse on, and game controllers and their 12 feet of cable aren't easily stored.

G-Force Rating—A unit of inertial force on a body that is subjected to rapid acceleration or gravity, equal to 32 feet per second per second at sea level; also written *G-force*. (Source: Dictionary.com.) In our case, this is the amount of force your computer components will have to withstand when you are driving.

G/ms—The amount of G-force per millisecond. Some vehicle shocks can easily have over 100 vertical Gs in a fraction of a second, so it is important to know what a device can withstand. See the sidebar "Measuring Gs in Your Vehicle" if you want to measure the G-forces in your car.

Choosing Computer Equipment for the Road

Let's take a look at some of the components we will be installing and how they need to measure up to the G-forces they may experience on the road.

Hard Drives and Optical Drives

The equipment you will be installing that is most sensitive to car travails is home computer equipment. Hard drives can crash given a hard enough shock. Standard optical (CD and DVD) drives don't usually hold onto a disk well enough to guarantee consistent reading (let alone burning!), and your car's vibrations don't help matters. Since home and office computers are usually assumed to be stationary, computer manufacturers keep their costs down by leaving out any sort of advanced equipment protection (sometimes referred to as *hardening* the equipment).

Laptops, on the other hand, are road warriors, literally. Their CD-ROM drives tend to have special spring-loaded spindles to prevent a CD or DVD from moving around while spinning, as shown in Figure 6-1. Their hard drives are specially designed to withstand über-shocks. I recall a few years ago when I was in an analyst meeting with IBM. They showed me their then-new 1-inch 340 MB compact-flash (CF) "microdrive," a miracle of engineering. IBM explained to me that this digital-camera-ready CF drive could be punted like a football while it was writing and there would be absolutely no data errors. They built similar technology into their TravelStar® line of laptop (2.5-inch and smaller) hard drives to protect the drive's data. In this book, we will follow their lead and only use laptop storage devices in computer-based projects (although you can still use desktop hard drives, but I don't recommend it). See Table 6-1 for a comparison of G-shock ratings for laptop and desktop hard drives.

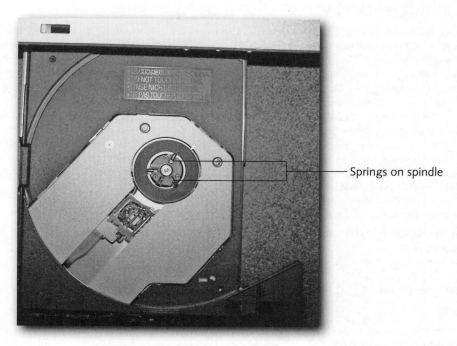

FIGURE 6-1: Spring-loaded spindle in laptop optical drive.

Table 6-1   Desktop versus Laptop Hard Drive G-Shock Tolerances

Hard Drive	Type	Size	Max G-Shock Rating (Operational, Gs/2ms)	Non-operational, Gs/2ms
Hitachi DeskStar 7K80	Desktop 3.5"	80 GB	55	350
Hitachi DeskStar 180GXP	Desktop 3.5"	180 GB	55	350
Hitachi TravelStar E7K60	Laptop 2.5"	40–60 GB	200	1,000
Hitachi TravelStar C4K60	Laptop 1.8"	20–30GB	500	1,200

When shopping for laptop hard drives, you may see what appears to be both IBM and Hitachi versions of the TravelStar product line. There's actually only one TravelStar. IBM's storage division was purchased by Hitachi in 2002.

Cartridge-Based versus Disc-Based Consoles

Adding a game console to your vehicle is easier overall because you don't have to build anything—you generally just need power, available video jacks, one or more displays, and cables. However, since today's game consoles tend to use optical discs like CDs and DVDs, the games have a tendency to skip. Recall that consoles are made to be stationary, not moving around and not compensating for a bumpy ride. There are some slight modifications that may need to be made in order to make your disc-based game console, such as the Nintendo Game Cube®, the Sony Playstation®, or a Microsoft Xbox® road-ready. These include modifying the drive (possibly installing a different drive or placing small tabs on the corners of the tray mechanism to prevent the disc from moving up and down (many computer optical drives already have these tabs), and mounting the console so it doesn't move much, if at all. Note that if you are planning on installing a cartridge-based console into your vehicle, such as an older Nintendo or Sega, you generally don't need to worry much about the cartridge slot and cartridge grip.

Formula for measuring file size for CDs (plug in your values for the words in italics):

(((*Bit Depth* * *Hz*) / 1024 Kbits) / 8 bits) * 2 audio channels * seconds = file size in Kbytes/sec

Formula for measuring file size for MP3s (plug in your values for the words in italics):

((Bits per second / 8 bits) / 1024 bytes) * seconds = file size in Kbytes/sec

Table 6-2 Standard CD versus MP3 CD Data Rates for 150 Seconds of Audio		
Audio Source	*Data/Second*	*Avg. Song Size*
CD Audio (44.1 KHz 16-Bit Stereo Audio)	(((16 bits * 44100 Hz) / 1024 bits) / 8 bits) * 2 audio channels* 150 secs = 172 Kbytes/sec	25,800 Kbytes
128 Kb/s Stereo MP3	((128,000 bits/8 bits) / 1024 bits) * 150 secs = 15 Kbytes/sec	2,344 Kbytes

Why Do CDs Skip?

Although G-shocks are the most noticeable force in your car, the more common enemy is actually vibration. Even if you've coated your car with antivibration wax, you're still going to deal with some vibes. Since hard drives and optical disc readers rely on precisely placed heads to read digital data from spinning platters, vibrations (and yes, shocks) constantly move those heads away from their targets. The result? In hard drives, slow response time because the drive controller has to realign the actuator. In optical readers, it's skipping.

To accommodate some vibration (and to some extent, shock), today's hard drives have technology in them that tries to predict movement from vibration using various sensors, and moving the actuator to accommodate. In the case of optical media, this is what the buffer is for, such as the 10-, 20-, 40-second and greater anti-skip protection you've probably heard of on portable CD players.

If you're wondering why MP3 CDs generally don't skip (if you're lucky enough to have one of those portable players), look at it from the data size point of view:

With an audio CD, the data is completely uncompressed and takes up around 20–40 megabytes per song (see Table 6-2 for formulas you can use to calculate file sizes). Memory isn't cheap enough (yet) to put 64-megabyte buffers in portable equipment, so manufacturers use more affordable buffers, such as 512 kilobytes to 2 megabytes. When the disc spins up, the system reads as much as it can into the buffers and streams the music out of the buffer (also called a *look-ahead cache*). If vibration or shock moves the heads while they're reading more data into the buffer, music continues to play from what's still in memory while the heads quickly realign themselves to refill the buffer. If the buffer runs out of music before the heads have recovered, the CD will appear to skip. There will always be a slight delay when you first try to play the CD or change tracks because the drive prefills the buffer.

Now, with MP3s, songs tend to be in the 2.5- to 5-megabyte range. Well, 512 kilobytes of an MP3 into the buffer could be one-fifth of the song, giving the computer plenty of time to play out the buffer while heads get realigned and the buffer gets refilled. It is also much easier to fill the buffer and play from it with an MP3 track, since much smaller amounts of data need to be read. As memory gets even cheaper, more buffer memory could be shipped in portable players and entire tracks could be kept in memory, and discs may not need to spin much at all!

Measuring Gs in Your Vehicle

Have you ever been to the drag races or stock car races and seen the technology those guys have in their roadsters? They have neat-o gauges, accelerometers, and turbo-boost meters. Every time I see those I want them—it's a ton of fun to drive with a bunch of gizmos running in front of you. Those amateur and professional racers know how to better tune their driving based on what those gauges say, and for this book I purchased a Beltronics Vector FX 2 to test the G-force ratings in a few cars to get more accurate results.

The FX 2, shown in the sidebar figure, is capable of telling you how long it takes your car to go from 0 to 60 miles per hour, G-force ratings, lap times, and more, even though I only used it for the G-force ratings for this book. With some extra software (around $25) it even lets you download the data to a Palm handheld or a PC, enabling you to check your results while you're in your car! So if you want to really get some of those spec numbers you see in auto magazines yourself, and you want another cool gadget in your car that makes people go "Whoa, what does that do?", pick one of these things up for about $249. They're not too hard to find—I bought mine at Circuit City. The software for downloading your performance statistics, however, you have to buy from Beltronics' online store at www.beltronics.com.

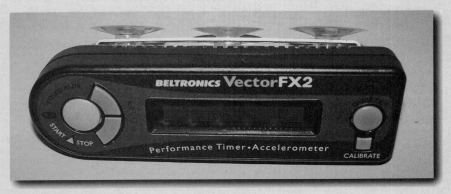

The Beltronics FX 2.

Mounting and Angling Storage Devices

Most computer cases mount CDs and hard drives horizontally and tightly bolted to a metal case. Since the enclosures don't move, there's very little concern over shock and vibration. As we have previously discussed, cars are completely different. When taking turns, your car has to shift its weight to the outside to make the tires grip. The weight is shifted in the computer case as well. When your car hits a bump, that energy is transferred into the car's frame, as well as into the computer's case, and ultimately to the hard drive and other electronics in the case.

When a car hits a bump, for example, there could be well over 100 vertical Gs in a fraction of a second. To mitigate this, you *could* mount all storage devices from rubber bands so they aren't easily affected by shocks, but that's a tad extreme. By mounting devices properly, you can mitigate bumps and transfers of weight and energy.

Did You Know

Exhaust systems are connected via a big rubber donut on cars because they are so long that if the front hits a large bump, the exhaust could be split in half because of harmonic resonance (refer to the Seattle-Tacoma bridge incident).

Mounting Storage Devices

When mounting a hard drive or optical device, you need to accommodate for the worst-case regular driving shock generator: turning *and* hitting a bump. When mounting the hard drive, make sure you mount it vertically and horizontally to the dashboard, as shown in Figure 6-2. This takes into account body roll and shock from bumps. Furthermore, use rubber mounts or shock-absorbing foam under the drive or to its side to absorb at least some of the shock. It also helps to use thick rubber washers when mounting drives and devices to the case to help reduce some shock. This is especially true in drive bays. These materials can be purchased at any hardware store.

Mounting Peripheral Cards

Peripheral cards are a bit different, because they generally are mounted at one end of the card and socketed. Like storage devices, mount these so they are parallel to the dashboard, but do not mount them vertically because the side-to-side motion could snap the card (and ultimately ruin other components in the computer).

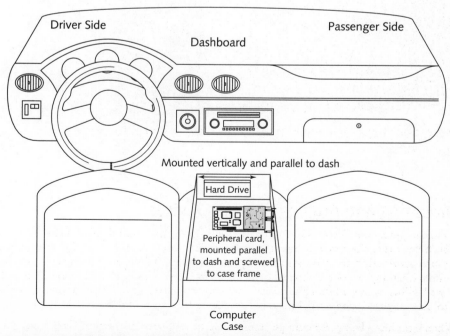

FIGURE 6-2: Example of a hard drive and peripheral card properly mounted.

A company called Analog Devices sells G-force accelerometers to IBM and Sony for use in their products. For IBM, it is used in their laptops, while Sony uses the sensors in some Walkmans®. These sensors instantly realize when a laptop has gone weightless (i.e., it is being dropped), and immediately tell the hard drives in those units to park their heads to prevent data loss.

Don't use a car computer to store sensitive, irreplaceable critical data. There is no guarantee what will happen in your car, be it heat, accidents, break-ins, or other such event. Important files, such as your entire music collection, should always be left in a safer location, such as on your home computer, and backed up regularly.

Summary

In this chapter you learned about the physics of your car's motion, selecting equipment to mitigate those natural forces, and saving your equipment from harm. You also learned how to plan for properly mounting these devices in your vehicle. When working on the projects later in this book, please keep in mind how your equipment will be used and how it was originally meant to be used. If you know this going into a project, your creation will last longer and you'll spend more time having fun instead of fixing!

The User Interface

part

Choosing a Display Device

The majority of projects in this book require some sort of visual user interface. In most cases this is a screen that is near you or your passengers. In this chapter I will help you choose a display device that suits the type of project you will be building. Many of these suggestions can be used with other projects based on what your billfold will tolerate, but if you can save up for the right display you will enjoy your experience much more!

Remember, This Is a Car

When choosing a screen for your vehicle, don't forget that you're putting all this stuff in a car. You generally aren't going to put a 20-inch television in there (well, you might, but we're not going over that). Most car video screens are between 4 and 7 inches, although I have seen flip-down 15-inch screens. These screens have traditionally been in a 4:3 aspect ratio (sometimes called *full frame*, and meaning the display is 4 arbitrary units wide by 3 units high), although newer screens are starting to be 16:9 (16 units wide by 9 units wide), or *widescreen* due to the popularity of DVD players in cars (and soon, the high-definition television craze).

The small size of these displays also means that you have to take special consideration into *what* you display. For example, when building a computer into your vehicle, it's better not to have very small text on the screen if you're going to glance at its contents while driving. With a video game console it may not matter, because chances are you're not playing that while driving, and the graphics are usually made to be very large and visible for quickly responding with action during game play.

Warning *Never* play video games while driving. Your job is to drive your car and keep your passengers safe!

Keep in mind that you need to keep your eyes on the road while driving. Don't put screens in your vehicle in places where they can easily distract you. In some states it is actually illegal to have a display on your dashboard (see Appendix A, "Legal Concerns," on these issues). Also, as a general rule of thumb, if a display takes your eyes away from the road for 3 seconds or more, it is considered too distracting, and a limit of 1 second may start to become the industry standard. As large displays start appearing more often in vehicles, drivers may get more and more distracted, so please try to build your projects in a fashion to keep you and your passengers safe at all times!

Analog versus Digital Displays and Connectors

There are two different types of display signals, *analog* and *digital*. (You may already be familiar with these terms and what they mean. If so, skip down a bit; otherwise, read on!) When it comes to display devices, these terms represent how the signal is transmitted to the display. Common analog connectors include *coaxial*, *composite* (such as RCA-style), *S-Video*, and *component*. Common digital connectors include *VGA, SPDIF, DVI, and optical (such as Toslink)*. Component and optical connectors are unique in that a digital signal can travel over them as well. For example, the only standardized way to get high-definition television (HDTV) over an analog cable is via component video cables. Optical audio connectors enable analog and digital signals to travel and be decoded by an appropriate receiver as well.

Let me explain the different types of connectors:

- **Composite Video (RCA)**—Composite video cables send the chroma (color) and luminance (brightness) signals on the same wire. This usually results in an inferior video signal quality, but on smaller displays, and especially with game consoles, that's not as noticeable. Oftentimes you will see color *bleeding* or *smearing* when composite video signals are displayed. Technically, this is called *crosstalk* between the two signals, which weakens both. Larger displays and analog converted computer-resolution images generally look terrible with composite video.

- **S-Video (*Separate-Video* or *Super-Video*)**—S-Video cables separate the luminance signal from the video signal, offering a much higher-quality image than composite and basically eliminating the bleeding and smearing commonly seen in composite. S-Video usually comes with DVD players, modern camcorders, and Super VHS (S-VHS) decks. Standard VHS decks do not generally ship with S-Video because their video resolution is already so low. S-Video is generally good for about 400 lines of vertical resolution, making it ideal for displaying DVDs when your display device doesn't support component video or digital video.

- **Component Video**—Component, as its name implies, separates the red, green, and blue video signals into their purest form for a pristine image. Component video cables are also the only standardized analog cable that can be used for transmitting both analog and digital (such as HDTV or progressive-scan video feeds) signals to a display (such as a television set).

- **VGA**—Short for *video graphics array*. See the sidebar "What Are VGA, XGA, and Other Graphics Adaptors?" for more details.

- **DVI**—Digital video interface transfers the video image digitally, is very fast, and supports pixel-to-pixel addressing. It also uses very expensive cables to go with it ($80 to $109 depending on where you shop, still around $40 at 15 points over cost from my research). DVI connectors are commonly found on new LCD displays and HDTV sets for pure digital signals and are the highest-quality video signal transfer method for HDTV today (well, in 2004 anyway). See Figure 7-5 later on in this chapter.

- **Optical (Toslink, Fiber-Optic)**—Optical cables can be used for transmitting any type of digital data from one device to another without any loss. Just as high-quality digital audio is stored on low-cost CDs, a low-cost fiber-optic cable literally carries these digital signals without wires from one device to another. A key advantage is that optical cables are impervious to many types of interference, such as electrical noise, static, and hum. They are also immune to being shorted out. Note that copy protection issues abound with this transfer method, and issues surrounding this are still being hashed out.

- **In the Future**—Wireless video transmitters are being developed, using optical and ultra-wideband RF transmission to keep cable and display costs down and reduce or eliminate cable clutter. Some industry analysts even say cables may be old-fashioned by the end of this decade, but only time will tell.

Analog Video Connection Types

The descriptions and figures that follow give some examples of the different analog connectors.

Figure 7-1 shows an analog composite RCA-style video cable and the port it plugs into. Composite cables are often included with game consoles, with higher-quality analog video such as S-Video being sold as add-on equipment. Just like most RCA-style audio, cables are red for the right audio channel and white for the left; a composite video signal cable is usually colored in yellow.

FIGURE 7-1: An analog composite RCA-style video cable and the port it plugs into.

In Figure 7-2 you can see a composite video connector as well. Many DVD players come with both composite and S-Video connectors because of their high-resolution video sources (the DVD), while most VCRs only come with composite video ports. Super-VHS, or S-VHS, decks almost always come with both composite and S-Video as well, because of S-VHS's higher video resolution. S-Video cables tend to cost about the same amount as composite video but provide a markedly better video quality because of the separation of luminance (a.k.a. "Y" signal) and video signals, practically eliminating the bleed you see in a composite video signal. If you don't have component video but you do have S-Video, this is a much better choice for quality video reproduction. Whereas composite video cables are yellow, S-Video cables are often black in color.

FIGURE 7-2: An analog S-Video cable and the port it plugs into.

Component video separates the red, green, and blue video signals into their purest form for a pristine image. Component video cables are also the only standardized analog cable that can be used for transmitting both analog and digital video signals (such as HDTV or progressive-scan video feeds) to a display (such as a television set). See Figure 7-3 for a set of component video cables and the connectors they usually plug into (often labeled as HD input, component input, or progressive scan input).

FIGURE 7-3: A set of component video cables (Y, Pr, and Pb), and the connectors they plug into.

Digital Video Connection Types

The descriptions and figures that follow here are some samplings of the various types of digital connectors.

Figure 7-4 shows a standard VGA connector. These cables also support S-VGA and XGA, as well as others. Figure 7-5 shows a DVI connector. Many new HDTV sets have these connectors on them as well so they can be used as computer displays since they are capable of displaying such high resolutions.

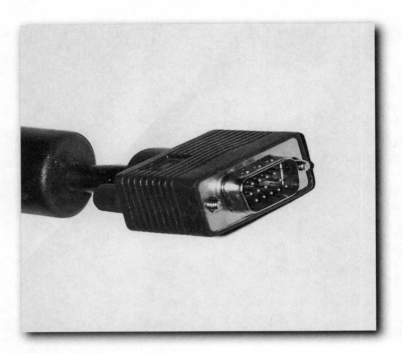

FIGURE 7-4: A VGA connector.

Figure 7-6 shows an optical cable and the jack it plugs into (top left). Note that when you are not using an optical jack you should use an optical terminator (bottom left) in its place.

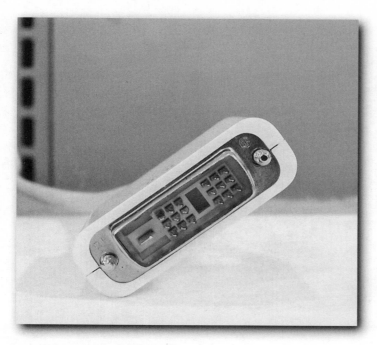

FIGURE 7-5: A DVI connector cable.

Warning If you are planning on having a multiple-VGA computer display configuration in your vehicle and plan to use the two displays for an *extended desktop*, make sure the graphics card you use has two VGA cables instead of a VGA and a DVI. If you use a DVI-VGA adapter, Windows will not let you have an extended desktop! You can still mirror the displays, however.

Tip Be wary of displays that promise VGA resolution but only give you analog connectors! These screens are often cheaper than VGA displays but don't come with the right cables for VGA connections! However, if you ask the manufacturer whether there is a VGA cable you can buy for the display, you may actually get a VGA-capable display at a great price!

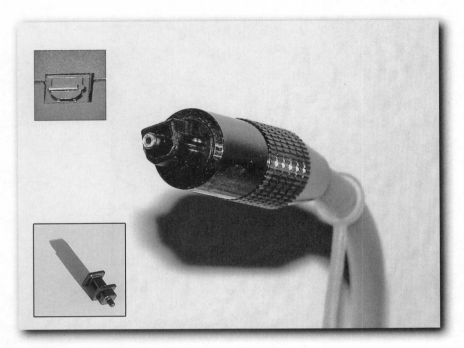

FIGURE 7-6: An optical cable and jack.

Choosing a Display: Head Units with Built-In Video Monitors

If you are in the market to have an all-in-one display and audio solution for a gaming or computing device, then a head unit with a built-in display may be ideal. As of the writing of this book, no head unit has a computer video input connector (i.e., VGA, S-VGA, etc.), but they do have composite and sometimes S-Video connectors. These solutions tend to be expensive—well beyond $1,000. eBay is a good place to find deals on these types of units. The advantage, especially if working with gaming systems, is that everything is in one unit, and the higher-end units support multiple displays and can be complete systems that you just plug the game or computer system's video into, provide a power source to, and play.

According to the head unit manufacturer Alpine, it is illegal in all 50 states and 11 Canadian provinces to have a motion-video display running in sight of the driver. Some of these in-dash units will *shut off* the video display when the car is in drive or in gear (passengers can still use video)! Find out if the one you are looking at does this before you fork over lots of money! And yes, there *are* ways to override the video inhibitors, but I will not go over those in this book because I don't want to get sued. Of course, if you searched the Web . . . (ahem)

What Are VGA, XGA, and Other Graphics Adaptors?

For years, computer users have heard many different graphics terms defining the resolution of their displays and their graphics cards. Some of us may remember good 'ol CGA, which stood for *color graphics adapter*, featuring a whopping four colors. Real history pundits will remember *Tandy Enhanced Color Graphics*, which sported an amazing 16 colors! Well, low and behold, more colors came to be in the form of EGA (enhanced graphics adapter), and finally what we have come to use as a catch-all phrase today—VGA, or *video graphics array*. Terms such as S-VGA (super video graphics adapter) and XGA (a term originally coined by IBM to compete with VGA but now just a term for resolution of 1024 × 768 or higher, meaning *extended graphics adapter*) are occasionally used to define higher resolutions, but most folks tend to know what VGA is and that's about it.

Are you curious what all of these resolutions mean? Sidebar Table 7-1 provides a list of graphics acronyms and what they mean.

Table 7-1   Graphics Adaptor Acronyms

Acronym	What It Means	What It Supports
VGA	Video Graphics Array/Adapter	A computer graphics/video standard that originally shipped with IBM PS/2 computers that supported a resolution of 640 × 480 and up to 16 colors. These days it means a resolution of 640 × 480 with at least 16 colors.
S-VGA	Super Video Graphics Array/Adapter	A computer graphics/video standard that originally meant a resolution of 800 × 600. Today it can mean a resolution of 800 × 600, 1024 × 768, 1280 × 1024, and 1600 × 1200.
XGA	Extended Graphics Array/Adapter	A computer graphics/video standard developed by IBM that features resolutions up to 1024 × 768 and up to 16-bit color (65,536 colors). This signal can be transmitted over a standard VGA cable.

Many of these video standards are managed by the Video Electronics Standards Association, or VESA for short. VESA has a wealth of information pertaining to display standards and regulations on their Web site at www.vesa.org.

Of all the components you're going to need for this book's projects, the display is the one that will likely be the most important to install. Heck, you can have any reputable store's personnel install it for you if they have an install bay, and that may be the easiest if you already know which cables need to be run. Just have them leave those out for you, and you'll be ready to plug stuff in and start playing! Multiple-screen systems, which we will come to shortly, require a bit more work to install, but keep in mind you can do that at the store or by yourself as well. Figure 7-7 shows a Kenwood All-in-One unit.

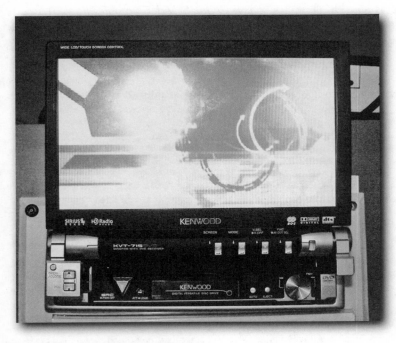

FIGURE 7-7: Kenwood All-in-One unit.

Note This book will not show you how to install a stereo into your car. (There are too many cars out there to cover this, and plenty of books about it. There are also plenty of retailers who will usually install one for under $100 in labor and parts.) Oftentimes when you purchase a new head unit the dealer or store will advertise free installation. This usually means the *labor* is free, but the parts needed, such as a wiring harness and adapters, are not, so be prepared to still spend up to $50!

Did You Know A somewhat new type of display making headway into the display market is organic electroluminescent, or OEL, displays, which require no backlight. Pioneer is "pioneering" this technology, which is often showcased at the Consumer Electronics Show held in Las Vegas every year.

Tips for Buying a Used LCD Display or Head Unit

Margins are so high on car LCD displays, and especially head units, that buying them used is often better and gives you the same quality as a new product. Be aware that the two most expensive fixes for an LCD display are a cracked screen (just go get a new one) and a failed backlight. Here are some tips when shopping for a used display or head unit:

- Watch out for dead pixels. These usually look like bright or dark, dead spots on the display. Show a white image on the display to see if any dark spots can be seen, then show a black or dark image and look for a bright white pixel. For many manufacturers, more than three of these constitute a defect covered by warranty (of course, this standard may change). A dead pixel doesn't mean the display is going bad; rather, it is a sign of a defect during the manufacturing process.

- When purchasing a head unit, make sure there is a mounting harness/bracket for your vehicle and that any adapters you will need are available. Since you may not be able to return a used item, it is a good idea to know whether it is actually compatible with your car.

- Verify that all necessary cables, parts, and adapters come with the unit. If the unit isn't too old (possibly back a year or two), see if local stores carry it and check a new system's box to find out what the contents *should* be and verify what you need. Some of these parts can be expensive if you can't find them used and have to get them from the manufacturer. Also, make sure that all cables and wires have no bent pins, kinks (hard bends), or frays in the wires.

- Determine whether the original manufacturer's warranty is still valid on the unit. If the owner has an extended service plan, make sure they transfer it to you. Most extended service plans are transferable to new owners, and the process is usually as simple as filling in a form on the back of their extended warranty card or making a phone call.

Computer Displays for Cars

Adding a computer to your car is a different beast alltogether when compared to simply adding a DVD player or game console. Computer displays have a demand for higher resolution, and the operating systems depend on that resolution being available. Sure, you can make font sizes bigger and window borders larger, but you still run into the same quandary—the high-resolution digital monitors are expensive! We're talking around $699 for manufacturer's suggested retail price (MSRP), and $400 or so on eBay. I suggest a couple courses of action:

- If you're only going to use the computer for playing back audio and video files, just get an analog display. These solutions are cheaper to begin with, and fairly inexpensive to expand.

- If you're going to use the computer for actual computing, such as accessing e-mail and the Internet, playing games, using GPS, and so forth, then buy a digital display. You *could* get by with an analog display and S-Video, but if you really want to enjoy a car *computing* experience, the digital displays are really the only way to go.

Choosing and Positioning Displays for Both Computers and Standard Video Devices

There are a few ways to approach choosing a display for the device in your car. You can mount the display on the dash, in the dash (using custom work), buy an in-dash display, or have displays in the seats (more on that particular topic later in this chapter). Of course, if you opt for an all-in-one unit, you're pretty much limited to your dash.

Issues with Installing a Display on Your Dash

Installing a display on your dash is a fairly simple process. In many cases you can literally stick the item to your dash with included adhesive. After a year I have yet to have an issue with the display mount coming loose on the dash. This is similar to how a radar detector may be mounted.

Make sure if you use adhesive that you completely clean and dry the area to which you will be adhering the mount, and use a little rubbing alcohol (90%+ alcohol) to make sure all grease is removed. I would not recommend doing this on a wood or leather surface, however, because the mount will not only look bad on it, it will likely destroy the surface if the mount is ever removed. See Figure 7-8 for an example of a car with a display from Xenarc (no, that's not a planet, www.xenarc.com) mounted on the dash. Also in Figure 7-8 you will see there is a sun blocker on the window behind the screen—this is intended to reduce glare and can be picked up at any auto components store for under $5.

 Warning

Keep in mind that installing the display directly on your dash can easily interfere with your visibility when driving. A 7-inch display can be quite a large obstacle to look past, especially when the display is flashing text and graphics.

Installing a Flip-Down Display

Often seen in minivans facing the passenger seating area, flip-down displays are convenient video displays if people in your back seat need a close-up look at a display, such as for when watching a DVD. This saves the cost of installing a video display in the back of every seat, and you can still have a display up front using a simple video switch. It may be best to have a professional installer put one of these in. However, if you want to do it yourself, the instructions are fairly straightforward. Figure 7-9 shows a flip-down display using an Audiovox overhead unit.

FIGURE 7-8: A dash-mounted display.

Installing an In-Dash Computer Display

I have been able to find only two VGA-capable computer displays for cars, and one of those wasn't shipping at the time I was writing this book. The other was a hand-made unit from Digital Worldwide (www.digitalww.com). I decided to install this unit into my vehicle because it is a touch screen (so I can just tap music I want to hear) and can tilt toward the driver or passenger. It has about a seven-day lead time for them to build it for you, but it's worth the patience!

FIGURE 7-9: A flip-down display.

Installing Displays in Car Seats

If you are going to have multiple displays embedded in your car seats, you actually have a number of options. There are many do-it-yourself kits you can purchase at retail and specialty stores.

My local Best Buy had a very nice selection of screens, and one of them was actually a replacement for the headrests—just take out your old one and put the new one (with the built-in display) in, as shown in Figure 7-10! This was a much more expensive option, on the order of $1,500, although many manufacturers are starting to announce similar replacement headrest displays. This competition will bring prices down to a much more comfortable level in 2005 and beyond.

FIGURE 7-10: A replacement headrest display.

Installing a display into your headrest yourself isn't difficult and may only be a couple hundred dollars per display. Many mobile displays come with mounting brackets so you can just latch on to the support bars (sometimes called adjustment bars) under your headrest (see Figure 7-11). In the case where you want to install the display directly into your headrest, the keys are planning how to cut into the headrest (or the seat in the case that you have no separate readrest) and properly placing the mount. Most displays will have instructions for both types of mounting. There are so many headrests and ways to mount that I can't cover them all here. Suffice it to say, if you have adjustable headrests, it's far easier to just use the included brackets for the display(s) you buy and attach them to those support bars. Using multiple video sources is explained in more detail later in this chapter.

FIGURE 7-11: A display attached to the support bars on a headrest.

Note Many mobile video displays can be found on eBay for less than $100, and often two for under $200. Although these displays are not VGA resolution, they are ideal for having multiple displays for gaming and DVD playback in your car.

Many displays have the ability also to feed audio over infrared to infrared-based headphones for keeping peace and quiet in the car when you're driving and your passengers are demanding entertainment. Choosing this option can enable your passengers to play games while you listen to the radio. This type of setup would require you to directly feed audio from an audio switch to an auxilliary input on your displays so they can switch to the separate audio (and possibly video) source while you listen to yours. More expensive head units can support multiple displays and multiple audio and video sources themselves, but these are much more expensive.

One way to get around purchasing an expensive multisource head unit is to purchase both an A/V (audio/video) switch (~$49) and an Audio/Video Distribution Amplifier (~$45, see Figure 7-12) from Radio Shack. Use the switch to determine the input source, and the distribution amplifier to feed the audio and video feeds to the various displays in your car. To switch among the different A/V sources, simply change the input setting on the switch, and it will send the correct feed to the distribution amplifier, which will then send the amplified feeds to the displays.

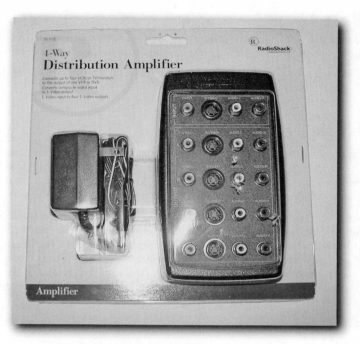

FIGURE 7-12: An Audio/Video Distribution Amplifier.

Tip

Consider some displays support multiple A/V inputs, so you could have more than one switch and distribution amplifier and feed each amp's output to the multiple A/V inputs on each display. This would allow passengers to switch between different video sources easily, such as the game console and a DVD.

Building Your Own Displays

There are many prebuilt displays you can purchase, but sometimes you need to come up with a custom solution. For example, you made need a larger screen than is typically available for cars, or a motorized in-dash enclosure. Sometimes you may just want to build everything yourself, like all the computers you spec and design for your own use. If you decide to build your own display, make sure the display takes the following items into account:

- **Heat**—Refer to Chapter 4, "It's So Hot in Here: Dealing with Heat."

- **Physics**—Refer to Chapter 6, "Physics Man, Physics: Preparing Home Electronics for the Road."

- **Durability**—Make sure bumps and vibrations don't make the screen come loose or fall out of place.

- **Visibility**—Make sure the screen is visible in broad daylight as well as at night.

- **Practicality for car use**—A 23-inch LCD may be cool, but what's its purpose in a car when it's so close to your face? Be careful becoming an open invitation to thieves.

- **Power usage**—You generally won't put plasma displays in your car, because of the sheer amount of power they require.

Installing Multiple Displays

If you are installing a computer or video entertainment system into your car, you may end up requiring multiple displays for all of your passengers to watch a movie. Sharing a single video source is generally an easy thing to do and requires only a video splitter if you only have one video source, and a video switcher and splitter if you're using more than one video source.

Having multiple displays usually means one in the back of each passenger seat and possibly one in the front seat. Using a distribution amplifier (about $50) and splitter, we can feed the signal to up to four screens in your vehicle. (Amplifiers capable of working with more than four sources are available, so feel free to look for those if you need them.) Now this usually requires some special power rigging, so refer to Chapter 3, "Giving Your Creation Life: Power Considerations" to learn about the many solutions you have available for powering devices in your vehicle.

Using Multiple Video Sources

If you are going to be switching among multiple analog video sources, you have a couple of choices. If you are going to have only a couple of inputs, it might be easier to purchase a display with a built-in video switcher and multiple video inputs. However, if you want to keep costs down, you can still purchase a video switcher and plug all items into the video switcher and then connect the single output into the display.

Multiple digital sources and multiple analog sources can be a lot more complex, requiring much more expensive video distribution amplifiers. Generally, however, you will have only a single digital source in your vehicle (such as your computer) so you should be able to get by with a display that has a single digital input and multiple video inputs. I installed such a device into my own vehicle, a Xenarc display with three analog video inputs and one VGA input, plus touch-screen capabilities, for about $400, as shown in Figure 7-13.

If you are going to have multiple digital and analog displays in your vehicle, you will have power issues because most digital-analog distribution amps require a separate power supply (which digital or analog specific switches usually do not because they are generally considered consumer items rather than professional items), as well as new cost concerns. A composite and S-Video switch may only run you around twenty dollars, while a product with those two plus component and optical switching is around $80 to $100. All of these switches usually include both the video and audio plugs so you can switch audio sources when you switch your video source as well.

FIGURE 7-13: Multiple display input connectors.

You can pick up the analog switches at any store that sells TVs, such as Radio Shack, Best Buy, CompUSA, Good Guys, and other similar stores. However, the professional video switches generally are only found at higher-end stores. I have found a shortcut to getting the high-end switch capabilities for less. There are game system switches that support most digital formats that run in the $80 range, such as the System Selector Pro from Pelican (www.pelicanacc.com). It's amazing how a usually expensive device geared normally for professionals becomes affordable when it is instead targeted toward a more cost-concious market such as gamers! See Figures 7-14 and 7-15 for samples of an analog A/V switch and the Pelikan digital-analog switch I purchased. This one is the MadCatz Ultra System Selector (www.madcatz.com) and requires no external power supply. The video selector is separated from the input sources and can be mounted on your dash or any surface with the convenient suction cups on the bottom. This helps you hide the cables while still having easy access to the video source selector.

FIGURE 7-14: The Pelican System Selector Pro has eight A/V ports on the back with a built-in optical audio switcher as well.

FIGURE 7-15: An analog video–analog switch you can pick up from practically any store.

Although most people will not use a higher-end device such as the Pelican System Selector Pro in their cars, those building show cars may want a system like this to really show off awesome displays.

Building a Screen Sock

In my first car going into this book, a Mazda Protégé 5, I had removable headrests, and I could install replacement headrest displays, mount speakers onto the headrest support bars, or cut into my seats (and easily find replacements). In my new car, a Dodge SRT-4, the seats are all one unit, with no adjustable headrest. I didn't want to cut into my brand new car's seats, and they would be expensive to replace if I messed up, but I still wanted to have screens on them. So I came up with an idea: screen socks. By using fabric I could buy at any fabric store and a little sewing (thanks to my step-mother for doing this!), I built a "sock" that goes over the top of my seat, and the screen is attached to the sock. Using elastic and the weight of the screen to keep the screen mounted, I could run any cables I wanted. In the following subsection, I will tell you how I did it (do not do this project while in your car, please—do it at home or in a workshop with a table and an environment you don't mind messing up a bit).

I found it is much easier to hand-sew the socks than to use a sewing machine. Your mileage may vary.

My screen sock idea is also useful for moving your screens into the trunk in order to prevent break-ins.

What You Need

To build the screen sock, you will need the following components:

- Elastic strips of appropriate length (see Figure 7-16)

- Vinyl or other fabric (replace the word *vinyl* with whatever material you use—black vinyl went best with my car's seats), with cloth backing for friction (see Figure 7-16)

- Scissors, sewing kit (thread, needle)

- Ruler

- Tape measure or tailor's flexible measure

- Razor

- Glue gun with super glue (sometimes called "heavy duty" glue), or appropriately sized screws, depending on how you want to approach attaching the screen (this will depend on your fabric—if it's thick, screws are okay, whereas with thinner fabrics, while you still want something robust, you will likely have to use a super glue, preferably with a hot glue gun)

FIGURE 7-16: Appropriate lengths of fabric (see Step 1 in the next subsection on how to measure these properly).

Making the Sock

Step 1: Measure Vinyl and Elastic

Measure a piece of vinyl large enough to go from the front of your seat's headrest piece to its back plus a few inches for the screen, and wide enough to cover the widest area of the headrest portion, as shown in Figure 7-17. Then, cut a piece of elastic the depth of the headrest portion of the seat, as shown in Figure 7-18. Remember: Measure *twice*, cut *once*!

FIGURE 7-17: Measuring from the front to the back of the headrest portion of the seat.

Step 2: Cut Vinyl and Elastic

Cut the vinyl and elastic based on the measurements you made in Step 1.

FIGURE 7-18: Measuring the depth of the seat.

Step 3: Sew the Elastic to the Vinyl

Now fold the piece of fabric over your seat, and there should be a little offset between where the fabric begins at the front of the seat to where it ends. The elastic needs to run straight across from where the fabric is beginning on the front to where that lines up on the back, so make a mark so that the elastic lines up properly when you finish the sock; then sew the elastic into the vinyl, as shown in Figure 7-19.

FIGURE 7-19: Note the offset of the elastic on the fabric and make appropriate markings before sewing.

Before attaching the screen, make sure you get all the information you need off the back of it (and store it in a place you can remember). Items such as model number and serial number, as well as manufacturer and any phone numbers, should be retrieved before attaching the back to the sock; otherwise, you may have to tear the screen off to get those numbers again.

FIGURE 7-20: The finished sock, sans display.

Attaching the Display

Now that you've made the sock (see the finished version in Figure 7-20), you need to attach the display to the vinyl. How you mount the display will depend on the display you purchased, so you may have to improvise my steps here. The ultimate goal is you don't want the display to come loose from the fabric.

Step 1: Score the Back of the Display

With the razor, score the back of the display along the sides and any flat areas that protrude outward, as shown in Figure 7-21. Scoring the plastic helps the glue bind to surfaces more effectively. (Remember this from middle school?)

Scored sections

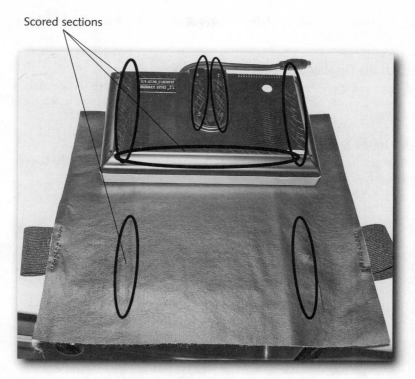

FIGURE **7-21: Scoring the back of the display and the fabric.**

Step 2: Score the Same Area on the Fabric

Now, for the same perimeter area on the fabric where the display will rest, score that area lightly with the razor—don't cut all the way through the plastic, as shown in Figure 7-21. Just lightly scrape to prepare the surface. The hot glue will melt the vinyl surface a little, giving an even stronger hold with the scoring in place. If you cut through the vinyl, be careful when gluing, so the glue doesn't seep through and stick to the other side of the sock.

Caution

Before gluing, make sure you have full access to the power and video ports on your display. If you need to run a cable from the back, do so *before* you glue, or you may not be able to get power or video to the display.

Step 3: Apply the Glue to the Display

Plug in the glue gun and insert the super-glue stick. Follow the instructions of the glue gun so you know when you can apply the glue. Be careful, it's hot! Also, be careful not to get the glue into any vents, power sockets, display connectors, or on the screen itself (if you do get glue on the screen, get it off quickly, before it hardens!). Now, apply the glue to the display on the areas you scored, keeping in mind the warnings just discussed. Immediately proceed to Step 4.

Note

Alternatively, you could use rivets or another solution to mount the display to the fabric. The glue is just one of many ways to do this.

Step 4: Attach the Display to the Fabric

Immediately after you apply the hot glue, attach the display on the scored surface of the sock. Push down a little (but not hard) to make sure the glue bonds properly. Let the display sit there for at least a minute.

Step 5: Glue in the Spots around the Display

After the initial glue has been applied, fill in the edges under the display with the hot super glue, as shown in Figure 7-22. This helps keep the display stable.

Gaps get filled in with glue

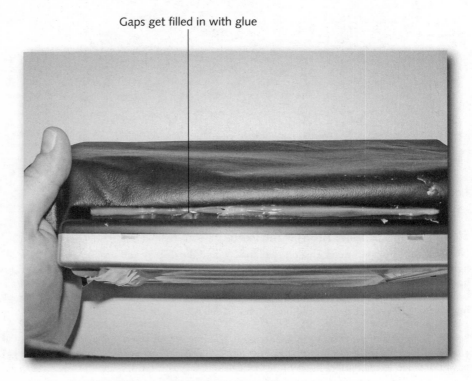

FIGURE 7-22: Filling in the gaps along the edges of the display with glue.

Step 6: Wait for the Glue to Harden

Now that you have applied the glue, wait at least two hours for it to harden. Do not move the display or sock while the glue is hardening.

Step 7: Test Drive!

When the glue has hardened, apply the sock to the car seat, attach it appropriately in your car to power and video sources, and take it for a test drive. Figure 7-23 shows the screen sock attached to the seat in my car. Drive on bumpy roads and try quick stops (with nobody around you, of course), to make sure the sock stays in place and that the display remains fixed to the sock.

FIGURE 7-23: The finished screen sock successfully applied to the seat.

Summary

This chapter discussed the various types of analog and digital connectors, the different displays and display-positioning options you have, and how to switch between multiple video sources. Displaying video in your car can make or break a long road trip (especially when nobody is telling good jokes), so I encourage you to install video solutions in your car for passenger entertainment!

Choosing an Input Device

The input devices you use in your car for computers, videos, or game devices need to be optimized for a car's environment. In this chapter I discuss the different types of input devices you may have in your car, issues with each, and the technologies that make them convenient for mobile use.

Keyboards, Mice, and Programmable Buttons

The majority of the time, interacting with a computer in a vehicle is spent performing simple gestures—pressing the Play button, tapping a song in a list, switching video sources. Very little time is spent by the driver doing any actual typing. Passengers, on the other hand, may get more interactive, such as entering the address of a Web site into a Web browser. However, once the page loads, they're back to the simple gestures of clicking and dragging.

How Will You Connect?

Today you have a lot of choices between wired and wireless device solutions. In the case of wired, the solution you purchase will either be PS/2, serial, or USB. With wireless, you have choices of RF (radio frequency), Bluetooth, or infrared. Since you are a geek, I will assume you already know what PS/2, serial, and USB ports are. To minimize clutter and distraction, I recommend going as wireless as possible, and the only usable input device solutions in a car tend to be RF or Bluetooth solutions (see later sections for more information on wireless technologies). Infrared input devices (wireless audio headphones are an exception) tend to be a bad choice because you will likely want to keep the input device's transceiver out of the way, and infrared devices need the transceiver visible in order to work. If you decide to go with a wired solution, pay close attention to Chapter 5, "Working with Cables," to make sure your cable lengths are within spec and that you hide and route them appropriately.

---

in this chapter

- ☑ Choosing an input device

- ☑ Wired and wireless solutions

- ☑ Adding game controllers

- ☑ Adding custom key panels and alternative input devices

Note Refer to Chapter 18, "Syncing Portable Music Players," for a project detailing how to add a USB hub to your car's center console.

Warning Be careful how many USB devices you attach to your machine, especially if you end up adding a hub. Many car computers will be built with minimal power supplies, so adding four or more devices to your machine may strain the power supply. It is best that, before you install the device for long-term use, you test it and find out whether you can use it with all of your other devices. Modern operating systems, such as Windows 2000, Windows XP, and Mac OS X will tell you if you don't have enough power for the device you are connecting. This shouldn't damage components if you just realize that you can't use a device when devices such as a removable hard drive and a digital camera and a memory stick and a USB hub are all plugged in at the same time. However, you could lose data if you're moving data back and forth from a storage device and the power level fluctuates!

Choosing a Mouse

Simple interactive activities tend to be performed by a mouse, touchpad, or trackball when you are at home or on a laptop. These are usually desk-based devices, or at least must be kept on a solid surface such as a tray in the back of an airplane seat.

Did You Know Years ago, Apple Computer realized how important simple gestures were to a user experience, and the Macintosh was born. The Macintosh operating system was actually built so you could use the entire computer with nothing but a mouse. The Macintosh's mouse-based interface was, to some extent, mimicked after systems seen by Apple engineers at Xerox PARC (Palo Alto Research Center).

Cars don't usually have the luxury of desk space. Keyboards and mice can't just sit around on the dash or they'll slide around when you take turns or hit bumps. You need a place to keep all of these devices so they are both accessible and easy to put away. Enter wireless.

Wireless mice run using radio frequency to communicate. It seems there are many different mice you can choose from, but the problem still remains that most mouse solutions are made to sit on a desk. A company called Gyration recognized this and designed a mouse (see Figure 8-1) that actually uses a gyroscope to work based on gestures you make in the air with your hand. For example, to move the mouse left, you just move your hand left (while holding the Gyration mouse, of course).

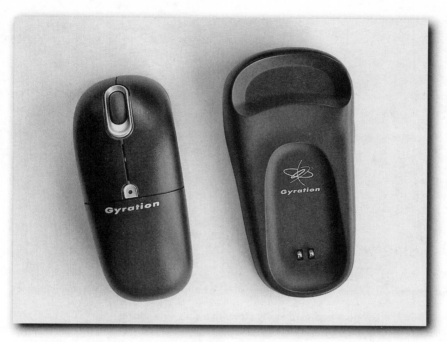

FIGURE 8-1: The Gyration mouse, which easily stows in the center console or glove compartment.

This proves incredibly convenient, and the mouse can be easily placed back into your center console and used later. Gyration even allows you to program gestures on the mouse to run programs and activities on a car computer, such as launching a media player or a Web browser. I haven't found any other products that do what the Gyration unit does. The Gyration product comes with both a programmable wireless keyboard (see Figure 8-2) and mouse for under $100, making it a good place to start if you're putting a computer in your car.

Can I Use Touchpads and Trackballs?

True enough, touchpads and trackballs can work vertically and can be mounted on your steering wheel, the dash, and other places. The inconvenience here is there weren't (last I checked) any wireless versions of trackballs or touchpads. If you can find one, however, it's also a good solution.

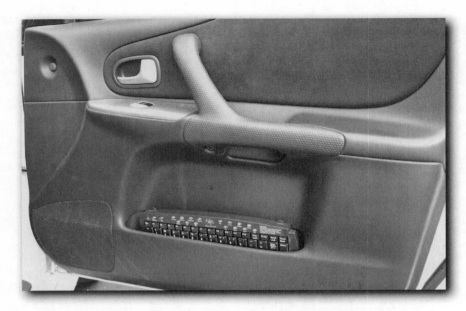

FIGURE 8-2: The Gyration keyboard easily stows in a car's side pocket.

Displays with Touch Screens

It can be cumbersome to use a mouse while the car is in motion, even with the Gyration product mentioned above. To this end, when you decide on your display device, you can purchase one with a touch screen built in. This is the ideal solution for a car, since you can just use a finger on the screen to tap to click, double-tap to double-click, drag, and more, all without using a mouse (and making faster selections, keeping your eyes on the road). VGA touch-screen solutions are readily available from companies such as Xenarc (www.xenarc.com) and Digital Worldwide (www.digitalww.com). Digital Worldwide actually sells motorized enclosures and in-dash touch-screen solutions that I have had excellent success with in my car computer solutions. I even wrote my car music player, Cartunes (www.cartunes.ws) to work with these high-resolution touch screens, so I can simply tap the music I want, just like a radio.

For more information on choosing displays, refer to Chapter 7, "Choosing a Display Device."

Choosing a Keyboard

Although choices for mice are limited due to the nature of where mice are usually operated (i.e., on a desk or other horizontal flat space), keyboards can be used anywhere without changing their form factor. A wired keyboard still doesn't make much sense since keyboards are generally large and need to be stowed away when not being used in a car environment. You can't always just unplug the keyboard (or other devices) if the computer is mounted in your dash, and finding a long enough keyboard cable, or running an extender, is fraught with trouble, such as when the extender becomes unplugged or the connector gets tangled. It's too much work to use a wired keyboard, and basically any wired input device on a computer for that matter, in a car environment. Hence, wireless is really your only option here.

Wireless keyboard solutions abound, and so do the technologies they use. Choose a keyboard you are comfortable with, but make sure it can be easily stowed away when not in use. A full-size keyboard may be too big to stow in a side pocket. Even though it may slide under a seat with no problems, people stepping on the keyboard may damage it. The Gyration product I mentioned earlier works very well. There are many mini keyboards to choose from, a very durable one being the Mini Virtually Indestructible Keyboard from GrandTec USA, which can even be rolled up and is impervious to liquid spills!

If you decide not to use the Gyration, which uses a proprietary radio frequency, pay attention to what technology your keyboard uses to transmit its signal. Common solutions are Bluetooth®, infrared (often called IrDA), and proprietary solutions. Right off the bat I'd like to suggest staying away from infrared, which uses light to transmit the device signals to a receiver, as discussed earlier. The odd angles at which passengers may hold the keyboard, including using a keyboard behind a seat, will make an infrared device almost worthless for use around the entire car. Any radio frequency (RF) based technology, however, such as proprietary ones used by the Gyration and others, and Bluetooth (which is just a standardized short-range RF technology running in the unlicensed 2.4 GHz band) can pass through material (such as seats) and be used anywhere in the car, almost regardless of where the signal transceiver is located.

Did You Know

For those of you wondering where the funky name *Bluetooth* came from, it stems from the great influence Baltic-region companies have had on the Bluetooth standard. Harold Bluetooth was the king of Denmark in the tenth century CE/AD.

Choosing a Bluetooth keyboard over a proprietary device will probably not make a difference, although your operating system may have better support for the Bluetooth device. If you decide to build a Macintosh® or Linux computer into your vehicle, for instance, there is probably a shortage of drivers for many of the wireless devices that are available, which usually only come with drivers for Microsoft® Windows®. Some newer Macintoshes have built-in support for Bluetooth, so those devices that support it may be the only alternative you would have. Mac OS X users may luck out in finding an open-source third-party driver on the Internet or at a user group meeting, especially if the device is a popular one.

Tip

When you use a wireless or Bluetooth keyboard *and* you decide to deploy a wireless Internet connection in your vehicle (or even in your home) using 802.11a, b, or g, you may encounter some interference. Both Bluetooth and 802.11x wireless technologies operate at the 2.4GHz frequency (802.11a can also operate at 5.2GHz and 5.8GHz as well, depending on your configuration). Many of the proprietary wireless solutions also run in the 2.4GHz band because it is unlicensed, meaning nobody has to pay for approval for their device to use the frequency. Specifically, this frequency range is called the Industrial Scientific and Medical, or ISM, band. Keep this in mind when planning what devices to deploy in your vehicle. Many wireless devices enable you to change the channel, or frequency, your device broadcasts on in case you encounter interference. Sometimes this is as easy as moving a switch on the device itself (as with game controllers and some keyboards) or pressing a button, and other systems may require you to run a separate software configuration utility on a computer.

Using and Programming Custom Button Panels

Although a keyboard and mouse may be the most common methods of interacting with a computer, you can also purchase programmable button panels and assign actions to them. For example, maybe you want a few buttons on your dash for radio, GPS, CD, DVD, Web browser, e-mail client, and a few key shortcuts, such as traffic reports, favorite song playlists, and news. Using a programmable keypad mounted on your dash, you could have simple one-button access to all of these features without using a mouse or lots of keyboard commands. I will show more on how to install these in the project chapters as I use them for some projects. If you want to start shopping around, do a search for "programmable keypad" on the Internet, or try a company like Kinesis at www.kinesis-ergo.com to get a feel for what you can do.

Another interesting solution I came across was a "knob" from Griffin Technology (www.griffintechnology.com) called the PowerMate that looks like one of the dials on a high-end stereo system. The PowerMate lets you program the device to enable "dialing" music, or using the device for video editing, and pushing the dial in for selecting items. It's very cool—check it out on their Web site as a solution for easily selecting music and then pushing the dial to make it play.

If you have any programming skills, it is pretty easy to write custom applications that let you control the various components of a car computer and customize your interface to suit your needs. Microsoft's Visual Basic (http://msdn.microsoft.com/vbasic/) makes this almost too easy, making it possible to interact with serial data coming from your engine into a serial port on your computer, access and play music and video files, and perform other similar tasks all in an application you design. There are so many components available for Visual Basic (and also the entire .NET framework, which includes C#, J# and C++) that almost anyone with programming skills can take most of the projects I present and make them smarter and cooler!

Choosing a Game Controller

You have a wide range of options when it comes to controllers for game consoles. Since the controllers are fairly standardized—meaning they can't use more power than the console is willing to give them and need to follow certain specifications for interoperability with games, other controllers, and the game system itself—you will find many solutions that don't require any additional power other than charged batteries to run. This makes wireless game controllers very convenient, and since you don't need another AC (alternating-current) outlet for them, they are basically as simple to install as wired controllers.

With game controllers, like other wireless devices, you need to watch what technology is being used. For wired controllers it obviously doesn't matter. With wireless, however, many game controllers used infrared to transmit the gaming signal to a receiver. It is better to use an RF technology that doesn't utilize infrared, because the game console will usually be either out of sight or at a poor angle for infrared light to reach the console's receiver. The technology used should be printed clearly on the controller's packaging, and any store representative should be able to tell you what's used prior to your making a purchase.

Can I Still Use Wired Devices?

In your initial configuration of a car computer, and in the case that you are just deploying a game console, wired input devices may work out just fine. For example, game controllers can be disconnected and neatly tucked under a seat or put in the trunk where they won't get damaged. Wireless doesn't really affect them. So, if you want to keep using wired devices, I would suggest only using them for noncomputer applications.

You can pick up game controllers, both wired and wireless, at practically any store that sells game consoles. Just find one that's comfortable. Realize that you can move the game controllers (and sure enough, the console) back and forth from your car to your home, regardless of which type you buy.

Infrared devices may have trouble in a vehicle in bright sunlight situations. Keep this in mind if a device's remote control is not working. It is best to put the device in a darker location anyway, because of heat concerns, but it may help out with the bright-light condition issue as well. For a different analogy, you can't play laser tag outside on a sunny day because the infrared transmitters on the guns wouldn't be able to transmit light to the other players' receivers (the sun would overpower the light being emitted from the guns). Infrared transmitters on remotes aren't any more powerful, either. Generally in a car environment you shouldn't have any real trouble, but sunroofs, lack of tint, and convertibles could very well cause issues. Like I said earlier—stick to RF solutions wherever possible.

Performing Input with Speech Recogition

The most obvious question here should be "How well does speech recognition work in a car?" With all of the ambient noise and the stereo running, the prospect of accurate speech recognition is usually low. This doesn't mean you can't do it, and many higher-end cars today actually use noise-cancellation sound waves to reduce the amount of noise in a vehicle, which acclimates the environment for more effective speech recognition. If you aren't using your stereo all the time, it's entirely feasible to attempt dictation, voice commands, and so forth. Programs such as Microsoft Office, IBM's Via Voice, and Dragon Systems software all do an excellent job. If you already have Microsoft Office XP or above, it comes with speech recognition built in (most people I tell this to never knew!), and it works pretty well. You can even program voice commands to perform many of the operations I suggested earlier for programmable keypads (favorite song lists, news, GPS, and so forth).

Microphone placement in relation to the sound source is key with speech recognition. Keep it close to the user's mouth or where their voice will be projected. I don't know of any wireless microphones that would be considered budget items, but you can find wireless mics at any audio speciality store that may work well. There are also wireless headsets that should work fine, with some having built-in noise cancellation features for noisy environments, and that can be moved from passenger to passenger for their own use. You can usually pick up these head-sets at any place that sells cell phones, as well as many retail computer stores like Best Buy and CompUSA.

In 1998 Microsoft showed off the AutoPC platform, a Windows CE–based system for vehicles that would interact with its PocketPC (and once called PalmPC) products. You could sync your calendar and contacts and then be told via text-to-speech technology about upcoming appoint-ments. Using speech recognition you could tell the stereo to change audio tracks and switch to the radio. The technology itself never really sold well, didn't have much developer support, and for a while Clarion was even selling an AutoPC product (for about $1,000 without even DVD support!) and has since pretty much faded into history, like Microsoft Bob®. Now that comput-ers in vehicles are again getting exposure in the press, we may see a rekindling of the AutoPC platform from Microsoft, with a richer developer toolset and support for their latest technologies, which would surely make the product more palatable for developers, and possibly for auto man-ufacturers as well.

Do not position any device, regardless how small, on a surface where an airbag may deploy. For example, if you mount a keyboard on your steering wheel and the airbag deploys, you, and pos-sibly your passengers, could be seriously injured or even killed by the blow! Even if you don't have an airbag, try to keep things that could fly around in an accident away from your face and head. There isn't any really good reason to mount a keyboard on your steering wheel, since you should-n't be typing while you drive. A touchpad or trackpad shouldn't be too much of a problem because you can mount those without much, if any, interference while you turn the wheel, but if something is going to get in the way of your driving duties, it's best to find another solution.

Summary

This chapter discussed input devices and how to choose the right solutions for your car. In addition, we went over some safety precautions and how to determine when it is okay to use wired input devices in lieu of wireless. Installation and positioning of these devices should be obvious in most cases, and most input devices will work with more than one project in this book, such as mice and keyboards, whereas gaming controllers tend to work only with the sys-tem they are designed for.

Foundation Projects

part

Building a Single-Source A/V System

Approximate project cost: $390 with display; $240 without display

In-car DVD players are one of the most popular after-market add-ons. The problem is that you are usually limited to just that—DVD players (and sometimes VHS players). What it all boils down to is installing screens and connecting them to an A/V (audio/video) device. In this chapter you will install a single-source A/V system into your car. In this case, it will be a *slimline* (very small and thin) DVD player, but it could just as easily be a VHS deck, camcorder, digital camera video output, or any video game system—the list goes on. Before moving forward with the project in this chapter, I recommend you read Chapter 3, "Giving Your Creation Life: Power Considerations," which covers power requirements; Chapter 7, "Choosing a Display Device," which covers options for displays; and Chapter 5, "Working with Cables," which covers installing cabling in your vehicle.

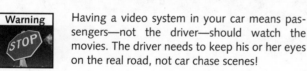

Warning

Having a video system in your car means passengers—not the driver—should watch the movies. The driver needs to keep his or her eyes on the real road, not car chase scenes!

What You Need

Here are the items you will need to do this project:

- Slimline DVD Player (approximately $40), as shown in Figure 9-1

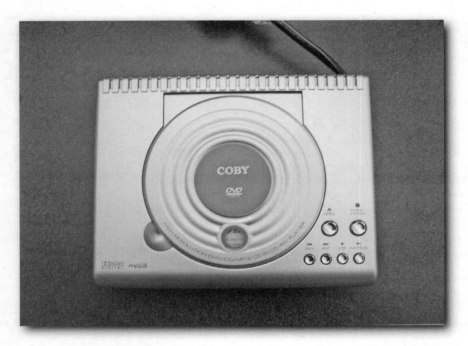

FIGURE 9-1: Slimline DVD player.

- Display to see the DVD player's output (varies on what you decide to install, see Chapter 7, "Choosing a Display Device")
- Left and right Monster cable stereo audio cables and composite video cable as shown in Figure 9-2 (these usually come with DVD players and other A/V devices, otherwise $40 for all from any local store that sells A/V equipment)

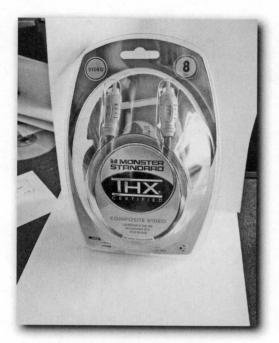

FIGURE 9-2: Monster Standard shielded A/V Cables.

- A/V switch to switch between computer and video audio (optional, $49)
- 350-watt AC (alternating-current) inverter to power video system and display ($60)
- Six to eight 1-foot-long Velcro® strips, as shown in Figure 9-3, half hook sides and half fuzzy sides (that's how they usually come anyway; pick them up at any hardware or home improvement store, $6)

FIGURE 9-3: Velcro strips.

- Scissors and a ruler or measuring tape (free from you or your neighbor Ned)
- Video distribution amplifier if you need to feed video to multiple displays (around $45)
- DVDs for your passenger's viewing pleasure (you could really show off with a copy of the Knight Rider® series)

Planning What to Install

Throughout this book I have emphasized the importance of planning, so the first step is to make some decisions about what you're going to install and why and how you're going to install it . . . let's do that now.

Choose the System to Install

You likely already know what system you want to install. I will assume you want to install a DVD player for this example, although any reasonable A/V device will do. You will want to find a device made for mobile environments, and, in this case, a portable DVD player will do.

You can usually pick these up new for no more than $40, and many times for less on eBay. There are two types you can buy—those with a built-in screen and those without. The ones without a screen will be most usable for your car, and you likely won't need the screen if you already have one. However, if you want to remove the device and use it as a portable DVD player elsewhere (on a plane, for example), the ones with screens are often not much more expensive, possibly on the order of $50 extra. You may also be able to save some money by taking a unit with a screen apart and retrofitting that to your car as the display device, but that could get ugly and you likely will still have to purchase a new screen enclosure.

Choose the Display

See Chapter 7, "Choosing a Display Device" to learn about the different types of displays you can install. The display used in the general-purpose PC project in Chapter 11, which supports both VGA and composite/analog inputs is ideal if you will be installing both a computer and a game system in your car. If you won't be installing a computer, choose a decent in-dash or on-dash analog display, which usually runs under $150 on eBay with the mounting kit. I picked up two quality displays for $179 plus shipping—check it out in Figure 9-4.

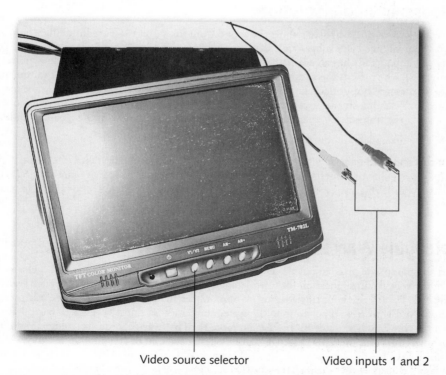

Video source selector   Video inputs 1 and 2

FIGURE 9-4: Display I used in my car and the associated A/V inputs attached to it.

All DVD players come with a composite video output port and both left and right stereo audio output ports. Some also come with S-Video and component (YPrPb) outputs. In practically all A/V configurations in your car, you will only be able to use the composite video signal, although some higher-end displays (read "very expensive") may allow S-Video and component. Composite should be fine in practically all scenarios, however, because the screens are so small you won't see much of a difference, and it's a heck of a lot cheaper to buy and implement composite cable solutions.

In regards to audio, you will likely always use the left and right audio RCA-type jacks and connect them as discussed later in this chapter. If you want something more than two-channel stereo audio you will have to buy a processor for such sound and a higher-end head unit. Oftentimes the Dolby® Digital processors and digital audio connections you can put in a car are overkill due to the road noise and compact size of most cars, so unless you have a lot of money to spend, it's tough to justify more than two channels of sound. Indeed, investing those funds into higher-quality speakers and high-end head units can greatly improve the sound fidelity in your car, while still costing less than multichannel sound implementations and giving you more enjoyment bang for your hard-earned bucks.

Choose an Audio Solution

You will likely want the ability to hear the sound from the system you are installing. In order to do this you will need a new head unit that has auxiliary audio input capability unless your current head unit already has an auxiliary input, or an FM radio audio transmitter (shown in Figure 9-5), which feeds the audio from your A/V device to an FM channel you can tune in on your current stereo. Your decision on which to install will depend on whether you want to replace your existing stereo (if you can; some cars make this difficult), or want to save money by just getting the transmitter. Your audio fidelity will be much higher with the auxiliary audio inputs.

Most cars and head units only support two-channel stereo audio. SRS® WOW® effects are usually meant to enhance two-channel sound. Don't worry if you have a Dolby Digital or DTS DVD playing—your DVD player will downmix the audio (i.e., merge the channels) for you automatically.

Determine Where to Install the System

Find an appropriate place to put the DVD player where the unit is accessible and cables won't get in the way. An ideal location for top-loading systems is the axle hump in the back seat of many cars. For side-slot- or tray-loading systems, under the driver or passenger seat is preferred as shown in Figure 9-6. If positioning the system under a seat, put it far enough back that when the tray is fully extended it reaches no more than halfway past the seat's edge (and preferably, not at all). This prevents passengers from kicking the unit or stepping on the tray while loading a DVD. Any place you put the DVD player, you can usually Velcro it there so it won't move, and your passengers can change DVDs very easily.

FIGURE 9-5: An FM radio audio transmitter can be quite convenient if you don't want to spend money on a new head unit.

Note Keeping a DVD player or other video device in the trunk isn't a good idea because you'll lose the ability to control the unit with the remote control (which usually uses infrared), and you'll have to pull over to change the DVD or other media.

Tip If you place the DVD player under the seat, make sure you inform your passengers that it's there so they don't kick the unit.

Do You Need to Configure an A/V Switch?

If you are installing more than one A/V device, such as the DVD player and a Game Cube, you will likely need an A/V Switch so you can switch the different audio sources with your stereo's auxiliary audio input. Figure 9-7 shows an installed A/V switch on the front console of my car.

FIGURE 9-6: The DVD player located under the driver's seat.

So why use an A/V switch when you're only switching audio? The A/V switch will allow you to use your display with multiple gaming systems if you decide to add them, as well as switch between your audio from your computer and your games. The A/V switch can also let you listen to music from your computer while your video is fed to video displays in the back seat (see Figure 9-8), which usually will have their own A/V switch built-in.

FIGURE 9-7: The installed A/V switch.

If you're going to be driving video to more than just a single display in the front, you'll need to install an A/V distribution amplifier so the audio and video signals can be effectively transmitted to each display, as well as the head unit (or audio transmitter, if you go that route). Weak video signals will result in poor video quality, and you want to do it right the first time. You'll likely not need anything more than a four-way amplifier, which can drive up to four screens; these can be picked up at any Radio Shack or similar A/V electronics store. Keep in mind that amplifiers require power, so you want to mount the device near your AC inverter.

FIGURE 9-8: The seat-back displays let passengers play games or watch movies while you use your GPS in the front.

Installing the DVD Unit

Now that you have the information you need, let's address installing the DVD player (these steps will likely be the same for any A/V device you decide to install).

Step 1: Configure the Stereo to Receive Audio

Like I said earlier, you probably want to hear your DVDs while you watch them (as a passenger, of course). In this case you have a couple of options:

- Use the built-in auxiliary input of your head unit.
- Use an FM audio transmitter if you don't have the luxury of an auxiliary port.

The location of the auxiliary audio port will vary from head unit to head unit, so I can't cover all models here. Follow the instructions in your respective manual to plug the audio inputs from either your video switch or your DVD player into those respective ports. Some factory head units have a port built into the glove compartment or center console (see Figure 9-10), while many third-party head units have RCA-type stereo jacks coming from their backsides (see Figure 9-9). If you don't have an auxiliary jack, you can easily build one with a faceplace and a dremel, as described in the next section, "Installing Auxiliary A/V Jacks."

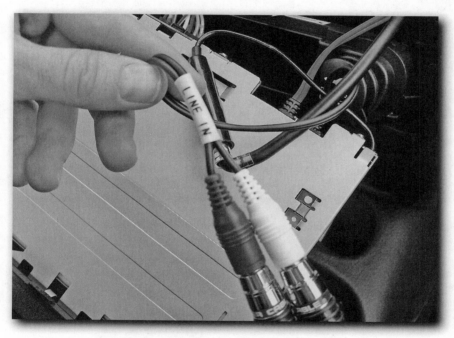

FIGURE 9-9: The auxiliary audio input from a third-party head unit.

FIGURE 9-10: The auxiliary audio input in a minivan.

Warning Your car or audio input device auxiliary audio input port may only be a phono jack instead of separate right and left RCA jacks, as shown in Figure 9-9. In that case you will need a *stereo Y-adapter*, which usually runs for under $5. Make sure you buy a stereo solution, or you will only receive monaural sound!

Note Some head units require you to enable the auxiliary input before you can use it. If you have a factory head unit (one such manufacturer requiring this is Saab—what a Saab story), you may need to pay your dealer to enable the auxiliary feature.

If you are using an FM transmitter, plug your A/V device into it, set the frequency, and continue to the next step (we'll test audio later).

Installing Auxiliary A/V Jacks

Sometimes you may want the ability to temporarily plug into any A/V device and use it in your car. For example, maybe you're on the way to the gym and you want to listen to your iPod® in the car and then disconnect it and listen to it while you work out. Maybe you want to quickly connect your digital camera so passengers can start going through the photos they just took on a bigger screen. Adding auxiliary A/V jacks in your car enables you to do just that. Another benefit to auxiliary A/V jacks is you can build an easily accessible location in your car for connecting A/V devices, instead of having to take apart your dash every time you need to connect or disconnect a device. Let's go over how to add a set to your car.

Determine Where to Install the Jacks

In this example I installed the A/V jacks into my center armrest compartment so I could simply plug in my iPod and then leave it in there in shuffle mode until I got to the workout center. This compartment in my Dodge SRT-4 is easily removable by taking out a few screws, so I could take it upstairs, modify it, and then bring it back downstairs and reinstall the modified unit. Your mileage may, of course, vary.

What You Will Need

In addition to the obvious audio and/or video receiver (such as a head unit and a video display), you will need the following to complete this project:

- In-line Triple Phono Plug Coupler with left audio, right audio, and composite video jacks (around $7, see Figure 9-11). If you want only audio inputs, not video, get a Dual instead of Triple phono plug coupler.

FIGURE 9-11: Phono coupler.

- Dremel tool with #561 multipurpose bit to cut plastic (around $39 if you don't already own one, see Figure 9-12).

- Glue gun with heavy-duty or super glue stick (around $20 for glue gun, usually comes with the sticks).

- Monster® stereo audio and composite video RCA cables, or similar well-shielded cable solution (around $40).

- Vice grip or similar device to hold the object you're cutting into.

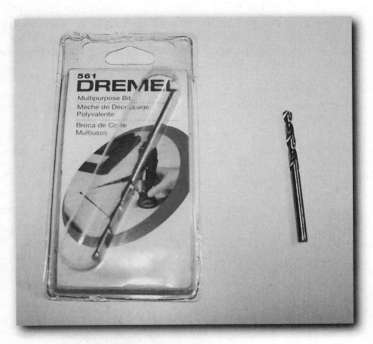

FIGURE 9-12: Dremel 561 drilling bit.

Installing the Jacks

Now that you have what you need, let's cut into the compartment.

Step 1: Prepare the Glovebox

Remove the compartment tray from your car (or whatever you decided to install the coupler into) and take it to your workspace. Do not try to do this project in your car—you need room to work. In Figure 9-13 you can see the removed compartment tray.

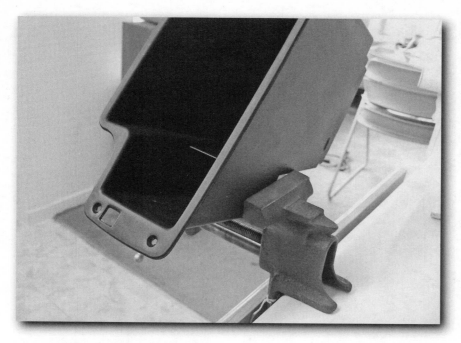

FIGURE 9-13: The removed compartment tray.

Step 2: Measure and Cut the Glovebox

Use a pencil and ruler to measure and draw a rectangle the width and height of the coupler on the plastic where you want to insert the coupler. This is where you will be cutting to make room for the coupler. I did this close to the top of the compartment but far enough away from the slot for the locking mechanism, as shown in Figure 9-14. Fill in (shade) the rectangle with the pencil so you can clearly see where you need to cut while you are cutting. (If you just do a single line, you can lose sight of where you need to be, and it's just plain easier filled in.)

FIGURE 9-14: Use a pencil to mark out where the coupler will reside in the plastic.

Before cutting, make sure you have protective eyewear and that you are comfortable and educated in using a Dremel tool. You can seriously injure yourself if you aren't familiar with this type of tool, and I don't want you to get hurt!

Once you've measured the hole, place the compartment in the grip and use the Dremel and the drilling bit to cut out the square. The easiest way to do this is to drill holes in the four corners of the rectangle, and then, in a sideways motion, cut out the sides of the rectangle, as shown in Figure 9-15.

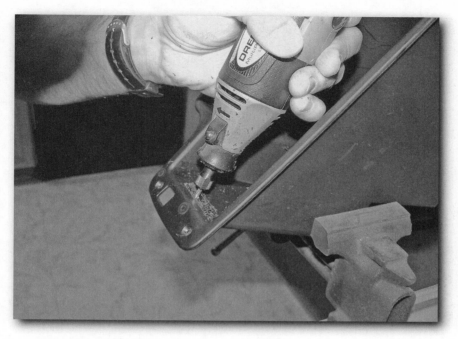

FIGURE 9-15: Cutting the plastic.

Step 3: Mount the Coupler

Once you've cut out the rectangle, place the coupler into the opening so the metal jacks and some of the coupler's plastic are visible from the backside of the compartment. This is where the cables running to your head unit and display will terminate. The other side, showing in the compartment, is where your auxiliary devices, such as an iPod or portable DVD player, will connect to, as shown in Figure 9-16.

FIGURE 9-16: The coupler properly inserted.

The rest of this step involves using the glue gun to mount the coupler in the plastic. If you prefer to use a different method of mounting the coupler, such as a mounting plate, do so and proceed to Step 4.

Using the glue gun (which should be heated and ready to go), carefully place glue between the openings in the plastic and the coupler, forming a seal, as shown in Figure 9-17. Be careful not to get any glue on the connectors themselves, because this may prevent your cables from plugging into them. Do this on both sides of the compartment and allow the glue to harden (about one to two hours).

When the glue has hardened, you can use tempura paint or another solution to paint the glue so it matches the interior of the compartment.

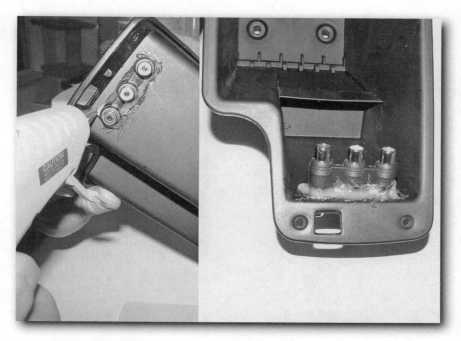

FIGURE 9-17: Applying the glue.

Step 5: Run the Cables to Your A/V Solution

Now that the coupler is mounted, connect the Monster cables to the back of your head unit and display (or to your video distribution amplifier if you are using more than one display). Use electrical tape on those connections to prevent them from coming loose because of vibration in your car. Then run the other end to where your coupler will be and connect those ends to the appropriate connectors on your coupler (usually white for left audio, red for right audio, and yellow for composite video), using electrical tape to keep the connections solid.

Step 6: Test!

Now that everything is connected, hook up a device and try out your new jacks! Figure 9-18 shows the finished product installed in the center armrest compartment.

FIGURE 9-18: The finished product.

Step 2: Run the A/V Cables

Now that you're set up to hear the audio, you need to run the audio and video cables. If you are using an A/V switch, run the audio and video cables from the DVD player to your switch. Once those cables are firmly connected, run the audio cables from your switch to your stereo's auxiliary input or audio transmitter and the video cables to your display. Follow the instructions in Chapter 5, "Working with Cables," on how to properly run cables in your car.

If you are not using a switch, run the audio cables from the DVD player directly to your stereo's auxiliary input or audio transmitter and the video cables directly to your display. Again, follow the instructions in Chapter 5 on how to properly run cables in your car.

Step 3: Apply Velcro

Before installing the system you need to make sure it won't move. If you are using a different method than Velcro to secure the system from moving, you can skip this step.

Measure and cut out hook-side (not fuzzy-side) strips for the two sides of the bottom of the DVD player (or possibly all four for your specific system), as shown in Figure 9-19. Make sure you don't cover up any doors or latches you need to reach!

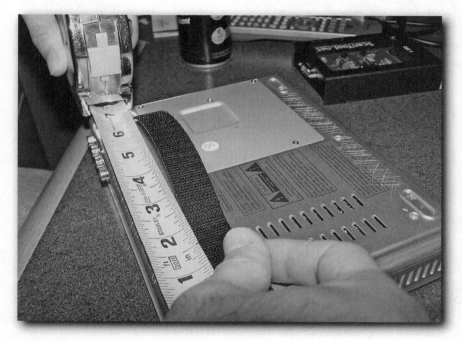

FIGURE 9-19: Measuring and cutting the Velcro.

With a razor blade or scissors, score the plastic bottom edges of the DVD player in a criss-cross pattern so the Velcro sticks well (remember this from middle school?), as shown in Figure 9-20.

FIGURE 9-20: Scoring the bottom edge of the DVD player.

Apply the Velcro as close to the edges as possible, as shown in Figure 9-21.

Step 4: Install the System

Now that the Velcro has been applied, place the system under the passenger's seat, or the location you decided to install it, as shown earlier in Figure 9-6. Make sure the disc slot is unobstructed and easy to reach for your passengers. This is especially important with DVD players with a slide-out tray—you don't want to position them where the tray can't fully eject!

FIGURE 9-21: The Velcro applied to the DVD unit.

Step 5: Play

Now that everything's connected, turn on your car and play a DVD!

You should generally have your car running while you play a DVD or use any nonstock-powered device. If your car isn't running, your A/V system can be quite a drain on your battery, and your AC inverter may very well let you know by whining loudly about the power consumption. It's okay to show off the DVD player without the car running, but just remember you've turned your car into a gas-powered, not a battery-powered, video player.

Do not sit in an idle car and watch a movie while the engine is running. Extended periods inside an idle car while it is running can expose you to carbon monoxide, sufficient amounts of which can kill you.

Summary

In this chapter you installed a DVD player and configured the appropriate A/V components for use in your car. DVD players are an awesome entertainment addition to any car and will provide hours of entertainment for your passengers! Keep in mind, of course, that you can instead install a game system such as a Playstation® 2 or a Microsoft Xbox® and get DVD playback *and* gaming capabilities all in one unit. See Chapter 10, "Integrating a Game Console," for more details on installing a game system in your car.

Integrating a Game Console

Approximate project cost: $480 with display; $330 without display

Gaming systems are one of the most enjoyable add-ons you can have in your car. From entertaining your passengers to keeping the kids quiet to playing DVDs, game consoles today have a lot of capabilities that complement the entertainment systems in a car.

In this chapter you will install a game system into your car. You can choose any game system you like, but the example used in this chapter will be the Nintendo Game Cube®. Once you have the A/V (audio/video) side of this project installed, of course, you can put in any game system you like, often as easily as unplugging the first system from the AC (alternating-current) inverter, removing the exposed game system, and replacing it with another.

Another perk to modern game systems is their high-end multimedia capabilities. Sony's Playstation® 2 comes with built-in DVD playback, and Microsoft's Xbox sports the same with an inexpensive add-on. The Xbox even lets you rip your CDs to its internal hard drive and play your music, all without installing a computer. With game systems such as the Xbox and the Sony Playstation 2 now running under $200, they are an ideal choice if you want an affordable and capable media center solution in your car.

Warning Having a game system in your car means your passengers should play it, not the driver! The driver needs to keep his or her eyes on the real road, not the one in Mario Kart!

in this chapter

☑ Installing a game console

☑ Using game consoles as media centers

☑ Feeding game video to multiple displays

What You Need

- Nintendo Game Cube or other game system (around $99)
- Left and right RCA cables and composite video cable (these come with the Game Cube, otherwise $40 for all from any local store that sells A/V equipment as shown in Figure 10-1)

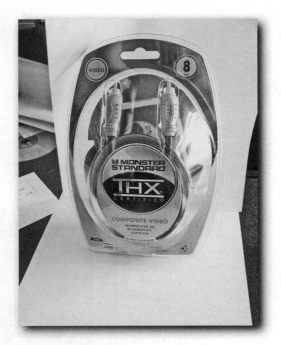

FIGURE **10-1: Monster Standard shielded A/V cables.**

- A/V switch to switch between computer and game audio (optional, around $49)
- 350-watt AC inverter to power gaming system and display ($60)
- Display to see the game system's output (varies on what you decide to install, see Chapter 7, "Choosing a Display Device")
- Wireless game controllers (around $25 each)
- Scissors and a ruler or measuring tape (free from you or your neighbor Ned)
- Six to eight 1-foot-long Velcro®, strips as shown in Figure 10-2, half hook sides and half fuzzy sides (that's how they usually come anyway; around $6)
- Video distribution amplifier if you need to feed video to multiple displays (around $45)
- Games (such as Mario Kart Double-Dash)

FIGURE 10-2: Velcro strips.

Planning What to Install

Throughout this book I have emphasized the importance of planning, so the first step is to make some decisions about what you're going to install and why and how you're going to install it . . . let's do that now.

Choose the System to Install

You likely already know what system you want to install. In this project I will assume a Nintendo® Game Cube® is being installed, although practically any game system can be substituted in the steps used in this chapter.

So why did I choose a Game Cube over other systems? The Game Cube is compact, its spindle is easily accessible via a top-loading mechanism (so I don't have to worry about where the tray will end up), and it uses very little power compared to the monstrous power-hungry processors in the Xbox and the first-generation Playstation 2, although Sony's redesigned, compact, and incredibly thin Playstation 2 console is very portable, making it another great choice for space-limited in-car use. The Game Cube also is the only game system with Mario Kart, one of my favorite games, and fantastic for road trips to keep both adults and kids entertained. If you are going to use an older cartridge-based system, most of the power concerns shouldn't be a big deal. (If you haven't already, see Chapter 3, "Giving Your Creation Life: Power Considerations.")

Choose the Display

See Chapter 7, "Choosing a Display Device" to learn about the various types of displays you can install. The display used in the general-purpose PC project in Chapter 11, which supports both VGA and composite/analog inputs is ideal if you will be installing both a computer and a game system in your car. If you won't be installing a computer, choose a decent in-dash or on-dash analog display, which usually runs under $150 on eBay, including the mounting kit (see Figure 10-3). All gaming systems for at least the past 10 years have come standard with composite output capabilities. This is fine for a car environment. There is no reason to spend the extra money for the S-Video or component video add-ons, even if you want to add DVD, the screens you will likely use in a car are usually no larger than 14 inches in size, and you won't be able to tell much of a difference when playing games (or DVDs, too, in the case of Xbox and Playstation 2).

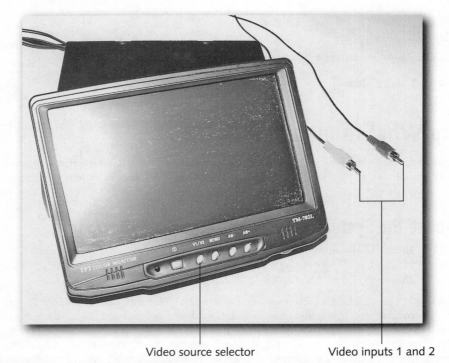

Video source selector   Video inputs 1 and 2

FIGURE 10-3: The display I used in my car and the associated A/V inputs attached to it.

Choose an Audio Solution

You will likely want the ability to hear sound from the system you are installing. To do this, you will need a new head unit that has an auxiliary audio input capability, unless your current head unit already has an auxiliary input or an FM radio transmitter, which feeds the audio from your A/V device to an existing FM channel you can tune in on your current stereo, an example of which is shown in Figure 10-4.

Your decision on which to install will depend on whether you want to replace your existing stereo or save money by just getting the transmitter. Sometimes you don't have the option to install a new head unit, likely because the head unit in your car is difficult to replace, or your car may not have a removable head unit (i.e., just a "command console" that controls everything from air conditioning to the use of the car stereo). Audio fidelity will be much higher feeding through the auxiliary audio inputs.

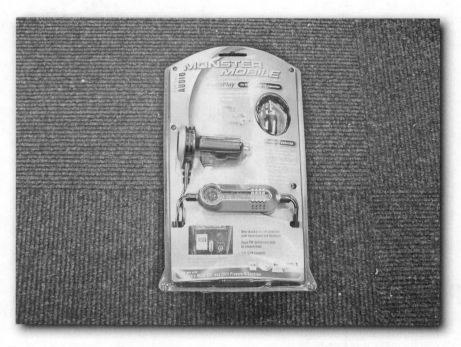

FIGURE 10-4: An FM radio audio transmitter can be quite convenient if you don't want to spend money on a new head unit.

Determine Where to Install the System

Find an appropriate place to put the Game Cube where the unit is accessible and cables won't get in the way. An ideal location is the axle hump in the back seat of many cars, as shown in Figure 10-5. If you place the Game Cube on the axle hump you can usually Velcro it there so it won't move, and your passengers can easily change games.

FIGURE 10-5: Game Cube located on the axle hump in the back seat.

Do You Need to Configure an A/V Switch?

If you are installing more than one A/V device, such as a computer and a Game Cube, you will likely need an A/V switch so you can switch the different audio sources with your stereo's auxiliary audio input (see Figure 10-6).

FIGURE 10-6: Installed A/V switch.

So why use an A/V switch when you're only switching audio? The A/V switch will allow you to use your display with multiple gaming systems if you decide to add them, as well as switch between your audio from your computer and your games. The A/V switch can also let you listen to music from your computer while your video is fed to video displays in the back seat (similar to Figure 10-7), which usually will have their own A/V switch built in.

If you are going to be driving video to more than a display in the front, you will need to install an A/V distribution amplifier so the audio and video signals can be effectively transmitted to each display as well as the head unit. Weak video signals will result in poor video quality, and you want to do it right the first time. You will likely not need anything more than a four-way amplifier, which can drive up to four screens; these can be picked up at any Radio Shack or similar A/V electronics store. Keep in mind that amplifiers require power, so you want to mount the device near your AC inverter.

FIGURE 10-7: Seat-back displays let passengers play games or watch movies while you use your GPS in the front.

Installing the Game Console

Now that you have the information you need, let's address installing the game console.

Step 1: Configure the Stereo to Receive Audio

You probably want to hear your games while you play them (in the passenger seat, of course). In this case you have a couple of options: You can use the built-in auxiliary input of your head unit (such as the set of cables coming from the back of the one in Figure 10-8), or you can use an FM audio transmitter if you don't have the luxury of an auxiliary port, as discussed in the planning section earlier under "Choose an Audio Solution."

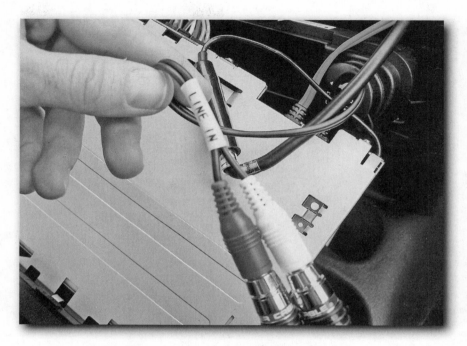

FIGURE 10-8: Auxiliary audio input from a third-party head unit.

The location of the auxiliary audio port will vary from head unit to head unit, so I can't cover all models here. Follow the instructions in your respective manual to plug the audio inputs from either your video switch or your game system into those respective ports. Some factory head units have a port built into the glove compartment or center console (the jacks from a minivan are shown in Figure 10-9), while many third-party head units have RCA-type stereo jacks coming from their backsides. If you don't have an auxiliary jack built into your car, you can easily build one with a faceplace and a dremel, as described in the section "Installing Auxiliary A/V Jacks" in Chapter 9, "Building a Single-Source A/V System."

FIGURE 10-9: Auxiliary audio input in a minivan.

Your car or audio input device auxiliary audio input port may only be a phono jack instead of separate right and left RCA jacks, as shown in Figure 10-8. In that case you will need a *stereo Y-adapter* (see Figure 10-10), which usually runs for under $5. Make sure you buy a stereo solution, or you will receive only monaural sound (this will be clearly marked on the adapter's packaging)!

Some head units require you to first enable the auxiliary input before you can use it. If you have a factory head unit (one such manufacturer requiring this is Saab—what a Saab story), you may need to pay your dealer to enable the auxiliary feature.

If you are using an FM audio transmitter to feed audio to your head unit, plug your A/V device into it, set the frequency, and continue to the next step (we'll test audio later).

Two black lines denote stereo

FIGURE 10-10: Stereo Y-adapter cable. Note that the extra line denoting the adapter is stereo instead of mono.

Step 2: Run the A/V Cables

Now that you're set up to hear the audio, you need to run the audio and video cables. If you are using an A/V switch, run the audio and video cables from your game system to your switch. Once those cables are firmly connected, run the audio cables from your switch to your stereo's auxiliary input or audio transmitter and the video cables to your display. Follow the instructions in Chapter 5, "Working with Cables," on how to properly run cables in your car.

If you are not using a switch, run the audio cables from your game system directly to your stereo's auxiliary input or audio transmitter and the video cables directly to your display. Again, follow the instructions in Chapter 5 on how to properly run cables in your car.

Step 3: Apply Velcro

Before installing the system you need to make sure it won't move. If you are using a different method than Velcro to secure the system from moving, you can skip this step.

Measure and cut out hook-side (not fuzzy-side) strips for the two sides of the bottom of the Game Cube (or possibly all four for your specific system), as shown in Figure 10-11. Make sure you don't cover up any doors or latches you need to reach!

FIGURE **10-11: Measuring and cutting the Velcro.**

With a razor blade or scissors, score the plastic bottom edges of the Game Cube in a criss-cross pattern so the Velcro sticks well (remember this from middle school?), as shown in Figure 10-12.

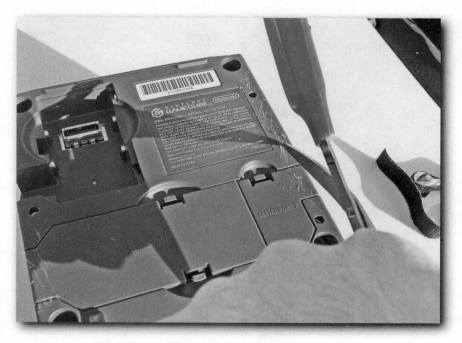

FIGURE 10-12: Scoring the bottom edge of the Game Cube.

Apply the Velcro as close to the edges as possible, as shown in Figure 10-13.

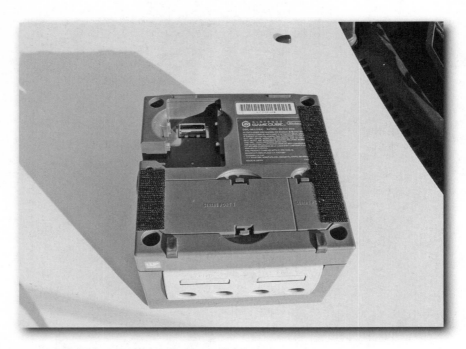

FIGURE 10-13: Velcro applied to the Game Cube.

Step 4: Install the System

Now that the Velcro is applied, place the system on the axle hump in the back seat of your car, or the location you decided to install it, as shown in Figure 10-14. Make sure the cartridge or disc slot is unobstructed and easy to reach for your passengers. This is especially important with game systems with a slide-out tray, such as the Xbox and Playstation 2—you don't want to position them where the tray can't fully eject!

FIGURE 10-14: Installed Game Cube.

Install the Game Controllers (Optional)

This part is simple—plug in the game controller(s). I strongly suggest you use wireless game controllers because they don't have any cable clutter and it's easy to pass them around the car without bugging the driver. If you haven't already, see Chapter 8, "Choosing an Input Device," which discusses wireless devices. Make sure you buy the RF wireless controllers (see Figure 10-15), since infrared solutions won't work very well in a car environment. You also need to make sure the channel used by each controller you add is unique—all of which should be explained well in the manual that comes with game controllers.

RF Game Controller   RF Receiver

FIGURE 10-15: Wireless game controller installed.

Test and Play

Now that everything's connected, turn on your car and play!

Note | Generally, you should have your car running while you play your game. If your car isn't running, your game system can be quite a drain on your battery, and your AC inverter may very well let you know by whining loudly about the power consumption. It's okay to show off the game system without the car running, but just remember you've turned your car into a gas-powered, not a battery-powered, Game Boy®.

Summary

In this chapter you installed a game system and configured the appropriate A/V components for use in your car. You also considered using a game system as a media center for your car, since the newer systems support many different media types (audio, video, gaming, and sometimes more). Game systems are an awesome entertainment addition to any car and will provide hours of fun for your passengers!

Adding a General-Purpose PC

Approximate project cost: $1,500 with screen; $1,000 without screen

Having a PC in your car is one of the coolest, geekiest toys you can show off. In this chapter you will build and install a Car PC, using the skills and information gathered from the first eight chapters. Since this is the Extreme Tech series, I assume you know how to put a PC together. If you don't, find a professional to build the PC for you (so you have someone to blame if it doesn't work) or pick up a book to learn how to do it, such as *Building a PC For Dummies, 4th Edition*, ISBN #0-7645-4247-8.

The computer you build in this chapter will be a *general-purpose PC*. A general-purpose PC is good, all-around, for anything you will likely want to do in your car. It uses little power, has plenty of storage space, plays DVDs, and lets you play games. Although it's not geared for high-end gaming, the general-purpose PC should be plenty for most people—heck, I'm a super geek and it's what I use!

Buying a Car PC versus Building Your Own

You can, of course, completely skip the step of building a computer and just buy one premade for your car. Many manufacturers of Car PC parts also sell ready-made systems. Normally these pre-built systems come with Windows XP and a 40-gigabyte hard drive but lack the unnecessary amenities home PCs often ship with, such as encyclopedias and productivity software. It's also convenient if you aren't comfortable building a computer, since you'll get a warranty and someone to turn to if you have trouble installing the PC in your car (parts missing, power issues, and so forth).

So You Want to Build Your Own?

Of course, my solution for the motherboard and processor isn't the only one. I encourage you to try other solutions to fit your needs. For example, you may want an AMD Athlon XP 3200+ in your car and a different motherboard. However, should you decide to go with a different motherboard/processor combination, please make sure you take into account heat issues and power issues. (See Chapter 4, "It's So Hot in Here: Dealing with Heat," for details on how to beat the heat, and Chapter 3, "Giving Your Creation Life: Power Considerations," to get a grasp on power issues.)

If you decide to go out on your own, here are a few tips to keep in mind:

- **Use mobile versions of the desktop processors you want to use.** For AMD these are called Mobile Athlons®, and Intel has their Pentium 4M (M is for Mobile). Intel also has an entire line of processors called the Pentium® M series, often bundled with their Centrino® chipset, which includes wireless networking capabilities.

- **Watch the power consumption!** You generally shouldn't put an Athlon 64, 2 gigabytes of RAM, and a 1-terabyte RAID array in your car. This will require too much power and generate too much heat. See Chapter 3 for power issues related to the equipment you install in your car. Note also that just because you *can* install something doesn't always mean you *should*.

- **Choose solutions based on what you need.** If all you're going to do is DVD playback, Internet surfing, war driving, and possibly some games, there's no reason to go overboard on the processor, memory, storage, and so on. The computer we build in this chapter will be capable of doing everything you like want to do with a car computer, and more.

- **Remember, this is a *PC* residing in *your* car.** You aren't building a desktop PC for your home, so keep this in mind as you decide to purchase certain parts and accessories. See the first eight chapters of this book for details on what equipment you should consider when purchasing for your car.

Following is a list of some manufacturers from whom you can buy prebuilt Car PCs and many related Car PC parts. For additional resources for parts, software, and more for Car PCs, check out Appendix C, "Additional Resources."

- Xenarc, www.xenarc.com
- Cappuccino PC, www.cappuccinopc.com
- CaseTronic, www.casetronic.com

I personally tried the Car PC solution from CaseTronic, and it works great. CaseTronic has their own custom low-profile heat-sinks and makes a computer package with a low-power-comsumption, well-performing 1.2-gigahertz Via C3 processor and 40-gigabyte hard drive for under $1,000. I installed it into my car with no problems, as shown in Figure 11-1.

FIGURE 11-1: CaseTronic Travla computer installed in my car.

Building Your Car PC

In this book I assume that you know how to put a computer together. If you don't, there are plenty of books out there that will show you—for the most part, it's just putting the pieces together (it's not like the old days, when you actually had to pay attention to what you were plugging things into).

All of this project should be done indoors. There is no reason to do anything outside of your home but installing the computer into your car. This way you can have easy access to all of the computer's ports, all of your software, plenty of working room, and Internet access to make sure everything's up to date.

Determining a Car PC Form Factor

There are two types of Car PCs you can build—*trunk-based* and *slimline*. The first is the most common—using standard PC cases that are somewhat large and can take full-size PC parts. These types tend to be placed in the trunk since they generally won't fit under a seat (and even if they did fit they'd be in your passengers' way).

The second type is the slimline form factor, where you use a much smaller case that can easily fit under most car seats (and sometimes in your center console above or below your stereo head unit). The slimline form factor is convenient since you don't have to get in and out of the car to work with it, such as when you need to swap DVDs. The drawback to the slimline, though, is it can't take full-size PC components, so the devices you install will tend to be more expensive laptop parts, such as 2.5-inch hard drives for storage and PC cards and external USB devices for extended functionality instead of being able to add internal PCI cards.

If you want to have ample expansion opportunities and are satisfied with having your Car PC in your trunk, the trunk-based form factor is the way to go. It's also the only viable option for using higher-speed processors and more advanced cooling systems (although the processor we will use for the general-purpose PC in this chapter is designed for mobile scenarios and will run very cool). If you're looking for a compact, chic, under-the-seat or in-dash solution you'll find it in the slimline. Slimlines, as I mentioned earlier, are very similar to laptops—not very expandable but very convenient, and they have everything you should need.

Requirements for a Trunk-Based Car PC

What you will need:

- "Pizza-box" computer case that can fit conveniently in the trunk, such as the Cooler Master (~$120, see Figure 11-2).

- Via EPIA-MII Mini ITX mainboard (a.k.a. motherboard), 1.2 GHz Via C3 processor, heat-sink, and fan (~$234 from Mini-Box.com, shown in Figure 11-3).

FIGURE 11-2: Cooler Master case for a trunk-based PC.

FIGURE 11-3: Via EPIA-MII mainboard.

- 256 megabytes of RAM (~$50, you can put 512 megabytes if you like, but nothing more should be necessary).

- 40 GB laptop hard drive (~$99, or higher capacity, as you desire).

Note You can opt to use cheaper, higher-capacity, desktop-type 3.5-inch hard drives if you choose. However, only the laptop drives were designed to withstand the shocks and heat your computer will likely be exposed to in a car, whereas home-bound desktop drives generally are not.

- IDE DVD-ROM/CD-RW combo drive (~$85, shown in Figure 11-4) with Mini-IDE to 40-pin IDE converter (~$20).

- Windows XP Home Edition (~$99, Professional is preferred if you're going to be implementing the music sync project in Chapter 17, "Syncing Music Library with Your Existing Home Network," ~$199). You can use Linux or any other operating system, of course, but in this book I will be focusing on Windows-based solutions since they are the most popular and have the most extensive commercial software and driver availability.

FIGURE 11-4: Slimline CD-ROM drive.

■ A PS/2 keyboard and mouse (or USB if you desire). See Chapter 8, "Choosing an Input Device," for details on choosing a keyboard and mouse for the car. In this project we will use the Gyration wireless product I recommend in that chapter. Windows XP automatically installs the drivers for the Gyration, so it should work once Windows comes up. (~$119).

■ A VGA display device, such as the Digital Worldwide (www.digitalww.com) TWW-7VGT (~$450), the Digital Worldwide fully motorized, in-dash display DWW-700M (~$500), or the Xenarc (www.xenarc.com) 700TSV. These displays come with both an AC (alternating-current) adapter and cigarette lighter adapter for easily working with them at home and in your car (meaning you shouldn't need a separate display). You can use a composite/analog display device and a VGA-to-composite adapter (such as those available from AVerMedia QuickPlay™, www.avermedia.com), but the video won't be very clear and you'll wish you had spent the money on a better display. See Chapter 7, "Choosing a Display Device," for more information on selecting displays.

■ A low-power (120–180 watt) AC power supply, for working on the computer at home (~$50).

■ The Mini-Box PW200M 200-watt DC-DC power supply, for when the computer is in your car (~$50, the 200 watts of power may seem like overkill, but is a good idea to install now for future expansion, shown in Figure 11-5).

FIGURE 11-5: Mini-Box PW200M power supply.

■ The Mini-Box ITPS auto power sequencer and low-dropout regulator, for enabling your Car PC to turn on and off properly when the car's ignition is switched (~$40, shown in Figure 11-6).

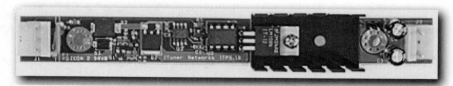

FIGURE 11-6: Mini-Box ITPS auto power sequencer and low dropout regulator.

Requirements for a Slimline, Under-the-Seat PC

What you will need:

- Small computer case that can fit under a seat (see Figure 11-7), such as the Travla C134 (~$149) or the slightly larger yet more practical (and easier to install stuff in) Travla C158 (~$159, shown in Figure 11-8).

FIGURE 11-7: Travla C134 case for the slimline PC (cramped, but could fit in the dash!).

- Via EPIA-MII Mini ITX mainboard (a.k.a. motherboard), 1.2 GHz Via C3 processor, heat-sink, and fan (~$234 from Mini-Box.com, shown in Figure 11-3).
- 256 megabytes of RAM (you can put 512 if you like, but nothing more should be necessary, ~$50).
- 40 GB laptop hard drive (or higher capacity, as you desire, ~$99).
- IDE laptop slimline DVD-ROM/CD-RW combo drive (~$85, shown in Figure 11-4) with Mini-IDE to 40-pin IDE converter (~$20).

FIGURE 11-8: Slightly larger yet still compact Travla C158 case for the slimline PC.

- Windows XP Home Edition (~$99, Professional is preferred if you're going to be implementing the music sync project in Chapter 17, "Syncing Music Library with Your Existing Home Network," ~$199). You can use Linux or any other operating system, of course, but in this book I will be focusing on Windows-based solutions since they are the most popular.

- A PS/2 keyboard and mouse (or USB if you desire). See Chapter 8, "Choosing an Input Device," for details on choosing a keyboard and mouse for the car. In this project we will use the Gyration wireless product I recommend in that chapter. Windows XP automatically installs the drivers for the Gyration, so it should work once Windows comes up (~$199).

- A low-power (120–180 watt) AC (alternating-current) power supply, for working on the computer at home.

- The Mini-Box PW200M 200-watt AC power supply (~$50, the 200 watts of power may seem like overkill, but is a good idea to install now for future expansion), for when the computer is in your car, as shown in Figure 11-5.

- The Mini-Box ITPS auto power sequencer and low-dropout regulator, for enabling your Car PC to turn on and off properly when the car's ignition is switched, shown in Figure 11-6 (~$40).

- A VGA display device, such as the Digital Worldwide (www.digitalww.com) TWW-7VGT (~$450), the Digital Worldwide fully motorized, in-dash display DWW-700M (~$500), or the Xenarc (www.xenarc.com) 700TSV. These displays come with both an AC adapter and cigarette lighter adapter for easily working with them at home and in your car (meaning you shouldn't need a separate display). You can use a composite/analog display device and a VGA-to-composite adapter (such as those available from AVerMedia QuickPlay™, www.avermedia.com), but the video won't be very clear and you'll wish you had spent the money on a better display. See Chapter 7, "Choosing a Display Device," for more information on selecting displays.

Tip

The motherboard, power supply, and power sequencer can all be purchased from Mini-Box.com for about $235. You can pick up a standard 180- to 200-watt AC power supply from any CompUSA, Best Buy, or similar store for under $100 (or just take it out of an old computer for free).

Choosing the Power Supply

The computer you install in your car needs to come up when you start your car and automatically shut down when you turn your car off. To do this properly you will need a DC-DC power supply for your car and a power-stepping unit (PSU) plus low-voltage regulator (ITPS) to provide this functionality. Examples of these products are shown in Figures 11-5 and 11-6. Many Car PC manufacturers and parts resellers offer these types of Car PC power supplies, sometimes built into a single unit. A list of these providers is in Appendix C, "Additional Resources." The solution used in this chapter is from Mini-Box (www.mini-box.com), but there are many solutions available and all of them have their pros and cons. It's a good idea before you install a solution to check with what other people have used, because the solution you install in your car may vary from what's discussed in this chapter. A list of online forums is also provided in Appendix C.

You don't want to power a computer from an AC inverter. Instead, you want to power it directly from your power system (the battery and alternator). To learn how to provide power directly to your computer from your car's power system, refer to Chapter 3, which has a project covering exactly how to do that.

Preparing Your PC for Car Installation

Building a Car PC is similar to building any PC, except you will be using a laptop hard drive and will be installing the standard AC power supply and swapping it out later for the car-ready power supply. Everything else will be just like building a regular PC.

Step 1: Install and Activate the Operating System

Install Windows XP according to the instructions that shipped with it. When you're asked to name the computer, you can name the computer anything you want—I named mine CARPC. This part can take up to an hour.

If Windows XP has already been installed (in the case this was an existing computer, or you just outright purchased it), follow the prompts if you are required to register and make sure you activate Windows (it will annoyingly keep asking you to do so until you do).

When Windows finally comes up, make sure you activate it, or your operating system will run for only 30 days.

Also, once Windows is activated, open the Display control panel and set your resolution to 800 × 600, or 800 × 480 if that is all your display will support. You can use a higher resolution, but higher resolutions tend to be difficult to read while driving.

If you are installing a composite display instead of a VGA (video graphics array/adapter) display, try not to use any resolution higher than 640 × 480 (VGA converted to composite just doesn't look very good).

A shortcut around navigating to the Control Panel to change display settings is to simply right-click the desktop and select Settings, which will bring up the Display control panel.

Step 2: Install Necessary Drivers and Software

Once the operating system has been configured, you must install the drivers for all the devices you want to use with your computer. Install each device according to the manufacturer's instructions, and make sure it works. If there are special configuration settings you would like to make, like specific hotkey actions, game controller settings, monitor resolutions, etcetera, you should set those now and test them. Anything you set up now should work fine once you get it into the car (the only thing that changes is the power supply).

Alternative Operating Systems

So you don't want to use Windows XP? Maybe you want to use Linux? Here are some tips for choosing an operating system:

- Make sure it supports power management, often called ACPI, or *advanced configuration and power interface*. Your operating system should be able to respond to power management hardware capabilities built into your computer. In Windows XP this enables the processor to be throttled up and down as power needs require. It also enables a hibernation mode, where the contents of memory are written to disk when the computer is powered down, enabling the computer to be quickly restored to where it was when you turned the car off. If your operating system doesn't support power management or hibernation, you may find yourself having issues turning the computer on and off in your car and waiting for the computer to start up every time you start the car. Also, keep in mind that if your computer just shuts off every time you kill the ignition switch on your car, without following a proper shutdown procedure, you may start having problems with your file system, rendering your computer unusable until you run a disk utility.

- If you don't have hibernation support, make sure you *shut down your operating system every time—before* you turn your car off.

- Make sure there are drivers for all of the hardware devices you want to install. Most flavors of Windows already have drivers available in the operating system or a version for Windows will be included by the manufacturer. With Linux you may not find the driver from a manufacturer, but instead may have to find a third-party solution online using a search engine. Remember, if you use third-party drivers, you may not get access to all the functionality of the device.

- Make sure your application software will run on the operating system. If the application you want to install won't work with your operating system, consider a different software package or a different operating system altogether.

- A note on having multiple operating systems and *dual booting* (choosing which operating system to start when the computer turns on): For all practical purposes this should be avoided. Since you have to choose an operating system when you start the computer, you may find yourself unable to make the selection and therefore not start the operating system. Like I said in the first bullet point—it's better to have one operating system with hibernation mode support so you can quickly resume your computer to its desktop rather than waiting for it to boot every time. You want to minimize nonessential interaction with the computer while driving.

Step 3: Install Common Applications

Now that your drivers are installed, install all of the applications you are likely to use. It is important that you have antivirus on your car computer, and a firewall, especially if you are going to connect it to the Internet. Here are some common applications you will most likely need to install:

- Antivirus software (a free antivirus product is available from Avast at www.avast.com in their Avast AntiVirus product)

- DVD playback software (should come with the computer or DVD-ROM drive), such as PowerDVD™ or WinDVD™

- Music-playing software (such as CarTunes™, iTunes®, MusicMatch® Jukebox, and so forth)

- Web browser (Internet Explorer comes with Windows, but you may want to install Mozilla® or FireFox®, especially because of their tabbed browsing abilities)

Step 4: Turn on Hibernation Support

Hibernation enables your computer to save its state when you kill the ignition. When you next turn the car on, the computer will start up from where it was when you last turned the car off, saving you from enduring the boot process or having to relaunch applications every time you start your car.

To enable hibernation in Windows XP:

1. Click Start.

2. Click Control Panel.

3. Click Power Options.

4. Click the Hibernate tab.

5. Check the Enable hibernation box (see Figure 11-9).

6. Click Apply.

7. Click the Advanced tab.

8. Under Power Options, set both drop-down boxes to Hibernate (see Figure 11-10).

9. Click Apply.

10. Click OK, and your computer is all set up to act properly when turning the ignition switch on and off.

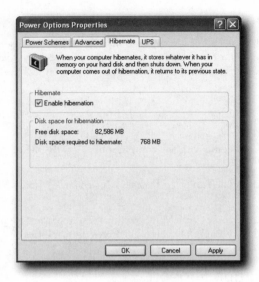

FIGURE 11-9: Select the Hibernate tab.

FIGURE 11-10: Select the Advanced tab.

Step 5: Update Your Software

Now that everything's set up, it's important to make sure you have the latest software on your computer. Since you aren't always connected to the Internet, make sure you update everything before you put the computer in your car, including:

- Windows and related drivers via Windows Update at www.windowsupdate.com

- Antivirus via your antivirus software's update feature

- Office software via Office Update at http://officeupdate.microsoft.com (if you installed Microsoft Office)

- Any other software you install

Other Neat Applications to Try

Before you put your new computer into your car, here's a list of some unnecessary yet very useful software you may want to install:

- CarTunes (http://cartunes.ws)—A media player I wrote specifically for Car PCs.

- Konfabulator (http://konfabulator.com)—Lets you customize your computer desktop with special objects called *widgets*. There are a *lot* of widgets you can download, from weather forecast widgets to clocks to media players—and you can even create your own. Originally, this feature was only for Macintosh, but now it's for Windows as well.

Installing the PC in Your Car

Tip If you are using the power sequencer, you must start your engine all the way to keep the computer working properly. If you just turn your key to the ON position and then a few seconds later to the Start position, the power sequencer often incorrectly will tell the computer to turn off as if the ignition had been switched to OFF. If this happens, turn your car off for two minutes and then start it and all should work fine again. Some newer versions of car power supplies attempt to prevent this issue, but keep this in mind if your computer isn't turning on after you start your car (and it had been working fine before).

Now that everything's configured, we're ready to place the computer in the car.

Adding a GPS Navigation System

You've probably seen those really cool GPS navigation systems in high-end cars like Lexus, Mercedes, BMW, and many SUVs. Those systems usually cost over $1,000 to have installed. Well, all they are is expensive single-purpose computers. With the PC you built in this chapter, you can add GPS for $129! *Microsoft's Streets & Trips 2005 with GPS Receiver* comes with the GPS receiver (it plugs into any available USB port) and a DVD full of detailed maps (see the following figure). Not only can you see where you're driving, you can get directions and see landmarks, lodging, and restaurants while you drive. Better yet, with an Internet connection, Streets & Trips will update its maps and give you traffic updates. Even the expensive solutions built into those high-end cars can't do that!

DeLorme (www.delorme.com) also offers an excellent GPS product, *Earthmate GPS*, for the same price as Microsoft's solution. DeLorme's solution also includes a USB GPS receiver (which, like Microsoft's solution, can be converted to work via Bluetooth), and even features voice prompts and speech recognition, as well as compatibility with DeLorme's other mapping products, such as TopoUSA and Street Atlas (which is included with the package).

You can find the Streets & Trips and Earthmate GPS products at Best Buy, CompUSA, and many places that sell computer software. Of course, you can also use any other GPS software and GPS receiver package that runs on PCs once you have a PC in your car, and the GPS units included with the software packages mentioned are often compatible with other GPS solutions.

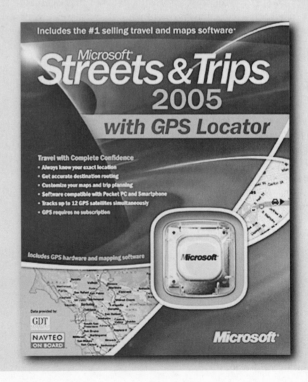

Step 1: Swap Power Supplies

Replace the standard computer power supply with the Mini-Box solution per the instructions from Mini-Box. Simply mount the power supply in your case along with the power regulator and that's it. To power your computer, and *before you go to Step* 2, follow the project steps in Chapter 3.

Note If you're using a power solution from a different manufacturer, that's okay. Now is the time to swap out the AC power supply for the solution you will be using in your car.

Step 2: Install the Display

After you have replaced the power supply, install the display you chose per the instructions from the manufacturer. See Chapter 7 for information on choosing a display. I recommend the Digital Worldwide (www.digitalww.com) DWW-7VGT (~$450) in-dash touch-screen display or their motorized DWW-700M solution (~$500) if your center console can support an in-dash unit the size of a car stereo (most cars can), which is sometimes called a 1-din or 1U size slot. If your car doesn't have an available slot for the display, you can just as easily mount a display on your dash, such as the Xenarc 700TSV (www.xenarc.com) on-dash touch-screen display. If you're into tearing your dash apart, you can also create your own moldings and build a display directly into your dash, but that's beyond the scope of this book.

See Figure 11-11 for a picture of the in-dash solution and Figure 11-12 for the on-dash solution. Both solutions use a USB interface to connect the display to your computer for input.

FIGURE 11-11: In-dash display from Digital Worldwide.

FIGURE 11-12: The on-dash display from Xenarc.

Step 3: Place the Computer

Now that you have your display installed, you can place the computer where you want to keep it. For the slimline PC, a good place is under the passenger seat. For the trunk-based PC, well, the trunk will do just nicely.

First, take some Velcro and run the hook (non-fuzzy) side of it along the bottom sides of the PC case, as shown in Figure 11-13. This will prevent the computer from sliding around, yet it will remain easy to remove.

Mount the PC on the carpet, far enough away from feet but open enough so you can open the DVD/CD-ROM drive and access the ports with no trouble, as shown in Figure 11-14 for the slimline PC and in Figure 11-15 for the trunk-based PC.

You may have to run an equal length of the the fuzzy side of the Velcro along your carpet to hold the computer if the hook-side you installed on the computer's bottom doesn't hook well on your car's carpet.

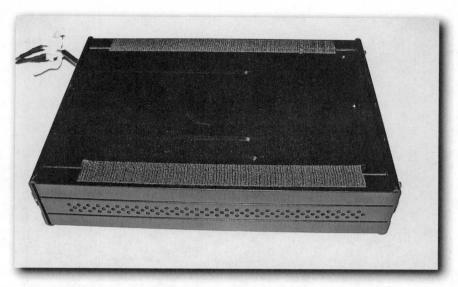

FIGURE 11-13: Velcro properly attached to the bottom of the computer case.

FIGURE 11-14: Slimline PC mounted under the seat with plenty of room.

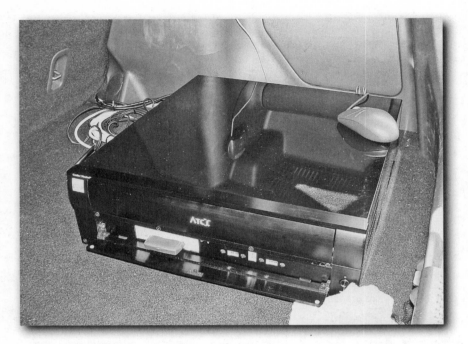

FIGURE 11-15: Trunk-based PC in the trunk with plenty of room.

Step 4: Connect the Display and Peripherals

Now that the computer is mounted, you need to run the cables to the PC. Follow the instructions in Chapter 5, "Working with Cables," to properly run the cables.

 Be careful not to let any wires cross the path of the seats or you may kink or tear the wires, which could cause a fire or shock hazard if you cut through a power cable!

Step 5: Turn It On!

Now that everything is connected, you should be able to turn your computer on and start using it!

Summary

In this chapter you installed a Car PC. Most projects in this book will build upon this project, letting you do many interesting things with your new geekmobile!

Installing a Media Center PC

Approximate project cost: $1,700 with screen; $1,200 without screen

An entertainment, or *media center*, PC can be just as useful as a media hub in a car as it is in your home, but you will use certain features more often in your car than you would at home. If you are looking at installing an easier-to-use, large-screen, menu-driven media solution for a minivan or RV, a media center solution is ideal because it can control your music, movies, photos, television, and even radio, all in one centralized location with an easy-to-use interface, as well as providing full computer capabilities when needed.

Recently, the media center PC has become the computer that sports all but the digital kitchen sink, capable of handling everything media-related in your entertainment system. With all these included features, however, come considerable power requirements. However, by thinking carefully about these higher power requirements and planning ahead, you can have practically everything a media center PC offers running in your car.

Choosing an Operating System

There are many operating systems you can choose from to provide access to all the components you want to install. One obvious choice is Windows XP, because there are drivers for nearly every peripheral component out there and lots of software that will let you play DVDs, work with photos, play audio CDs, and so forth. However, Microsoft and industry partners have worked together on a Windows XP *Media Center Edition* that slimlines the Windows XP interface to tie all media access together (see Figure 12-1), such as personal video recorder (PVR) functionality with television access, or the ability to use the PVR functionality while watching a DVD, so you don't miss your favorite shows while on the road. There's even a remote control! Windows XP Media Center Edition is a full version of Windows XP, and its easy TiVo®-like interface can be disabled when you want to do real computer work, but the slimline interface is very useful as an all-in-one centralized media management solution.

Warning If you decide to install a Linux or other non-Windows-based solution, make sure there are fully functional drivers for the devices you plan to install. The primary drawback to alternative operating systems is their lack of any or only partial support for hardware features, meaning what you buy may not do what's advertised when using components on non-Windows systems.

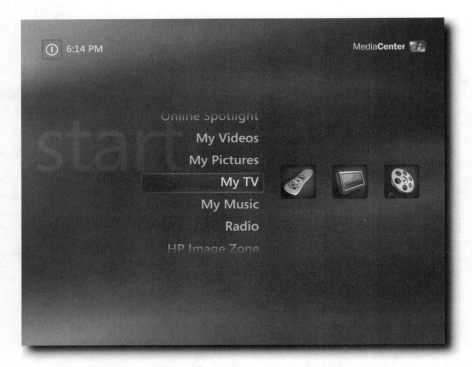

FIGURE 12-1: Screenshot of Windows XP Media Center Edition and remote.

Software Geared for Car PCs

If you don't want to pay extra for Windows XP Media Center Edition, there are, of course, open source, freeware, shareware, and commercial alternatives on the market that are specifically geared toward Car PC users. If you want to use Linux, you'll obviously need an alternative to Microsoft's solution. There are many free, powerful solutions out there, and many of them also sport full GPS integration, DVD playback, FM radio tuning, Web-browsing capability, and sometimes more. Download locations for these products are listed in Table 12-1.

Table 12-1   Car PC Software Solutions

Package	Download URL
CentraFuse	`www.fluxmedia.net`
FrodoPlayer	`www.frodoplayer.com`
MediaCar	`www.media-car.fr.st`
MediaPortal	`http://sourceforge.net/projects/mediaportal/`

Choosing Media Components to Install

Media is such a generic term that I can't cover every type you might want to install. In this chapter I will discuss many that you are likely to consider installing in your car, van, or RV. Keep in mind that, because you're installing a PC, you should be able to expand your system almost ad infinitum as new devices and media technologies become available, as long as you don't overburden your power supply (both the computer's and the car's).

Watch Your Power by Consolidating!

Many of the components you add to a computer can double-up for other duties. For example, a DVD-ROM or DVD burner can also double (or triple) as a DVD player, audio CD player, Video CD player, and regular data drive for computer applications. Television tuner cards can come with AM/FM tuners built-in as well, rounding out a media center solution with only two devices! The name of the game is not just functionality but power conservation. Also keep in mind that your internal PCI slots are limited, and most external USB media devices require an extra power supply, so it's crucial to make the most with what you have. See Chapter 3, "Giving Your Creation Life: Power Considerations," for tips on providing power to your media center solution and other devices in your car.

Choosing the Power Supply

The computer you install in your car needs to come up when you start your car and automatically shut down when you turn your car off. To do this properly you will need a DC-DC power supply for your car and a power stepping unit (PSU) plus low-voltage regulator (ITPS) to provide this functionality. Examples of these products are shown in Figures 11-5 and 11-6, in Chapter 11, "Adding a General-Purpose PC." Many Car PC manufacturers and parts resellers offer these types of Car PC power supplies, sometimes built into a single unit. A list of these providers is in Appendix C, "Additional Resources." The solution used in this chapter is from Mini-Box (`www.mini-box.com`), but there are many solutions available, and all of them have their pros and cons. It's a good idea before you install a solution to check with what other people have used, as the solution you install in your car may vary from what's discussed in this chapter. A list of online forums is also provided in Appendix C.

You don't want to power a computer from an AC inverter. Instead, you want to power it directly from your power system (the battery and alternator). To learn how to provide power directly to your computer from your car's power system, refer to Chapter 3, which has a project covering exactly how to do that.

Don't Overdo the Processor and RAM!

Since you will likely be doing only one or two tasks at a time with your computer, such as monitoring GPS directions while listening to music files, you don't need a power-hungry, high-performance processor or gobs and gobs of memory installed. Consider low power consumption, mobile-optimized processors (see Table 12-2) that have great media performance, such as the Intel Pentium M (often confused with Intel Centrino, which is just a mobile chipset, not a processor), the AMD Athlon M, or the Via C3, a fully x86-compatible processor that hardly requires a fan (see Chapter 11 for more information). When it comes to RAM, 256MB is actually likely to be enough, and 384 or 512 should suit your needs for a long time to come. Remember, with a car computer it's not what you have that counts; it's what you can *do* with it.

Your processor is hardly being maxxed out for most computing applications. Most of the time it is just "twiddling its thumbs," waiting for an application to make a request. A 1 GHz processor is likely fine for multitasking music playback, GPS navigation, and Web surfing all at once. An exception is software DVD decoding, which requires a good 40%+ of the processing power of a 1 GHz processor, but watching a DVD would likely be the only thing your computer is doing (since it's likely going to be playing full screen). This will save you money on the processor you purchase, as well as successfully keeping your power consumption under control.

Table 12-2   Power Consumption for Popular Desktop and Mobile Processors

Manufacturer	Processor	Speed	Wattage (W)
AMD	Mobile Sempron	1.6–1.8 GHz	21–25 W
Intel	Pentium M, 755, 745, 735, 725, 715	1.3–2.0 GHz	21–24.5 W
Intel	Pentium M Low-Power, 738	1.1–1.4 GHz	10–12 W
Intel	Pentium M Ultra-Low-Power, 723, 733	900 MHz–1.2 GHz	5–7 W
Intel	Mobile Pentium 4 with HyperThreading 538, 532, 518	2.8–3.2 GHz	76–88 W
Intel	Pentium III M	550 MHz–1.33 GHz	0.5–2 W

Manufacturer	Processor	Speed	Wattage (W)
Intel	Ultra-Low-Power Pentium III "Battery Optimized Mode"	500 MHz	0.5 W
Via	C3 "Nehemiah"	1.4 GHz	20 W

Buying a Prebuilt System

Have some extra cash lying around? It may be easier to just buy all of this at once in a simple media center PC offering from the store, or retrofitting a Car PC from the many resellers of ready-made Car PCs. Going the retail purchase route is ideal for those with RVs or mobile homes, because the environments are already like a home and should provide a cool enough environment with enough power that the purchased PC can be both the media hub and computer for the mobile environment.

Many media center offerings were available on the market as of this book's publication, including some which look just like standard component A/V (audio/video) systems you'd find in an entertainment system rack. Most major manufacturers build these systems, including Hewlett Packard®, Gateway®, and Dell®. See a retail store near you, such as Best Buy, CompUSA, Good Guys, and so forth, for media center PC solutions. Figure 12-2 shows an example Windows XP Media Center–based PC with front and back views and the remote unit.

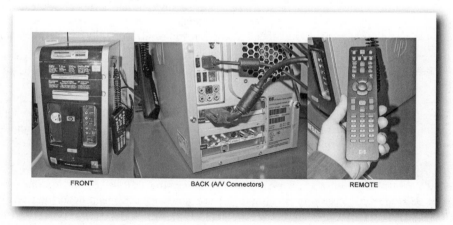

FRONT   BACK (A/V Connectors)   REMOTE

FIGURE 12-2: Media Center PC.

Adding a DVD Player

DVD playback functionality is simple to add because it's just a DVD-ROM drive with special DVD playback software installed on the PC. Make sure you get an internal IDE DVD drive—external players/burners were never meant for cars (not to mention that they are very bulky and require an external power supply). DVD burners are cheap enough these days that you might as well buy a "combo drive" that includes the burning capability, which will give you CD and DVD playback, as well as CD and DVD burning capabilities. Do not buy a slot-loading DVD drive for your car, because if a disc gets stuck, it can be a pain (and expensive!) to fix—the ones with a tray just like most computer drives will do nicely, and the drives made for laptops with the spring-loaded spindle are even better.

The DVD-video playback software is usually included with the DVD-ROM or DVD burning drive you purchase, and sometimes it's even included with the mainboard, or motherboard, you buy. If you do not receive DVD-video playback software, you can purchase any of a number of solutions at the store, such as Intervideo's WinDVD. Keep in mind, however, that these products can cost as much as $50, which is a lot of money to spend when you could instead find a different brand of DVD drive that actually comes with the playback software (which will likely be either the same price or cheaper).

Adding Television Access

Television access is easy to add, yet TV broadcast signals can often be hard to receive. Due to the speed your car may be traveling through areas wih large buildings or structures that may reflect or disrupt the TV transmitters' signal, your reception may be hazy or choppy. Up to 20 to 35 miles from the TV station, most TV signals are easily captured, although while driving near tall buildings or large structures, the signals may fade or become uneven. It will still be viewable, just don't expect the kind of clear reception you would normally receive when at a standstill.

You have a two choices when adding television access: an internal PCI expansion card or a USB solution. The PCI expansion card is going to use less power and use a lot less space (since it's installed inside your computer case), whereas the USB solution is easily removable but requires an AC (alternating-current) power outlet and additional space in your car (see Chapter 3 for more details). Depending on the mainboard you decide to install, you may be limited on the number of PCI and/or USB slots available.

 Tip You don't have to be limited to standard television signals in your car. Using the internal ATI HDTV Wonder PCI card (www.ati.com) or a similar external USB device, such as the Sasem OnAir USB 2.0 HDTV receiver (www.usbhdtv.com), you can receive high-definition television (HDTV) signals in your car for under $250. Although you may not be able to view the full resolution of HDTV in your car, you can still receive it with a better picture quality than the "standard" NTSC television you are used to, and continue to tune in "standard" NTSC channels with the same unit.

Table 12-3 shows a list of some good solutions for television access in your car. I've had good luck myself with these products, but there are many more out there I haven't used that may be fine as well.

Table 12-3   Products for Car TV Access

Card / Device	Type	Price Range	Notes
ATI TV Wonder	PCI Card	$20–$50	Great software. Can record TV, too.
ATI All-in-Wonder Series (see Figure 12-3)	AGP Card	$100–$400	Awesome replacement graphics card that has television tuning, AM/FM tuning, and video capture built-in. Also comes with DVD playback software. Don't install the higher-end solutions because they require too much power—the 8500 series is very good and not power hungry.
Hauppague WinTV	PCI o rUSB 1.1	$20–$75	The software is a little buggy. Can record TV, too.
Hauppaugue WinTV (see Figure 12-4)	PVR PCI or USB 1.1	$79–$99	Also has AM/FM tuner built-in, as well as television, composite video, and S-Video recording capability.

FIGURE 12-3: ATI All-in-Wonder series.

Tip   A great place to find products is by using Google's Froogle Web site (www.froogle.com). Froogle instantly searches a bazillion stores and tells you what is available and for how much. Try a search for "USB TV Tuner" and you'll see what I mean.

FIGURE 12-4: Hauppauge WinTV PVR.

See Chapter 16, "Adding Television Access," for more information on adding television to your car.

Adding an AM/FM Radio

Although you may already have one of these in your car (man, I hope so, since that also means you have an easy-to-access car antenna), you can also add AM/FM tuning capabilities to your car PC. Shopping your local CompUSA will reveal a number of solutions that will tune AM/FM via USB or PCI card, allowing you to not only listen to your favorite stations but record them as well. Some all-in-one solutions, such as ATI's Radeon All-in-Wonder series or Hauppauge's WinTV PVR, offer television tuning and video capture in addition to AM/FM tuning capabilities, and it's all integrated into a single software suite. Such integration is a boon because you want as simple an interface as possible when using these features in your car.

Standalone USB AM/FM tuner solutions are readily available, of course. You don't have to add television tuning capabilities to your car, especially if you want to save money by going an all-audio route. You can pick up USB tuners new in the store (although they're getting harder to find there) or on eBay, such as the discontinued D-Link NetEasy DRU-R100 (FM-only, ~$10) or XMPCR (for receiving XM satellite radio service, ~$120). I even found a mouse with a built-in radio tuner that may work quite well—the FM 2000 Radio Mouse—available at `www.compgeeks.com/details.asp?invtid=FMMOUSE&cat=MOU` (will wonders never cease). Extreme PC Gear also sells an FM tuner solution for $4.99 brand new, available at `www.xpcgear.com/usbfmradiogrn.html`.

Warning If you're going to add an AM/FM tuner, it should be tuned by your passengers. The interface for the PC tuners was never made for car environments and *will* take your eyes off the road. I generally recommend you use your car stereo for the AM/FM tuner when driving, although it's pretty cool to brag that you have both.

Adding a Digital Photo Reader

If you want to peruse digital photos while in your car, such as when you're on the way back from a trip, or you had the camera running while you were doing sprints, simply install a media reader, which lets you access the photos and movie files on any number of digital film cards, such as Compact Flash, Smart Media, SD, XD, Memory Stick, and so forth. These are readily available from any retail store that sells computers, and you can buy compact USB solutions, or even some that work internally and mount in a drive bay. If you follow the instructions for building a USB hub into your dash, as shown in Chapter 18, "Syncing Portable Music Players," the USB media reader solution is likely easier. This way, you can use a USB media reader in any computer you own (there's really no reason to have one in the car all the time).

Adding a PC Card Drive

A good solution for adding advanced capabilities to your PC without using limited PCI slots or dealing with lots of USB devices is to use what laptops use—PC cards (sometimes called CardBus or PCMCIA cards). These small cards can add Firewire, television tuners, cell phone Internet cards, media readers and more, and they just slide into a PC card slot. Although these drives are not cheap (on the order of $100), they are very useful, and the fact that you can simply "plug in" functionality that's fully powered by your computer is very handy, and you can share that functionality with any laptop you own as well. Figure 12-5 shows what a PC card drive looks like.

Note Make sure you buy a PC card drive and that it isn't just a PC card *media reader*. The readers don't provide all the functionality of a drive and may not accept the PC cards that provide additional functionality. Readers are meant more for reading files from the PC card storage devices, which were popular many years ago.

PC card drives are not easily found in stores (they just aren't a popular add-on), but they are easily purchased from online resellers, such as CDW (Computer Discount Warehouse, www.cdw.com). Here are two products to consider:

- Linksys Desktop PCMCIA solution (Model PCMRDWR, ~$100)
- Actiontec Internal Dual PCI Slot PC Card Reader (Model AD75000-70, ~$110)

FIGURE 12-5: PC card reader installed in my car PC with my Sprint PCS Vision cell phone Internet card installed.

Adding FireWire®

IEEE-1394, also known as *FireWire* or *iLink*, provides you high-speed access to storage, video cameras, and a number of other devices. To add it to your car, you will either have to install an IEEE-1394 PCI card (about $50) or a PC card solution and the PC Card drive described earlier. Note that 1394 interface cards will come with either miniature (four-pin) or full-size (six-pin) sockets. The six-pin socket provides DC power to many external devices (such as hard drives, so they don't require an external power supply), while the four-pin does not. Make sure you have a socket that matches the kind of socket you have on your own Firewire device. When in doubt, retailers such as Radio Shack offer four-pin to six-pin and six-pin to four-pin IEEE-1394 adapters.

Components and Tools Needed

What you will need:

- Flat pizza-box-sized computer case that can fit conveniently in the trunk, such as the Cooler Master ATCS (see Figure 12-6). The flat cases are easy to place in the trunk, easy to mount and secure, and are easily expandable with the peripherals you will likely want to use in a media center PC (~$120).

FIGURE 12-6: Cooler Master ATCS case.

- An appropriate motherboard (a.k.a. mainboard) for the processor you have chosen to implement, along with that processor, appropriate heat-sinks, and fans (price varies depending on what you decide to implement and which processor you choose, ~$120–$400).

- 256 megabytes of RAM (you can put 512 megabytes if you like, but nothing more should be necessary, ~$50). Most store-bought Media Center PCs ship with 512 megabytes standard.

- 40-gigabye full-size or laptop hard drive (or higher capacity, as you desire; ~$99). When choosing the drive, pay close attention to the G-force shock rating, and stay away from high-performance (i.e., 10K RPM and higher) drives because they generate more heat and require more power. See Chapter 6, "Physics Man, Physics: Preparing Home Electronics for the Road," for more information on the physics of choosing a hard drive.

- IDE DVD-ROM/CD-RW combo drive (*not* slot-loading, ~$85).

- Windows XP Home Edition ($99, Professional is preferred if you're going to be using the music sync project in Chapter 18, $199). You can use Linux or any other operating system, of course, but in this book I will be focusing on Windows-based solutions, since they are the most popular.

- A PS/2 keyboard and mouse (~$119, or USB if you desire). See Chapter 8, "Choosing an Input Device," for details on choosing a keyboard and mouse for the car. In this project we will use the Gyration wireless product I recommend in that chapter. Windows XP automatically installs the drivers for the Gyration, so it should work once Windows comes up.

- A VGA (video graphics array/adapter) display device, such as the Digital Worldwide (www.digitalww.com) TWW-7VGT (~$450), the Digital Worldwide fully motor-ized in-dash display DWW-700M (~$500), or the Xenarc (www.xenarc.com) 700TSV. These displays come with both an AC adapter and cigarette lighter adapter for easily working with them at home and in your car (meaning you shouldn't need a separate display). You can use a composite/analog display device and a VGA-to-composite adapter (such as those available from AVerMedia QuickPlay™, www.avermedia.com), but the video won't be very clear and you'll wish you had spent the money on a better display. See Chapter 7, "Choosing a Display Device," for more information on selecting displays.

- A low-power (120–180 watt) AC power supply, for working on the computer at home (~$50).

- The Mini-Box PW series AC power supply, for when the computer is in your car, shown in Figure 12-7 (~$50). Make sure you purchase the appropriate model for your processor and motherboard type (see www.mini-box.com for details).

FIGURE 12-7: Mini-Box power supply.

■ The Mini-Box ITPS auto power sequencer and low-dropout regulator, for enabling your Car
   PC to turn on and off properly when the car's ignition is switched (~$40, see Figure 12-8).
   Make sure you purchase the one appropriate model for your processor and motherboard type
   (see www.mini-box.com for details).

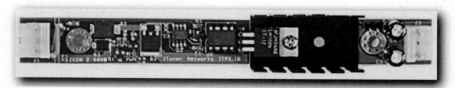

FIGURE 12-8: Mini-Box ITPS auto power sequencer and low-dropout regulator.

Preparing Your PC for Car Installation

Now that you have everything you need for your media center PC, including any PCI cards and USB devices you want to install, it's time for you to put it all together.

Step 1: Building the PC

Building a Car PC is similar to building any PC, except you will be using a laptop hard drive and will be installing the standard AC power supply and swapping it out later for the car-ready power supply. Everything else will be just like building a regular PC. If you aren't familiar with building PCs I suggest you either have a professional build the PC for you (all the parts they need are listed above), or learn how to do it yourself with a book such as *Building a PC for Dummies*, ISBN #0-7645-4247-8. Once you have built the PC and installed all the PCI cards, memory, hard drive, and other devices, continue to Step 2.

Step 2: Install and Activate the Operating System

Install Windows XP according to the instructions that shipped with it. When you're asked to name the computer, you can name the computer anything you want—I named mine CARPC. This part can take up to an hour.

If Windows XP has already been installed (in the case this was an existing computer, or you just outright purchased it), follow the prompts if you are required to register and make sure you activate Windows (it will annoyingly keep asking you to do so until you do).

When Windows finally comes up, make sure you activate it, or your operating system will run for only 30 days.

Also, once Windows is activated, open the Display control panel and set your resolution to 800 × 600, or 800 × 480 if that is all your display will support. You can use a higher resolution, but higher resolutions tend to be difficult to read while driving.

If you are installing a composite display instead of a VGA display, try not to use any resolution higher than 640 × 480 (VGA converted to composite just doesn't look very good).

A shortcut around navigating to the Control Panel to change display settings is to simply right-click the desktop and select Settings, which will bring up the Display control panel.

Step 3: Install Necessary Drivers and Software

Once the operating system has been built, you must install the drivers for all the devices you want to use with your computer. Install each device according to the manufacturer's instructions and make sure they work. If there are special configuration settings you would like to make, such as specific hotkey actions, game controller settings, monitor resolutions, and so on, you should set those now and test them. Anything you set up now should work fine once you get it into the car.

Step 4: Install Games and Common Applications

Now that your drivers are installed, install all of the applications you are likely to use. It is important that you have antivirus on your car computer, and a firewall, especially if you are going to connect it to the Internet. Here are some common applications you will most likely need to install:

- Antivirus software (a free antivirus product is available from Avast at www.avast.com in their Avast AntiVirus product)

- DVD playback software (should come with the computer or DVD-ROM drive), such as PowerDVD or WinDVD

- Music-playing software (such as CarTunes™, iTunes®, RealPlayer, Windows Media 10, MusicMatch® Jukebox, and so forth)

- Web browser (Internet Explorer comes with Windows, but you may want to install Mozilla® or FireFox®)

- Car PC–specific software, such as MediaCar, or any of the many others listed in the "Software Geared for Car PCs" section earlier in the preparation section of this chapter.

Now is also the right time to install your games. Install your games in "full" mode so all the files you need should be on your computer. Be sure to activate any applications that require online activation or registration *before* you put them in a car where Internet access will likely be limited.

Keeping CDs Available and Dealing with Copy Protection

Some games and software applications require the original CDs or data discs to be in the CD or DVD drive before you can run the program. Obviously you don't want to keep your original CDs or DVD collection in your car all day and night. Heat can warp the discs, passengers can scratch them, thieves may break into cars with discs in the open, and there are, of course, other issues with having lots of expensive discs in your car.

The common solution is to use a disc-imaging application to move the CD or DVD directly to the hard drive and mount that disc on a *virtual* CD or DVD drive. One of the most popular applications is Alcohol 120% from Alcohol Software (www.alcohol-soft.com) for about $60. Alcohol 120% is capable of reading and imaging many different copy-protected CDs and works very well. It even doubles as a CD-burning application. Once a CD or DVD is imaged, you can mount it on a virtual CD or DVD drive, and your applications should be tricked into thinking its original CD is available! Of course, it's possible that some games will work around this, but that leaves room for Alcohol Software to release updates. A similar application to Alcohol 120% is DriveImage from PowerQuest (www.powerquest.com), which sells for about $50.

Different applications use different copy protection methods, and Alcohol 120% supports most of them via "profiles," which define how to read copy-protected discs, as well as how to write them back to a CD (such as when you need a backup copy). I have found that many discs can be used if imaged with the "SafeDisc 2/3" profile, but you may have to tweak the disc read settings to get a good read. Looking online can help you find the right profile to use for copying your disc to an image. One popular site for finding such information is www.gamecopy world.com.

Keep in mind, the game manufacturers know these disc-imaging products exist and are finding ways to circumvent them. Unfortunately, with software piracy being such a large problem (estimates say more than $1 billion per year is lost in the game software industry due to piracy), they can't just issue copy protection that keeps honest people honest. Hence, you may need to make physical backup copies of your discs to keep in your car. Alcohol should help you properly image a disc and then write it back to a CD or DVD and use it in your car. This tactic should help get you around the game's lack of support for virtual drives and from keeping the original disc in your car. Your last resort may be to contact the manufacturer for another copy of the disc the game requires to run (possibly incurring a nominal fee).

Note   I don't condone piracy—neither should you! If you use an application like Alcohol 120% to image a disc, please don't distribute the image file. Software developers work very hard to bring you the programs you enjoy, and you (and others) should pay for the commercial and shareware programs you use.

Step 5: Turn on Hibernation Support

Hibernation enables your computer to save its state when you kill the ignition. When you next turn the car on, the computer will start up from where it was when you last turned the car off, saving you from enduring the boot process or having to relaunch applications every time you start your car.

To enable hibernation in Windows XP:

1. Click Start.

2. Click Control Panel.

3. Click Power Options.

4. Click the Hibernate tab.

5. Check the Enable hibernation box (see Figure 12-9).

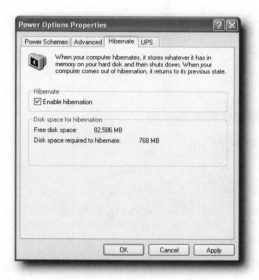

FIGURE 12-9: Select the Hibernate tab.

6. Click Apply.

7. Click the Advanced tab.

8. Under Power Options, set both drop-down boxes to Hibernate (see Figure 12-10).

9. Click Apply.

10. Click OK and your computer is all set up to act properly when turning the ignition switch on and off.

FIGURE 12-10: Select the Advanced tab.

Step 6: Update Your Software

Now that everything's set up, it's important to make sure you have the latest software on your computer. Since you aren't always connected to the Internet, make sure you update everything before you put the computer in your car, including:

- Windows and related drivers via Windows Update at www.windowsupdate.com
- Antivirus via your antivirus software's update feature
- Games
- Office software via Office Update at http://officeupdate.microsoft.com
- Any other software you install

Other Neat Applications to Try

Before you put your new computer into your car, here's a list of some unnecessary yet very useful software you may want to install:

- CarTunes (`http://cartunes.ws`)—A media player I authored specifically for Car PCs.

- Konfabulator (`http://konfabulator.com`)—Lets you customize your computer desktop with special objects called *widgets*. There're a *lot* of widgets you can download, from weather forecast widgets to clocks to media players—and you can even create your own. Originally, the product was only for Macintosh, but now it works with Windows as well.

Installing the PC in Your Car

If you are using the power sequencer, you must start your engine all the way to keep the computer working properly. If you just turn your key to the ON position and then a few seconds later to the Start position, the power sequencer often incorrectly will tell the computer to turn off as if the ignition had been switched to OFF. If this happens, turn your car off for two minutes and then start it and all should work fine again. Some newer versions of car power supplies attempt to prevent this issue, but keep this in mind if your computer isn't turning on after you start your car (and it had been working fine before).

Now that everything's configured, we're ready to place the computer in the car.

Step 1: Swap Power Supplies

Replace the standard computer power supply with the Mini-Box solution per the instructions from Mini-Box. Simply mount the power supply in your case along with the power regulator and that's it. To power your computer, and *before you go to Step 2*, follow the project steps in Chapter 3.

If you're using a power solution from a different manufacturer, that's okay. Now is the time to swap out the AC power supply for the solution you will be using in your car.

Step 2: Install the Display

After you have replaced the power supply, install the display you chose per the instructions from the manufacturer. See Chapter 7 for information on choosing a display. I recommend the Digital Worldwide (www.digitalww.com) DWW-7VGT (~$450) in-dash touch-screen display or their motorized DWW-700M solution (~$500) if your center console can support an in-dash unit the size of a car stereo (most cars can), which is sometimes called a 1-din or 1U size slot. If your car doesn't have an available slot for the display, you can just as easily mount a display on your dash, such as the Xenarc 700TSV (www.xenarc.com) on-dash touch-screen display. If you're into tearing your dash apart, you can also create your own moldings and build a display directly into your dash, but that's beyond the scope of this book.

See Figure 12-11 for a picture of the in-dash solution and Figure 12-12 for the on-dash solution. Both solutions use a USB interface to connect the display to your computer for input.

FIGURE 12-11: In-dash display from Digital Worldwide.

FIGURE 12-12: On-dash display from Xenarc.

Step 3: Place the Computer

Now that you have your display installed, you can place the computer where you want to keep it. If you're installing a slimline case, a good place is under the passenger seat. For a larger form-factor PC, such as the Cooler Master ATCS pizza-box-style case in Figure 12-6 and specified for this project, the trunk will do just fine.

First, take some Velcro and run the hook (i.e., nonfuzzy) side of it along the bottom sides of the PC case, as shown in Figure 12-13. This will prevent the computer from sliding around, yet it will remain easy to remove.

FIGURE 12-13: Velcro properly attached to the bottom of the computer case.

Mount the PC on the carpet, far enough away from feet but with enough room so that you can open the DVD/CD-ROM drive and access the front ports and buttons with no trouble, as shown in Figure 12-14.

Step 4: Connect the Display and Peripherals

Now that the computer is mounted, you need to run the cables to the PC. Follow the instructions in Chapter 5, "Working with Cables," to properly run the cables.

 Be careful not to let any wires cross the path of the seats or you may kink or tear the wires, which could cause a fire or shock hazard if you cut through a power cable!

Step 5: Turn It On!

Now that everything is connected, you should be able to turn your computer on and start using it!

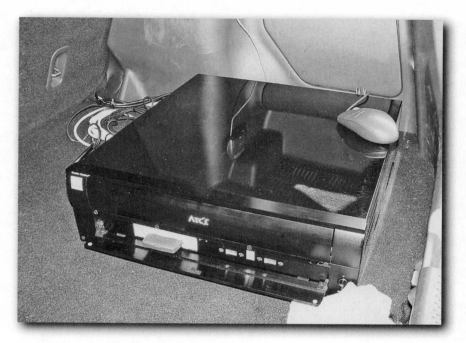

FIGURE 12-14: PC in the trunk with plenty of room.

Summary

In this chapter you installed a media center PC, giving you the ability to have a full entertainment system in your car for all your passengers to enjoy. Using both free and commercial software and only a couple extra devices (a tuner and video receiver in addition to a DVD-ROM), you can listen, watch, and play using your newly installed Car PC!

Installing a Gaming PC

Approximate project cost: $1,700

The greatest convenience of computers being so ubiquitous is their ability to be easily upgraded. Should you build a general-purpose PC, it can be pretty easy to improve the graphics performance with an AGP or PCI graphics card and possibly a higher-performance sound card. It's just as easy (and fairly cheap) to build your own performance gaming system, too. However, in a vehicle environment you are restricted by the amount of power, the size of the screen, and heat and radio frequency interference issues.

This chapter will discuss installing a gaming PC into your car. We will not go over how to build the PC, as I assume you already have the knowledge to build a PC if you purchased a book with the word *Geek* in the title! If you do not feel comfortable building a PC, please have a professional build one for you, following the specifications in this chapter and based on what you learned in Parts I and II of this book.

Tip

Regarding gaming PC power requirements, minimize power requirements by getting a lower-end processor with a higher-end graphics card. Sometimes buying a laptop and retrofitting it to a mobile environment can be just as effective for in-car gaming over building your own desktop form-factor system, especially since laptops are already optimized for their respective advertised performance level (i.e., gaming laptop, business laptop, personal laptop, and so forth) in mobile environments. See the sidebar "High-Performance, Low-Power Processors and Motherboards" for more details.

Choosing an Appropriate Processor

Many gamers tend to install the latest, greatest, fastest, most powerful processors in their systems. Sometimes they even have more than one! This tends to generate lots of heat, requires lots of power, and is usually entirely inappropriate for a mobile environment. For example, an Intel Pentium 4 desktop processor uses more than 80 watts of power and requires many fans and plenty of air flow to keep cool, unless an advanced liquid cooling system is installed. Advanced graphics cards can use just as much power, and possibly more.

Within a mobile environment you have to take a different approach. Instead of large screen sizes, plenty of available power, and plenty of space, all in a fully climate controlled environment, in a car you have exactly the opposite. These limitations actually work to your benefit, believe it or not. The smaller screen sizes enable you to use lower resolutions and still have an entertaining game experience, requiring less processor power and less graphics card capability due to the decreased amount of data to be processed. Also, because of the smaller screen, you probably won't notice as much detail, allowing you to use game settings for less detail. Since you won't need as much extra processor and graphics power, you can get lower-power (and often less expensive) processors, such as the Pentium M, Pentium III, or the mobile Pentium 4 or Mobile Athlon processors with their sizable caches but lower power consumption than desktop versions. You can also get lower-power (and cheaper) graphics boards and install them. Likewise, you can purchase slower hard drives or laptop hard drives, and possibly even flash memory disks.

Many consumers confuse Intel's Centrino® product offering with the Pentium M processor. The Centrino is just a chipset consisting of an Intel motherboard, Pentium M processor, and Intel wireless networking technology. When asking for just the processor, make sure you ask for the Pentium M.

Retrofitting a Laptop Instead of Building a Computer

Another option you might want to consider is buying a used laptop with acceptable graphics and gaming performance. This way you'll have all the parts you need with an already power-optimized system. Oftentimes you can find these systems on eBay with dead screens, which you won't need anyway if you already have a screen picked out. If you go the laptop route, and you need an analog output for your display, consider the AVerMicro QuickPlay USB (www.avermicro.com) solution, which enables you to send VGA (video graphics array/adapter) signals over analog (composite, S-Video, or component), with no configuration, just by plugging it into your USB and VGA cable.

Many laptop boards can be retrofitted to a small or slimline PC case and placed under the seat. You can also just keep the laptop in its original case. Either way, you will have to double-check the laptop's BIOS settings to make sure video mirroring is always on, since you will be using your own screens via the laptop's auxiliary VGA output instead of the built-in display (unless of course you decide to convert that to a screen as well). Some laptops may not allow you to permanently turn on the external video via the BIOS, but there may still be an option to do so—check with the manufacturer or search online.

Keep in mind that if you can't find a way to keep video mirroring on, and you can't retrofit the laptop's primary display to work in your vehicle, you may find yourself up the creek—so make sure the external video works *before* you install the computer in your car. A good way to force yourself to test the video capabilities is to do all laptop configuration, software installs, and so forth, via the external display (not just on the laptop's built-in one). Furthermore, consider that the Function key combination that usually toggles video on laptops may not work with the external keyboard you use, preventing you from just toggling the switch!

Don't Install Super-High-Performance PCs

Please keep the super-high-performance PC out of your car. Although they sound cool, they're likely going to be more trouble than they're worth. The liquid cooling systems, high-RPM hard drives, power-hungry processors, and performance RAM, RAID arrays, and multiprocessor graphics boards were never meant to travel at anything but zero miles per hour. High-performance PCs with all the extras can also exhibit radio interference, unsafe battery drain, and are basically not practical for cars. There's the coolness factor, but then there's common sense.

Keep It in the Trunk

Depending on what case you choose, the PC you will be installing in this chapter may likely be installed in the trunk, where it can stay fairly cool, unless you have plenty of room in your car for a full-size case. See Chapter 11, "Adding a General-Purpose PC," for details on slimline PCs, which can fit under a seat. Some higher-performance motherboard solutions won't fit in the slimline cases, even if you use PCI risers (cards that let you mount a card horizontally instead of vertically), due to their size and fan requirements. You likely won't need access to the drives much at all anyway, since you can image the discs you need, which is discussed later in this chapter.

Note If you are installing the PC in your trunk, and your car has a folding back seat, make sure to position the PC so you or a passenger can fold down the back seat and access the computer without opening the trunk. Keeping the drive trays and status LEDs facing the opening to your passenger compartment can be very convenient!

Tip Some motherboards are shipping with acceptable to very good chipsets on-board, so consider motherboards with the features you already want built-in when you go shopping. It's better to have the simpler, all-in-one solution than many expansion boards and the associated power management issues that come with them.

Components and Tools Needed

What you will need:

- Flat pizza-box computer case that can fit conveniently in the trunk, such as the Cooler Master ATCS (~$120, see Figure 13-1). The flat cases are easy to place in the trunk, easy to mount and secure, and are easily expandable with the peripherals you will likely want to use in a gaming PC.

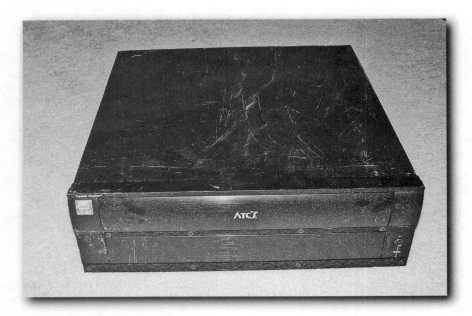

FIGURE 13-1: Cooler Master ATCS case.

- An appropriate motherboard (a.k.a., mainboard) for the processor you have chosen to implement, along with that processor, appropriate heat-sinks, and fans (price varies on what you decide to implement, ~$120–$400).

- 512 MB of RAM (you can put 1 gigabyte if you like, but nothing more should be necessary, ~$99).

- 40 GB full-size or laptop hard drive (~$99, or higher capacity, as you desire). When choosing the drive, pay close attention to the G-force shock rating, and stay away from high-performance (i.e., 10K RPM and higher) drives because they generate more heat and require more power. See Chapter 6, "Physics Man, Physics: Preparing Home Electronics for the Road," for more information on the physics of choosing a hard drive.

- IDE DVD-ROM/CD-RW combo drive (*not* slot-loading, ~$85).

- Windows XP Home Edition ($99, Professional is preferred if you're going to be using the music sync project in Chapter 18, "Syncing Portable Music Players," $199). You can use Linux or any other operating system, of course, but in this book I will be focusing on Windows-based solutions since they are the most popular.

- A PS/2 keyboard and mouse (~$119, or USB if you desire). See Chapter 8, "Choosing an Input Device," for details on choosing a keyboard and mouse for the car. In this project we will use the Gyration wireless product I recommend in that chapter. Windows XP automatically installs the drivers for the Gyration, so it should work once Windows comes up.

- A VGA display device, such as the Digital Worldwide (www.digitalww.com) TWW-7VGT (~$450), the Digital Worldwide fully motorized in-dash display DWW-700M (~$500), or the Xenarc (www.xenarc.com) 700TSV (~$450). These displays come with both an AC adapter and cigarette lighter adapter for easily working with them at home and in your car (meaning you shouldn't need a separate display). You can use a composite/analog display device and a VGA-to-composite adapter (such as those available from AVerMedia QuickPlay™, www.avermedia.com), but the video won't be very clear and you'll wish you had spent the money on a better display. See Chapter 7, "Choosing a Display Device," for more information on selecting displays.

- A low-power (120–180 watt) AC power supply, for working on the computer at home (~$50).

- The Mini-Box PW series AC power supply, for when the computer is in your car, shown in Figure 13-2 (~$50). Make sure you purchase the one appropriate model for your processor and motherboard type (see www.mini-box.com for details).

- The Mini-Box ITPS auto power sequencer and low-dropout regulator, for enabling your Car PC to turn on and off properly when the car's ignition is switched (~$40, see Figure 13-3). Make sure you purchase the one appropriate model for your processor and motherboard type (see www.mini-box.com for details).

FIGURE 13-2: Mini-Box power supply.

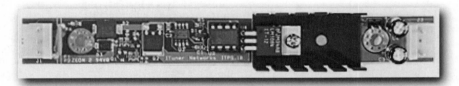

FIGURE 13-3: Mini-Box ITPS auto power sequencer and low-dropout regulator.

Preparing Your PC for Car Installation

Now that you have everything you need for your gaming PC, including any PCI cards AGP graphics boards, and USB devices you want to install, it's time for you to put it all together.

Step 1: Building the PC

Building a Car PC is similar to building any PC except you will be using a laptop hard drive and will be installing the standard AC power supply and swapping it out later for the car-ready power supply. Everything else will be just like building a regular PC. If you aren't familiar with building PCs, I suggest you either have a professional build the PC for you (all the parts they need are listed above), or learn how to do it yourself with a book such as *Building a PC For Dummies* (Wiley), ISBN #0-7645-4247-8.

Step 2: Install and Activate the Operating System

Install Windows XP according to the instructions that shipped with it. When you're asked to name the computer, you can name the computer anything you want—I named mine CARPC. This part can take up to an hour.

When Windows finally comes up, make sure you activate it, or your operating system will run for only 30 days.

Also, once Windows is activated, open the Monitors control panel and set your resolution to 800 × 600. You can use a higher resolution, but higher resolutions tend to be difficult to read while driving.

Step 3: Install Necessary Drivers and Software

Once the operating system has been built, you must install the drivers for all the devices you want to use with your computer. Install each device according to the manufacturer's instructions and make sure they work. If there are special configuration settings you would like to make, such as specific hotkey actions, game controller settings, monitor resolutions, and so on, you should set those now and test them. Anything you set up now should work fine once you get it into the car.

Step 4: Install Games and Common Applications

Now that your drivers are installed, install all of the applications you are likely to use. It is important that you have antivirus on your car computer, and a firewall, especially if you are going to connect it to the Internet. Here are some common applications you will most likely need to install:

- Antivirus software (a free antivirus product is available from Avast at www.avast.com in their Avast AntiVirus product)

- DVD playback software (should come with the computer or DVD-ROM drive), such as PowerDVD or WinDVD

- Music-playing software (such as CarTunes™, iTunes®, MusicMatch® Jukebox, and so forth)

- Web browser (Internet Explorer comes with Windows, but you may want to install Mozilla® or FireFox®)

Now is also the right time to install your games. Install your games in "full" mode so all the files you need should be on your computer. Be sure to activate any applications that require online activation or registration *before* you put them in a car where Internet access will likely be limited. The paragraphs that follow will go over how to get around keeping all your game CDs in your car.

Keeping CDs Available and Dealing with Copy Protection

Some games and software applications require the original CDs or data discs to be in the CD or DVD drive before you can run the program. Obviously you don't want to keep your original CDs or DVD collection in your car all day and night. Heat can warp the discs, passengers can scratch them, thieves may break into cars with discs in the open, and there are of course other issues with having lots of expensive discs in your car.

The common solution is to use a disc-imaging application to move the CD or DVD directly to the hard drive and mount that disc on a *virtual* CD or DVD drive. One of the most popular applications is Alcohol 120% from Alcohol Software (`www.alcohol-soft.com`) for about $60. Alcohol 120% is capable of reading and imaging many different copy-protected CDs and works very well. It even doubles as a CD-burning application. Once a CD or DVD is imaged, you can mount it on a virtual CD or DVD drive, and your applications should be tricked into thinking its original CD is available! Of course, it's possible that some games will work around this, but that leaves room for Alcohol Software to release updates. A similar application to Alcohol 120% is DriveImage from PowerQuest (`www.powerquest.com`), which sells for about $50.

Different applications use different copy protection methods and Alcohol 120% supports most of them via "profiles" which define how to read copy-protected discs, as well as how to write them back to a CD (such as when you need a backup copy). I have found many discs can be used if imaged with the "SafeDisc 2/3" profile, but you may have to tweak the disc read settings to get a good read. Looking online can help you find the right profile to use for copying your disc to an image. One popular site for finding such information is `www.gamecopyworld.com`.

Keep in mind that the game manufacturers know these disc-imaging products exist and are finding ways to circumvent them. Unfortunately, with software piracy being such a large problem (estimates say more than $1 billion per year is lost in the game software industry due to piracy), they can't just issue copy protection that keeps honest people honest. Hence, you may need to make physical backup copies of your discs to keep in your car. Alcohol should help you properly image a disc and then write it back to a CD or DVD and use it in your car. This tactic should help get you around the game's lack of support for virtual drives and from keeping the original disc in your car. Your last resort may be to contact the manufacturer for another copy of the disc the game requires to run (possibly incurring a nominal fee).

Note I don't condone piracy. If you use an application like Alcohol 120% to image a disc, please don't distribute the image file. Application software developers work very hard to bring you the programs you enjoy, and you (and others) should pay for the commercial and shareware programs you use.

High-Performance, Low-Power Processors and Motherboards

With heat and power consumption being such important items to keep in check when building a computer in your car, it should be comforting to know that processor, motherboard, and case manufacturers feel your pain. To this extent, processor manufacturers are releasing low-power, high-performance desktop processors into the marketplace based on their mobile offerings, while case and motherboard manufacturers are moving to more energy efficient computer form factors that require fewer fans.

In the case of processors, Intel's highly successful and very powerful Pentium® M processor lineup is now shipping in desktops. The Pentium® M offers comparable performance to the Pentium 4 product line while requiring much less power, and it's fully capable of actively stepping its speeds up and down based on power requirements. AMD has taken a somewhat opposite approach, offering its popular Athlon product in a mobile version called the Mobile Athlon instead of an entirely new processor, which can still be implemented as long as you have a compatible motherboard. Still other manufacturers provide processors geared for acceptable overall performance and exceptional media performance, such as the Via C3 line of processors, which can run fanless (and are an excellent fit for general-purpose and media center PC solutions).

As processors have become more capable and power-hungry, manufacturers have started to become more aware of the manufacturing costs of adding all of the fans, higher-capacity power supplies, and other necessary components to support such capabilities. For at least 10 years, these manufacturers have used the ATX and microATX form factors, adding fan after fan to keep these enclosures and the associated motherboards cool. A new technology making its way into systems and stores by 2005 is the *BTX*, or *Balanced Technology Extended*, form factor. BTX moves all of the power-consuming and heat-generating components, such as the processor, chipsets, and graphics processor to the center of the motherboard and case and has two big, slow fans blowing air over the components from front to back. This cools the components more efficiently and keeps the computer quiet. It also eliminates a number of extra fans, which ultimately will enable manufacturers to drop component costs.

When building a PC for your car, keep the lower-power-consumption processors and modern PC form factors in mind before you build. It will help you get the performance you desire using a more efficient and likely more reliable and longer-lasting solution.

Step 5: Turn on Hibernation Support

Hibernation enables your computer to save its state when you kill the ignition. When you next turn the car on, the computer will start up from where it was when you last turned the car off, saving you from enduring the boot process or having to relaunch applications every time you start your car.

To enable hibernation in Windows XP:

1. Click Start, then Settings.

2. Click Control Panel.

3. Click Power Options.

4. Click the Hibernate tab.

5. Check the Enable hibernation box (see Figure 13-4).

FIGURE 13-4: Select the Hibernate tab.

6. Click Apply.

7. Click the Advanced tab.

8. Under Power Options, set both drop-down boxes to Hibernate (see Figure 13-5).

9. Click Apply.

10. Click OK and your computer is all set up to act properly when turning the ignition switch on and off.

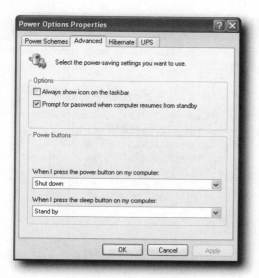

FIGURE 13-5: Select the Advanced tab.

Step 6: Update Your Software

Now that everything's set up, it's important to make sure you have the latest software on your computer. Since you aren't always connected to the Internet, make sure you update everything before you put the computer in your car, including:

- Windows and related drivers via Windows Update at www.windowsupdate.com
- Antivirus via your antivirus software's update feature
- Games
- Office software via Office Update at http://officeupdate.microsoft.com
- Any other software you install

It is imperative that you install the latest versions of your games, graphics card drivers, and Microsoft's DirectX (if you're using Windows) because many new games have issues with older graphics cards and DirectX versions. Since you won't always be connected to the Internet, now is the time to install all the updates so you can reduce crashes and improve performance. Furthermore, many game CDs actually have an older, more crash-prone version of the game— so make sure you go online and update all your games to get the best experience possible.

Other Neat Applications to Try

Before you put your new computer into your car, here's a list of some unnecessary yet very useful software you may want to install:

- CarTunes (`http://cartunes.ws`)—a media player I wrote specifically for Car PCs.

- Konfabulator (`http://konfabulator.com`)—Lets you customize your computer desktop with special objects called *widgets*. There are a *lot* of widgets you can download, from weather forecast widgets to clocks to media players—and you can even create your own. Originally, the product was only for Macintosh, but now it works with Windows as well.

Installing the PC in Your Car

Tip If you are using the power sequencer, you must start your car all the way to keep the computer working properly. If you just turn your key to the ON position and then a few seconds later to the Start position, the power sequencer often incorrectly will tell the computer to turn off as if the ignition had been switched to OFF. If this happens, turn your car off for two minutes and then start it and all should work fine again.

Now that everything's configured, we're ready to place the computer in the car.

Step 1: Swap Power Supplies

Replace the standard computer power supply with the Mini-Box solution per the instructions from Mini-Box. Simply mount the power supply in your case along with the power regulator and that's it. To power your computer, and *before you go to Step* 2, follow the project steps in Chapter 3, "Giving Your Creation Life: Power Considerations."

Note If you're using a power solution from a different manufacturer, that's okay. Now is the time to swap out the AC power supply for the solution you will be using in your car.

Step 2: Install the Display

After you have replaced the power supply, install the display you chose per the instructions from the manufacturer. See Chapter 7 for information on choosing a display. I recommend the Digital Worldwide (www.digitalww.com) DWW-7VGT (~$450) in-dash touch-screen display or their motorized DWW-700M solution (~$500) if your center console can support an in-dash unit the size of a car stereo (most cars can), which is sometimes called a 1-din or 1U size slot. If your car doesn't have an available slot for the display, you can just as easily mount a display on your dash, such as the Xenarc 700TSV (www.xenarc.com) on-dash touch-screen display. If you're into tearing your dash apart, you can also create your own moldings and build a display directly into your dash, but that's beyond the scope of this book.

See Figure 13-6 for a picture of the in-dash solution and Figure 13-7 for the on-dash solution. Both solutions use a USB interface to connect the display to your computer for input.

FIGURE 13-6: The in-dash display from Digital Worldwide.

FIGURE 13-7: The on-dash display from Xenarc.

Step 3: Place the Computer

Now that you have your display installed, you can place the computer where you want to keep it. If you're installing a slimline case, a good place is under the passenger seat. For a larger form-factor PC, such as the Cooler Master ATCS pizza-box-style case shown in Figure 13-1 and specified for this project, the trunk will do just fine.

First, take some Velcro and run the hook (i.e., non-fuzzy) side of it along the bottom sides of the PC case, as shown in Figure 13-8. This will prevent the computer from sliding around, yet it will remain easy to remove.

FIGURE **13-8:** Velcro properly attached to the bottom of the computer case.

Mount the PC on the carpet, far enough away from feet but with enough room so that you can open the DVD/CD-ROM drive and access the front ports and buttons with no trouble, as shown Figure 13-9.

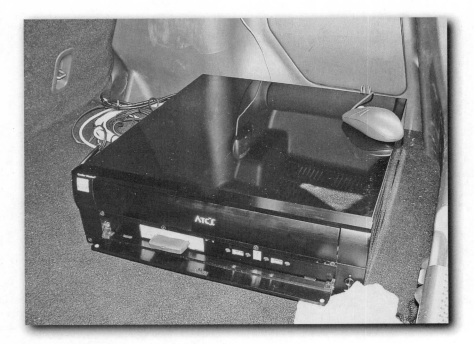

FIGURE 13-9: The PC in the trunk with plenty of room.

Step 4: Connect the Display and Peripherals

Now that the computer is mounted, you need to run the cables to the PC. Follow the instructions in Chapter 5, "Working with Cables," to properly run the cables.

 Warning Be careful not to let any wires cross the path of the seats or you may kink or tear the wires, which could cause a fire or shock hazard if you cut through a power cable!

Step 5: Turn It On!

Now that everything is connected, you should be able to turn your computer on and start using it!

Summary

In this chapter you built a Gaming PC and configured it for use in the car. Although you generally shouldn't be installing a performance powerhouse into your car, you can fully enjoy all the games out there within your car without spending a lot of money.

Advanced Projects

part

IV

Adding Internet Access

Approximate project cost: $200–$800

O ne of the most useful features to have on the road is Internet access. From checking sports scores to finding directions to chatting with friends to sending out that client e-mail you "kinda forgot about," Internet access opens up a world of possibilities. While you're driving, your passengers can use it, or your GPS can keep itself up to date and determine whether there are alternate routes to get around traffic. While parked you can send e-mail without driving back to the office, school, or home. In this chapter we'll discuss various wireless ways to get you connected, from using your cell phone to utilizing 802.11 (a.k.a. Wi-Fi) wireless hot spots, and even touching a bit on *war driving* through neighborhoods in our emerging wire-free world in search of free Internet access.

Warning
Do not surf the Internet and drive at the same time. Either pull over to the side of the road and park to surf the Internet (if it's legal to pull over), or let your passengers look items up for you. It is very dangerous to surf and drive!

in this chapter

☑ Choosing an Internet access method

☑ Wi-Fi, GPRS, and satellite Internet

☑ Building a USB hub into your dash

☑ War driving

Components and Tools Needed

Here are the items you will need to get the projects done in this chapter.

If you are adding Internet access via your cell phone:

- A cell phone with Internet connectivity capabilities (via Bluetooth®, for example), or a cell phone Internet access card, such as a PC Card or Compact Flash (varies, ~$200–$600)

- The software for the Internet connectivity via the cell phone (free, usually comes with the phone)

- The car computer to run it on
- Appropriate input/output (I/O) port available on your computer, such as one available USB port or Bluetooth capabilities, as required by the phone (see sidebar on adding a USB hub to your dash for another cool project!), or a compatible PCMCIA or Compact Flash drive

If you are adding Internet access via 802.11a, b, and/or g (a.k.a Wi-Fi):

- A Wi-Fi receiver (~$39–$99 for PC Card—a.k.a. PCMCIA or CardBus—versions, $25–$50 for USB)
- An operating system that supports the adapter and Wi-Fi access
- Wi-Fi access point ($99, this will vary by location, more on that soon)
- Available USB port, Bluetooth capabilities, or PCMCIA card slot as required by the Wi-Fi adapter

Choosing the Connection Method

Just because I will be giving you two options doesn't mean you can't use both. Wi-Fi and cell phone Internet access complement each other. You won't always have access to a Wi-Fi access point, and you can't use Wi-Fi while you are driving because of the short range of Wi-Fi networks. Then again, cell phone Internet access can be expensive, especially if you use it quite a bit. Let's go over how to choose which to use (I use both, by the way).

Cell Phone Internet Access

There are a couple of different methods for getting access to the Internet via a cell phone. One is to use the cell phone itself via either a serial/USB cable kit or built-in Bluetooth® for wireless access to the phone. The other is to use a special dedicated PC card made specifically for Internet access (some give you faxing and phone call capabilities as well). These cards all have different names, but they all use similar technologies named GPRS, PCS, EDGE, 1xRTT, and 3G.

Connecting via a Cell Phone

Being able to browse the Internet on your phone doesn't necessarily mean you can use it with your Car PC. To find out whether your phone supports Internet access via a computer, the easiest thing to do is to check the manual, and if that doesn't work, check with your cell phone service provider. Many lower-cost phones do not offer Internet access, whereas mid-range to expensive ones sport either Internet access via Bluetooth or via a connection cable.

Connecting via a Cellular/GPRS/3G/PCS Connection Card

Although connecting to the Internet via your cell phone may be possible, it is many times more convenient to have a separate connection card for Internet access. For example, I go to the local café and get work done while I use a Sprint PCS Vision Connection Card, and use my cell phone for phone calls. With Sprint I can't use the Internet and receive phone calls at the same time, so that was my only option. Other providers may be different. There are so many different providers that no single chapter could cover what each one does here. Your best bet to find out whether you would need a connection card in addition to your phone is to call your service provider.

Each service provider tends to use different technologies for providing data access. Keep this in mind, because cellular connection cards tend to work only with the provider stamped on them. These cards use technologies like 2G, 3G, GPRS, and others as described in the "New Term" sections that follow.

New Term

GPRS—General Packet Radio Service. A wireless packet data service used in mobile telephony solutions to transmit nonvoice data at speeds up to about 171 kilobits per second. GPRS complements Simple Messaging Service (SMS) because of its speed.

PCS—Personal Communications Service. This is a general term for personal communication services by a mobile phone or mobile voice/data device. Because it is such a generic term, PCS encompasses many technologies when they are used together in a single device, including CDMA, TDMA, GSM 1900, 1G, 2G, 2.5G, and 3G.

EDGE—Enhanced Data Rates for GSM Evolution. A global wireless data network based on GSM that provides higher speeds than GPRS, up to about 400 kilobits per second, or about 7.5 times the speed of dial-up.

1xRTT—A 3G wireless technology developed by Qualcomm running on the CDMA network offering up to 144 kilobits per second data rates. An updated version of the protocol, 1xRTT Release A will offer double that speed, or 288 kilobits per second data transfer. Another enhancement is also in development named 3xRTT. Sprint PCS and Verizon Wireless use 1xRTT. Sprint has called 1xRTT 3G in its promotions and has forecasted speeds of over 1 megabit per second being made available to cell phones and other mobile devices via its 3G network. The 1 in 1xRTT is due to the number of 1.25 MHz channels used by the technology.

3G—Third-Generation Wireless. A standard wireless data service to be used in future cell phones that provides multimedia and high-speed data access, improved voice quality, among other features. 3G was preceded by 1G (first-generation wireless) in the 1970s and 1980s and 2G (second-generation wireless) in the 1990s. Many phones today are actually deemed 2.5G, because they do not yet offer all of the features of 3G. 3G is expected to be rolled out in ubiquity in 2005.

Have Treo Will Surf

Owners of the Handspring® (now PalmOne®) Treo® 270, 300, and 600 series (including the Treo 650) can use a handy program to get Internet access virtually for free with their phones. *PdaNet*, from JuneFabrics (www.junefabrics.com), utilizes the data connection Treos use for their regular browsing and passes it on to your computer over Treo's USB cable, as shown in the following sidebar figure. PdaNet appears as a modem on your Treo. All you have to do is install the software for your Treo and your PC (all in a single, simple installation program), tap "Connect" on the Treo, and you're connected at up to 144 kilobits per second, or about 2.5 times the speed of dial-up. Those lucky enough to have the Treo 650 and a Bluetooth interface on their computer (easy acquired through $30 USB solutions) can wirelessly connect to the Internet via Bluetooth on the Treo 650 using the PdaNet software. As of the writing of this book, PdaNet did not support Macintosh, but there was a suggestion on its Web site to try using PdaNet with Virtual PC®, a product from Microsoft that lets you emulate a PC (including USB ports) on a Mac.

If you don't already have a Treo, this approximately $35 utility is an affordable alternative to a connection card with a separate account. The older Treo 300s can be purchased for under $200 (they make a great phone, too), and if you can share your service plan minutes with your current cell phone account, you can just add the Treo to your existing account and usually pay a lot less than a new connection card with a data plan.

There have been some rumors that providers may install a hack disabling use of PdaNet. Although this is possible, it's probably not a good idea, because that could cause any applications that need Internet access to cease functioning, and thus lower the value of the Treo. Of course, if something like that happens, you still have a great phone to use!

The problem with the connection card route is it usually carries with it a hefty price tag. Most will not feed off your cell phone's minutes because the cards tend to be data-only, although some may support voice call and fax capabilities. Therefore you have to have a separate phone number or service plan on the card, which is usually monthly and usually at least $20 per month. I pay $80 per month via Sprint for unlimited access, which ends up being more than $960 per year, so if you can find a way to connect via your cell phone and you don't mind missing calls, I'd suggest that route. Services providers offer dozens of data-rate and data-volume plans, usually topping out with unlimited access for between $80 to $100 a month.

Tip

If you are self-employed or work for a business that benefits from you having mobile Web access, the fees and the hardware for wireless access and cell phone data service plans may be partially or totally tax-deductible.

Also consider that connection cards are usually PCMCIA cards or Compact Flash cards. Most computers don't come with these types of drives, and PCMCIA drives may not fit in super-slim computer cases. You may be thinking that a Compact Flash card will work as long as you have one of those media readers. This is not necessarily true, because many of those readers do not support anything but storage devices, so check that your computer can handle the card you purchase *before* you purchase a card and/or activate a data account!

Did You Know

Handspring was founded by the original developers of the Palm Pilot PDA. They disagreed with the way the Palm business was being run and started another company that makes a competing device with the same operating system. Handspring became so successful that Palm bought back the company.

Wi-Fi and 802.11a, b, and g

The home and abroad stationary wireless technology of choice today is 802.11a, b, and g, also known as *Wi-Fi*. You can usually find Wi-Fi *access points* at local coffee shops, schools, college campuses, office complexes, and many times in home neighborhoods. The reason I say this is a popular stationary technology is due to 802.11, a network's often limited transmission range, and the fact that you are usually sitting and using Internet access. The 802.11 technology also wasn't designed for cell switching as cell phone networks do, which provides cell phones the capability to hand off the phone call between different "cells" as you drive to keep the phone call going. Basically, this means you won't be able to use 802.11 at 50 miles per hour, and thus limits the Internet access you may have for passengers while you drive.

A fun escapade with Wi-Fi networks, though, is what has been commonly referred to as *war driving*. This is the practice of driving around neighborhoods, business complexes, and other populated areas and looking for open Wi-Fi networks that you can use for Internet access (and hopefully not anything else, but hey, it's your call). You've probably heard of war driving on the news. It can be a lot of fun to drive around your town and find your neighbor's home network is open and tell them about it. I've played pranks before where I've gone to a college campus and found a networked printer and printed bad words just to get them riled up (I don't encourage such activities, of course).

So if you want to war drive, see the sidebar "Of Course You Know, This Means War (Driving)."

Why Is It Called 802.11?

Many people wonder what the heck the 802.11a, b, and g stand for. The IEEE (Institute of Electrical and Electronics Engineers), the same people who brought your IEEE-1394 (a.k.a. FireWire®, iLink®, and so forth) is an established standards body that has defined many technologies through its internal open working groups (WGs). The 802.11 technology is named for its IEEE working group number, 802.11. IEEE Project 802 is also called the LAN/MAN Standards Committee, or LMSC, and the 802.11 working group handles wireless LANs. Tens of millions of IEEE 802.11 devices have been deployed worldwide and are interoperable.

IEEE 802.11 has many flavors. The most widespread today is 802.11b (named after IEEE 802.11 working group B), which operates in the unlicensed ISM (Industrial, Scientific, and Medical) band at approximately 2.45 GHz, and can transmit up to 11 megabits per second (Mbps). Newly available 802.11 flavors include 802.11a and 802.11g. 802.11a and g support speeds up to 54 Mbps (in the standard, proprietary solutions claim faster speeds) and operate in the ISM band, as well as the newly unlicensed U-NII (Unlicensed National Information Infrastructure) band, which operates at 5.2 and 5.8 GHz.

Even though 802.11 is a standard, its availability is restricted in different regions of the world due to varying regulations. Generally, 802.11b in the United States has 13 broadcast channels available for use (3 optimal ones because they are nonoverlapping), and 802.11a in the United States supports 140 channels, with 12 nonoverlapping optimal channels. However, in France and Spain, the various channels available to 802.11b and g users is severely limited (1 nonoverlapping channel), while there are actually *more* channels available in Japan (13 channels, 3 nonoverlapping). Take note: Even though 802.11a provides so many optimal channels, the international legalization of its 5.2 GHz frequency use has not been standardized, so outside-U.S. deployments may run into broadcast legal issues. Another note: The 5.2 GHz U-NII spectrum is also used by microwave landing systems to help planes land in bad weather.

Choosing a Wi-Fi Adapter for Your Car

The type of Wi-Fi adapter you decide to install will depend on the type of computer you are installing and how gung-ho you are about installing Wi-Fi in your car. There are a few different types—USB, PCI (i.e., *internal*), PCMCIA, Compact Flash and Secure Digital Input/Output (SDIO).

If you are installing a slimline computer in your car, and you don't have many PCI slots (i.e., one or none), you should go the USB route. If your computer only supports USB 1.1, you will be limited to the 11 Mbps speed supported by 802.11a, b, and g. If you have USB 2.0, however, you can utilize the maximum 54 megabits (and possibly more with proprietary 802.11a and g systems from some manufacturers).

When selecting a USB solution, I decided on a slimline solution from Belkin® that was all-in-one and very portable. After installing a USB hub into my dashboard (see the section "Adding a USB Hub to Your Dash" later in this chapter), I simply plug it in when I need it, and unplug it when I don't. Since USB draws power from the bus, I don't keep the wireless adapter plugged in when I'm not using it. I also remove it when I'm not in the car because thieves may notice the device and decide to smash'n grab.

FIGURE 14-1: The Belkin slim 802.11g wireless adapter.

Another available USB solution is one of the less portable products that sports a removable antenna. These units have the advantage of supporting more capable antennas, such as the range extenders readily available at CompUSA, Best Buy, and many other computer stores. You can run these antennas to the platform near your rear window (possibly less enticing to thieves) to improve reception. Range extenders run anywhere from $20 to well over $100 and usually provide at least a 6-milliwatt (mW) receiver (most router and card antennas are 2 mW or less).

Warning

Do not splice your Wi-Fi antenna feed into your car's antenna feed! Many car antennas have very balanced input stages—sharing 802.11 can swamp the radio or cause damage of any attached satellite radio, interfere with antitheft systems that use cellular transmitters or LoJack® antitheft frequencies, possibly blowing not only the warranty but also voiding the insurance coverage. Some German cars have a GPS antenna going through that antenna also, and those systems are *not* expecting 600 mW of transmitter power appearing at many points in the spectrum!

If you're unsure as to whether you have USB 1.0, 1.1, or 2.0 slots in your computer, check your user's guide. Some computers have USB 2.0 slots (which are backwards compatible with USB 1.1 and 1.0), and then some have USB 1.1–only slots as well. I know it's confusing, but hey, I don't design motherboards. Also, the USB 1.1 and USB 2.0 cables look identical, so slots usually won't be tell-tale signs of what type they are. You can, however, look for the "USB High Speed" logo, which computers sporting USB 2.0 tend to have featured on stickers plastered to the front of their case.

If your computer has available PCI slots, your options are more plentiful, because there are numerous PCI (i.e., internal) wireless adapters that are pretty cheap (under $50), and very effective. Speed is also not an issue as it would sometimes be with USB, as I discussed earlier. The problem with the PCI solution is that the card is always drawing power and you can't easily share the card with multiple computers (such as a laptop). Since you probably won't be able to use the wireless while driving, there's no reason to have the continuous drain, so I recommend against the internal wireless solution.

FIGURE 14-2: A PCMCIA (i.e., PC Card) wireless adapter.

Note Don't use Bluetooth Wi-Fi adapters. In my experience, they're just not worth it for the car application because they're too slow (Bluetooth tends to be limited to 1 megabit/second data transfers).

The PCMCIA (shown in Figure 14-2), Compact Flash, and SDIO solutions can all support the high-speed wireless solutions, and just like USB they are removable. The problem with these solutions is that they are very specialized. PCMCIA drives usually come only with laptops, so there's no reason to buy a PCMCIA drive just for a wireless card (although it would enable you to use many of the cellular connection cards). Compact Flash and SDIO solutions are usually only for PDAs. If your computer has a drive capable of using SDIO or Compact Flash cards, then you may have a slight power advantage over the USB solutions, so long as the card adapter isn't itself powered by USB.

Caution Not all Compact Flash adapters will work with PCs for Internet Access. Be wary of buying a Compact Flash or other media card *reader*, because most of these will not allow you to use the cards for Internet access! If you want to use an SDIO card with your computer or device, make sure it specifically has SDIO capability.

Bluetooth-Capable Phones

Some phones support Bluetooth and thus also support data access by simply placing the phone next to a device, such as a computer, with a Bluetooth receiver. Bluetooth supports "classes" of devices, making it possible for a Bluetooth-enabled computer to automatically detect a Bluetooth-enabled cell phone and use its features, such as data access, voice calling capabilities, and so forth, automatically. Your cell phone manual should tell you whether your phone supports Bluetooth. If it does, great! Prior to using your phone's Bluetooth connection for Internet access you should make sure you can *pair* the two, meaning that the Internet access by your computer shares your cellular phone's data access plan.

Caution Just because a phone supports Bluetooth for data access, that doesn't mean it's free to use it for Internet access. There may still be separate data service charges when using the phone for data services, so it is important that you check with your service provider before connecting to the Internet via Bluetooth, because you may rack up data minutes, and a hefty bill, without even realizing it! As stated earlier, some phones and cellular phone service providers allow a PC to "pair" with it, sharing a net access plan. Some unlimited access plans are as low as $4 a month.

A Bluetooth *adapter* for a PC is an affordable device, usually selling for $50 or less. Some Macintoshes and notebook computers already have Bluetooth built in, so check before you buy. These adapters usually have a high profit margin, so if you can get a discount on the unit through a user group, you will likely save a few bucks. To find the Bluetooth adapter for a PC, simply go to the Networking aisle in your local computer store, such as CompUSA, Best Buy, Circuit City, and so forth.

So What's Bluetooth?

Bluetooth could be considered the next generation of an alternative to infrared technology. Infrared is commonly used today for line-of-sight (the devices have to see each other, with nothing in the way) wireless networking applications, such as PDAs or handheld devices communicating with a computer or base station. Handheld parking ticket generators may use infrared at the end of the day to transmit data to a main system. Infrared has served its purpose well over the years, but non-line-of-sight and greater-distance, yet low-power, low-cost multi-device solutions (infrared is one-to-one) are needed today.

If you're wondering where the funky name *Bluetooth* came from, it stems from the great influence Baltic-region companies have had on the Bluetooth standard. Harold Bluetooth was the king of Denmark in the 900s.

I am not going to elaborate much on infrared technology in this book because you won't use it much except for wireless headphones. The infrared standard is IrDA, controlled by the Infrared Data Association. It can transmit line-of-site to any other IrDA-capable device at many speeds, up to four megabits per second (sixteen Mb/s rates are in the works). IrDA provides a different level of security since (a) the devices must be able to see each other and (b) each device could encrypt the connection's data and always "see" who they're sending to without someone covertly listening in (e.g., in the other room). The technology is also deployed in millions of devices worldwide, including PDAs, cell phones, laptops, handheld devices, consumer electronics equipment, and more. It is both cheap and easy to deploy for uses such as information kiosks and remote control systems where the signal must go only to the device it's being pointed at (such as wireless headphones).

Bluetooth has a number of advantages for short-distance radio transmissions, such as handheld device communication, synchronization, printing, talking to cell phones (i.e., for an Internet connectivity), and many other uses. Unlike 802.11x, which generally has a 6 milliwatt (mW) transmitter, Bluetooth transmitters tend to only use 1 mW, greatly reducing the battery drain and transmission radius, thus helping to prevent Bluetooth devices from interfering with adjacent networks. Like 802.11b and 802.11g networks, Bluetooth runs on the unlicensed ISM band, so keep that in mind when deploying Bluetooth where an 802.11b or g network already exists.

Bluetooth is well-suited for transmitting small amounts of data between devices. Generally, Bluetooth devices transmit at 1 megabits/second, compared to 1–54 Mbps for 802.11x and up to 4 megabits/second for IrDA (an infrared standard). Bluetooth also has standard device classifications. As a result, Bluetooth devices can intelligently communicate with each other automatically, such as placing a Bluetooth-enabled cell phone next to a Bluetooth-capable laptop and automatically providing Internet services (after manually establishing a "peering" between them). In fact, you could describe Bluetooth as a wireless USB, with similar classes of wireless (akin to 802.11 being a wireless version of Ethernet).

Satellite Internet Systems: Not Worth the Money (Yet!)

Mobile satellite Internet access systems have been around for a number of years now, often requiring very expensive equipment and providing slow data speeds. Although the option has usually been only abysmal data throughput, along the order of a 9600-baud modem, new technologies and service providers have emerged to try to address such issues.

Satellite Internet access tends to be impractical because of the fairly expensive equipment and installation expertise necessary to make it work. The satellite must also be mounted on top of your car to receive a clear signal—something many people will not want to do and only invites thieves.

To install satellite Internet access you will need a dish, a service plan, a vehicle on which you don't mind bolting a satellite receiver, and a professional installer (let them take the blame if a mistake is made).

Similar to satellite television, you not only need to buy the equipment, you must sign up with a service provider, such as Hughes and their Direcway service. Of course, with the self-aligning dish, you should be able to receive both satellite Internet access *and* satellite television. Most people I have discussed this topic with, however, have told me *not* to install satellite anything in a vehicle because it's just plain unreliable. People I know have spent small fortunes to install neat-o technologies in their cars, and satellite appears to have been their least favorite.

The largest obstacle for satellite Internet access is that you must have a clear view to the southeast to communicate with orbiting satellites, requiring constant realignment of the dish, which must be mounted on the top of your vehicle. Should you be in a city, the Internet connection likely just won't work, unlike Wi-Fi and cellular connection cards, which use a terrestrial network much less dependent upon clear views of the sky. Remember, most people think of satellite as a residential service, a service provided to and from those huge satellites next to radio stations and on the tops of tall buildings, and a service for military personnel in the middle of the desert.

If you are considering installing satellite, it is fairly easy today to get a "self-aligning" dish. Searching on the Internet will bring up any number of providers of these satellites. One such provider is DataStorm. There is also a DataStorm users forum online so you can chat with other users of the product and see how their experiences have been.

Finding an installer should not be difficult. Any high-end A/V (audio/video) store in your area can probably recommend a custom installer for such services. Whether they are any good could be hard to judge. Keep in mind that just because you spend the money on satellite Internet that doesn't mean it will work everywhere you go. The same goes for Wi-Fi and cellular data providers, but their coverage area and performance is much more predictable.

Satellite technology is always improving, however. Future satellite transceivers may solve many of the line-of-sight issues experienced with satellites today. For now, unless you have a lot of money, stay away from it. More information on finding a reseller or installers is available in Appendix C, "Additional Resources."

The Federal Communications Commission (FCC) has mandated that consumer mobile satellites can only receive, not transmit, while in motion. It is a federal crime to transmit data while mobile, so if you get satellite Internet access (this does not apply to cell phone and Wi-Fi Internet service providers) you are only allowed to *receive* data when mobile. This regulation comes from a snafu in the late 1990s when a mobile satellite transmitted to the wrong satellite and wiped out all of Wal-Mart's data uplink for an entire day. If you are caught transmitting while mobile, it could lead not only to federal fines and jail time but also to litigation and prosecution by companies or entities your transmissions affect.

Future Technologies: WiMax and FLASH-OFDM

Yes, I know I said you wouldn't be using 802.11 while driving. But are cellular providers your only recourse for true mobile Internet access? Not if 802.16 (a.k.a. *WiMax*) and Flarion, Inc.'s FLASH-OFDM technologies gain broad deployments. These two competing technologies attempt to solve the distance and bandwidth problems of bidirectional wireless data transmissions over long distances (up to 30 miles per service cell) as well as the inevitable switching that must take place between each service cell while moving. The 802.16 technology is an IEEE standard, whereas FLASH-OFDM is a proprietary solution from Flarion, Inc.

The WiMax standard is not expected to be completed until 2006 or 2007.

Orthogonal Frequency Division Multiplexing (OFDM)—allows the signal to be maintained even in areas where tall buildings and structures tend to reflect many portions of the signal, creating what is called *multipath*. Multipath confuses many Internet connections, and OFDM is designed to ensure as stable and as clear a signal as possible while driving.

Initially intended to bring wireless broadband to the masses in homes and businesses, cell phone manufacturers are keeping an eye on these new technologies for possible integration into their own cell phones. Wouldn't it be convenient if your broadband service provider were the same for both your home *and* on the road? With these two competing technologies, that scenario may end up becoming a reality. There haven't been any large-scale deployments of either WiMax or FLASH-OFDM as of the writing of this book, although testing shows that these technologies do work. As with any technology, if it gains support, you will hear a lot about it. More information on 802.16 can be found at the IEEE Web site at www.ieee.org. More information on FLASH-OFDM can be found on Flarion's Web site at www.flarion.com.

Getting Connected

Now that we've covered the different access methods, let's go over how to get connected with each of the solutions discussed earlier in this chapter.

Connecting via Cell Phone

This step will vary based on your cellular phone data service provider and whether you are using a cell phone or a connection card.

Regardless of which access method you choose, you need to first install the software that enables your cell phone or communications card to talk to your computer. If you have a Bluetooth-capable phone, make sure your computer has all the software and hardware, such as a Bluetooth receiver, it needs in order to use the phone as a connection device. The user guide for the device you use should explain how to get connected and to verify that you are indeed connected.

Warning

Watch out for how long you stay connected! If you're not paying for an unlimited-usage Internet account, beware of staying connected for long periods of time and using up your minutes. Just because you're not surfing the Internet, that doesn't mean you're not using up your bandwidth. Automatic program update services and antivirus update services may start downloading their update files while you're connected, possibly using megabytes of your bandwidth allotment, and potentially running you over. Of course, your service provider won't let you know when you do this, until you get your bill that is!

Connecting via Wi-Fi

Although you probably won't be using Wi-Fi too often in your car, the nice thing to know is that it's easy to set up. With the ubiquity of Wi-Fi-compatible devices and the fervor for inherent operating system support for the technology, you basically just have to plug in a Wi-Fi adapter, possibly load a few drivers, select a network to connect to (if one is available), and connect. Windows XP and Mac OS X both have simple wireless network setup capabilities.

I will assume that you already know how to connect and use a wireless network and will not go into tremendous details regarding those steps. The following is brief recap of how to connect to wireless networks in Windows XP and in Mac OS X. If you need a more involved guide, pick up a copy of PC Magazine's *Home Networking Guide.*

Finding and Connecting to a Wi-Fi Network

Although this step will vary by operating system, the first thing to do is find a wireless network. In Windows, this is done by going to Start, Control Panel, Network and then double-clicking your wireless connection. Available wireless networks should appear in order of their name, or Service Station I.D. (SSID). Double-click the network and it should connect you (you should already know the name of your home network or other networks you trust to connect to). You may have to enter a network key, also known as a WEP Key, to gain access to encrypted networks.

On Macintosh computers you should be able to select a wireless network by its name/SSID from the Airport® menu on the top right of the screen, which looks like arched radio transmission waves.

Of Course You Know, This Means War (Driving)

So you want to war drive? Here are a few programs to help you get started. I won't go into detail on war driving, but it can be a lot of fun—just don't do it while on a date.

First, make sure you have a Wi-Fi adapter in your car. I used a fairly inconspicuous mini-adapter from Belkin (shown earlier in Figure 14-1). It's easy to remove, so I can use it with my laptop and other computers, it uses little power, and I didn't have to do any special wiring to boost its signal.

Second, you will need a Wi-Fi network scanner. The most popular of these is *Network Stumbler*, also called *NetStumbler*, a free program you can download from `www.stumbler.net`. Network Stumbler will scan for all available networks, whether they broadcast an SSID or not, and tell you the make and model of the network router, whether it is protected by WEP or it's an open network you might be able to use, and more. See the following figure to see some networks I came across at a stop sign in my dad's neighborhood.

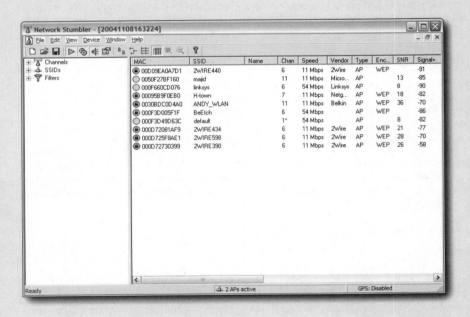

Despite warnings to the contrary, many people will install a wireless network and never enable the encryption the router supports. This means you can often connect to access points by simply parking yourself in a neighborhood; you can use their Internet connection and possibly even browse their network. Note that it is likely illegal to do this, being the equivalent of trespassing in some states, and there may be other legislation. Of course, there are legitimate networks you may be able to sniff out, such as those at local coffee shops and universities (if you're a student, of course).

Once you're connected, you can surf the Web, chat with your preferred instant messaging application, possibly use an Internet phone, such as those from Vonage®, and even update your car computer's software and antivirus definitions.

Some networks may also be encrypted. There are many tools you can use to crack the WEP keys in these networks, which I won't show you how to do. If you're curious as to how such utilities work, or you want to (ahem) learn how packets travel in a wireless network, try out AirSnort, BSD-AirTools, and WEPCrack. These utilities can be found by your favorite search engine, but keep in mind they can be less-than-honest tools and may compromise your computer, so it's your problem if you get in trouble using those applications.

Caution

CAUTION

Don't connect to networks that are not yours. Not only is there a possibility that you're breaking the law; you could get caught and be fined or imprisoned. I don't suggest snooping around wirelessly. Unless you're a security expert, you probably don't realize how many breadcrumbs you're leaving (such as your NETBIOS ID or MAC address). Also keep in mind that networks you do not control (and therefore should not trust) may be compromised and/or monitored by unscrupulous people. Don't go checking your bank statement, making credit card payments, and other private transactions just because you found an open network.

Adding a USB Hub to Your Dash

Approximate project cost: $100

I was getting tired of having to run USB cables to my computer under the seat. Having a USB hub on the floor didn't seem like a good idea either. I decided I could take my ashtray and a micro USB hub and add the hub directly to my car's dash. This made it easy for me to connect my iPod, removable storage devices, game controllers, and more to my car without dealing with a lot of messy cables. Here's how I did it.

What you will need:

- An ashtray that you don't care about messing up (or similar removable item that you can replace if you sell the car or mess up). Make sure the hub you buy can actually fit into the ashtray! (~free to $100+ to replace)

- A Dremel® tool (or similar rotary cutting tool or other tool capable of cutting metal) as shown in Figure 14-3, with a metal-cutting bit and a sanding bit, available from most hardware stores (~$40).

- A two- or four-port micro USB hub (~$20–$50, these are the small USB hubs, also called thumb-USB hubs). I chose a four-port for convenience. I also recommend that the hub be USB 2.0 instead of 1.1, because a 2.0 hub supports much faster devices and can also support USB 1.1 devices. Make sure the hub doesn't *require* a power adapter but can utilize an external power supply if needed (some even come with the external power adapter).

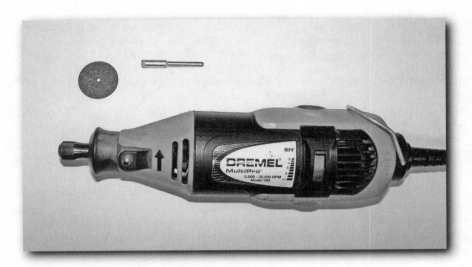

FIGURE **14-3: A Dremel® tool with an appropriate cutting bit.**

- A USB extension cable, of appropriate length to reach your car computer (~$10–$40).
- A hot-glue gun and the super-glue sticks to mount the hub in the ashtray so that it doesn't move (~$20).
- Electrical tape (~$3).
- An available USB 1.1 or USB 2.0 port on your car computer.

Prepare the Ashtray

The first thing to do is determine where and what you want to drill. Remove the ashtray (or whatever you chose to install this into) from your car. *Do not do this project in your car—it is too dangerous!* Measure the hub's perimeter so you know how big of a hole to make, and outline that in pencil where you are going to drill. I found that my ashtray allowed me to unscrew the plastic piece so I could drill the metal separate from the plastic.

Make sure that before you drill you remove any plastic or rubber pieces, if possible. This will prevent you from making melted areas in the plastic while you cut.

Drill the Metal

This is where the Dremel comes in. Make sure you do this in a well-ventilated area and wear hand, eye, and mouth protection. You don't want to breathe in the metal dust, you don't want to get bits in your eye, and you don't want to cut off fingers or cut yourself. If you don't know how to use a Dremel, or you aren't comfortable with using a cutting tool, ask a professional to do it for you.

Mount the ashtray in a vice grip so it doesn't move or fly around and injure you, injure someone else, or break anything. Make sure you don't bend any metal in the ashtray, because you want it to fit cleanly back into the dash when you're done with this project.

Choose the appropriate bit based on the Dremel or similar tool you've purchased. This will vary on the manufacturer but should be clearly outlined in the manual for a bit that cuts metals.

Now, cut a hole in the front of the ashtray so you can slide the hub in. After you've done this, cut a 1-inch by 0.5-inch hole in the back of the ashtray to run the USB cable through.

After cutting the metal, use a sanding bit (see Figure 14-4), if you have one, to smooth out the edges of the just-cut metal. The metal shouldn't be exceptionally hot after cutting or sanding, but I still wouldn't touch it for a few minutes.

FIGURE 14-4: A sanding bit for the Dremel tool.

Cut the Plastic

Using the Dremel, or other cutting device, cut out the area in the plastic you will be inserting the hub into. You have to be pretty precise about this because if you make the gap between the hub and the plastic too wide, it will be more difficult to fill in the gap with the super glue, and thus the hub may come loose. Try to use a low-RPM setting if using a Dremel, because high RPMs may quickly melt the plastic and make things a tad ugly.

Install the Hub

Now that you've cut everything, reattach any plastic you have removed and slide the hub into the hole. Make sure it is easy to access the back of the hub so you can run the extension cable, and make sure the connector on the back of the hub is not touching any metal in the ashtray.

Warm up the hot-glue gun with the super-glue stick. Once you have everything in place, use the hot-glue gun to put super glue on all sides of the hub, and hold the hub and the ashtray together for at least a minute, allowing the glue to cool a bit. Set the hub and ashtray down in a position where there's no tension or force on the hub, allowing it to stay in the desired final position until the glue cools (see Figure 14-5). I would wait about an hour here—go watch a movie or something.

FIGURE 14-5: The hub after being inserted in the ashtray.

Run the Cable to Your Car Computer

Now that the hub is in the ashtray, we need to test that it doesn't budge. Do this by plugging in a couple of USB devices or cables and then unplugging them. Don't try too hard, or you *will* break the adhesive—just use the force you would normally use for adding and removing a device from a hub. If the hub comes loose, you will need to reglue it, possibly with a stronger glue. If it is stable, run the extension cable through the hole in the back of the ashtray to the back end of the hub and connect the two. Tightly wrap some electrical tape around the two once they are connected so a passenger doesn't accidentally step on a cable to cause it to come loose. Run the other end of the USB cable behind your dash (or under your center console, depending on where your ashtray is located) and to your car computer and plug it in, preferably to a USB 2.0 port, but a USB 1.1 port will do.

Test Your Hub

This is pretty easy—turn on the computer and plug in a device as shown in Figure 14-6. If it shows up, it works! Try plugging a digital music player and synchronize your car computer with its music collection for use on the road (see Chapter 17, "Syncing Music Library with Your Existing Home Network"). When you leave your car, simply unplug your music player from the dash and take it with you! How cool!

FIGURE **14-6:** The finished product.

Secure Your Connection

Once you have a connection in your car, regardless of how you connect, make sure you turn on a firewall and keep your antivirus up-to-date. A car computer is just as vulnerable as any other computer, and if you perform advanced tasks, such as monitoring or programming your car's computer, the last thing you need is a hacker compromising your computer system. The last thing you want is a hacker hijacking your computer over the Internet. While a seemingly remote scenario now, it is possible for the hacker to take control of your machine and possibly control your engine computer and so forth while you drive.

Windows XP comes with a built-in firewall and so do many flavors of Linux. If you aren't running Windows XP or Linux, there are many free alternatives out there, such as ZoneAlarm and 602LANSuite. There are also many commercial firewall packages, such as Trend Micro Internet Security, Norton Internet Security, and many others available online and at your local computer store.

Summary

This chapter went over getting connected to the Internet via cell phones, cellular connection cards, and Wi-Fi, and where each is appropriate for use. It also discussed emerging technologies and even a few side projects to get some extra entertainment out of an in-car Internet connection.

Networking and Sharing an Internet Connection

Approximate project cost: $300

In this chapter we will go over how to set up a network in your car, including how to share an Internet connection. This is very similar to how you would set one up at home. Having a network in your car lets you have mobile LAN (local area network) parties, lets fellow associates connect to the Internet and get work done while riding with you instead of singing karaoke to the radio with you, and just amazes other people who get in your car and find out they can connect to the Internet.

If you have not done so already, go back and read Chapter 14, "Adding Internet Access," which covers many aspects of connecting to the Internet in your car that will save you time and money!

Minimum Hardware Needed

Only three items are needed to set up a wired network in your car: a switch ($40, see Figure 15-1 for a compact solution from CompUSA, although Netgear also makes a nice metal solution, and there are other manufacturers with similar products), Ethernet cables ($3–$10 each, see Figure 15-2), and one machine or more that has an Ethernet port (all modern laptops do, see an example port in Figure 15-3). If you want to go wireless, all you need are a wireless access point (WAP) for all the devices to connect to and a laptop with a wireless card. I suggest you go the wired-switch route, because with wireless you can run into bandwidth issues and must assume everyone has a compatible wireless card, whereas Ethernet will just work as long as someone has an Ethernet port in their laptop (and like I said, practically all of them do).

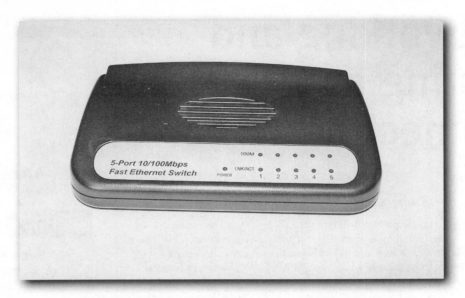

FIGURE 15-1: A mini-Ethernet switch is compact and easy to place in your car.

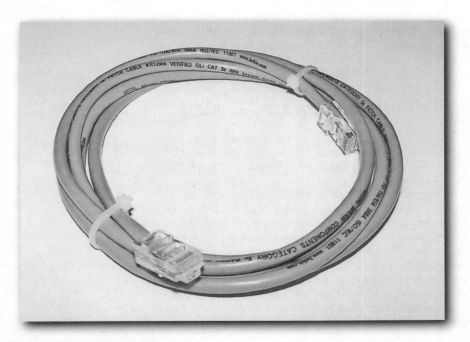

FIGURE 15-2: An Ethernet cable.

FIGURE 15-3: The Ethernet port on the back of a laptop.

Note   I will assume that because you are a geek you know where to buy Ethernet switches, but in case you don't, you can pick them up at any store that sells computers.

Computer versus Device Internet Sharing

If you want to share an Internet connection with other computers in the car, there are a couple of approaches: software- and hardware-based connection sharing.

The first approach—software-based Internet connection sharing—utilizes a *host* PC (such as your Car PC built in a previous project) that connects to the Internet, and all other devices in the car connect through that machine, which acts as a *router*.

New Term   Router—also known as a *gateway*. It routes the packets to and from the Internet for all local network (non-Internet) devices.

The second approach, a dedicated hardware-based router solution, which is usually found in homes, can be used to connect to the Internet and then share the connection just like the software-based solution. The hardware solution can also be used to share the connection wirelessly in the car by purchasing a router with a WAP built in.

Ultimately, the software-based solution is the most practical for sharing a connection in a car. Most cellular Internet providers require a PC with a CardBus or PCMCIA slot or Bluetooth® capabilities in order to connect, and if you already have a PC installed in your car, there's no reason to buy another hardware device when the computer can already do the same thing. Considering that the only practical mobile Internet connection solution today is through cellular Internet service providers, the Car PC using software-based Internet connection sharing and sharing the connection with other computers through a switch (and possibly wirelessly as well) is the best approach.

Not all Internet service providers allow you to share an Internet connection. Although you may be technically able to use the steps in this chapter, make sure you don't violate your provider's Terms of Service (TOS), ultimately getting your account shut off or charged unexpected fees.

Internet Connection Considerations

Before setting up Internet connection sharing, here are some important items to consider.

What about Bluetooth Phone Internet Access?

Although some phones support Bluetooth and Internet access through Bluetooth-capable phones, you can only pair the Internet connection to one computer, so you will still have to share the Internet connection through a host PC running Internet connection sharing software. This approach should work fine because Bluetooth transmits faster than most cellular Internet services, so you shouldn't experience any speed degradation.

Getting Internet Connection Sharing Software

Lucky for you, Internet connection sharing is built into many operating systems today. I will go over how to set this up in Windows XP later in this chapter. With Linux and Mac OS you also have many options—simply go to software download sites such as www.download.com or www.versiontracker.com and search for "Internet connection sharing."

You don't need a CarPC installed in your car to share an Internet connection—any laptop or PC will do. It's just much more convenient to have the CarPC set up for sharing the connection, since you only have to set it up once.

Note There's an issue with using Linux or Mac OS to share an Internet connection. Because they are labeled as "alternative" operating systems (please, don't shoot me), hardware manufacturers often don't write official drivers for them, so getting cellular Internet connection cards to work can be difficult depending on which Linux distribution you are running, or which version of the Mac OS is installed. There are often third-party drivers written by individuals or other companies to make these devices work, but there's no guarantee those drivers will support all of the device's features (although sometimes third-party drivers can be even *more* robust). The rule of thumb is always to make sure the hardware you want in your car will work with the operating system you decide to install.

Choosing an Internet Connection to Share

Cell phone connections are the easiest to share when mobile, because they work in many areas in the country, and they work at the speeds your car travels at. Stationary solutions, such as satellite and Wi-Fi are easy to share as well, but since you can't use them while the car is moving (distance is an issue with Wi-Fi, and two-way satellite is outright illegal to use when a vehicle is mobile), you're basically limited to the cellular connection solution. See Chapter 14 for more details on the Internet connection options you have.

Don't Forget about Antivirus and Firewalls!

The last thing you want to deal with is a virus or hacker intrusion in your Car PC. Make sure not only that your Car PC's applications and operating system are up-to-date but that it also has current antivirus software installed and fully updated, as well as an active firewall (most modern operating systems come with one built in). The same goes for any computers connecting to the network in your car—make sure they are current, otherwise don't let them connect, because they could possibly affect your computer and negate a lot of your hard work!

Setting Up Internet Connection Sharing in Windows

All versions of Windows XP have built-in Internet connection sharing that is simple to install. Basically, all you have to do is right-click a connection and turn sharing on.

What You Need

You will need the following items to set up Internet connection sharing:

- A PC with an Ethernet port and a cellular Internet connection card or Bluetooth compatible phone, such as your Car PC
- Any version of Windows XP, Service Pack 2 or later, with all the latest patches to prevent the host machine from getting infected while connected (~$99–$299)

- A wired Ethernet switch, such as the compact solution shown in Figure 15-1, if you are not using a wireless solution (~$40)

- Ethernet cables going to each machine in your car from the switch, or an Ethernet cable going to a WAP (~$80) for sharing the Internet connection wirelessly (~$3–$10 each, depending on where you buy them)

Note If you share an Internet connection wirelessly, any car or computer near you with a wireless card will likely be able to connect and use (or try to crack into) your car's Internet connection *and* network, so make sure all computers have an appropriate firewall installed to prevent intrusion attempts.

Step 1: Choose the Connection to Share

To choose the connection you want to share, open the Windows XP Network Connections dialog box by going to Start → Settings → Control Panel → Network Connections. The Windows XP Network Connections window will appear, as shown in Figure 15-4, and display all of your network connections. In this example, I am using the Sprint PCS Vision connection card, denoted as *Novatel Wireless Connection*—your connection may be named something else, so check your manual (although you will likely already know what it's called).

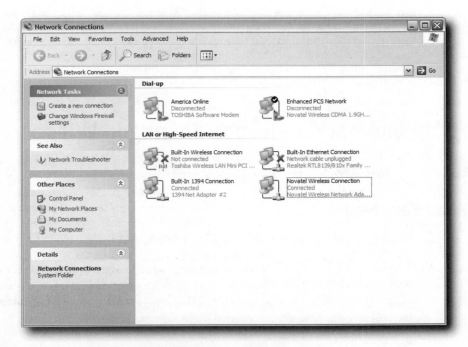

FIGURE 15-4: The Windows XP Network Connections window.

Step 2: Share the Connection

Once you have selected the Internet connection to share, right-click it and select Properties. The properties window for the selected connection will appear. Then select the Advanced tab, as shown in Figure 15-5.

When the Advanced tab appears, check the box next to "Allow other network users to connect through this computer's Internet connection."

FIGURE **15-5: The Advanced tab in the network connection properties dialog box.**

Do *not* check the box next to "Allow other network users to control or disable the shared Internet connection." There's no reason for client computers to control your Internet connection.

You will now have to tell Windows what port to share the connection through. If you are using an Ethernet (or wired) network, select *Built-In Ethernet Connection*. If you want to share the connection via an installed or built-in wireless adapter, select *Built-In Wireless Connection*.

Now that you have told Windows to share the connection, you need to tell it what services to share. Click the Settings button in the Internet Connection Sharing box (there's also one under Windows Firewall, which we won't be discussing here, although you should always have your firewall on, especially when sharing an Internet connection) and the Advanced Settings dialog box will appear, as shown in Figure 15-5.

Decide which services you want others to be allowed to use on the Internet. The most popular will be SMTP (sending e-mail), POP3 (receiving e-mail), HTTP (Web) and HTTPS (secure Web). There may be other ports you want to open, which can be added by clicking the Add button and filling in the appropriate fields. Table 15-1 shows popular application port numbers you may want to open.

Table 15-1   Common TCP and UDP Port Numbers

Application	Port Numbers (TCP)	Port Numbers (UDP)
AOL Instant Messenger (AIM)	5190	
Apple iTunes Music Sharing (Digital Audio Access Protocol, DAAP)	3689	3689
BitTorrent	6881–6889, 6969	
Blizzard Battle.net	4000, 6112–6119	4000, 6112–6119
HotLine	5500–5503	
iChat	5298	5298
ICQ	5190	
IRC	6667, 7000	
MSN Gaming Zone	28800–29100	28800–29100
MSN Messenger	1863 (for IM), 6891–6900 (for file transfers), 6901 (for voice)	2001–2120, 6801, 6901 (for computer to phone audio conversations); 6901 (for computer to computer audio conversations)
Real Audio and Video	7070	6970–7170
Yahoo! Messenger	5050 (for IM), 5000, 5001 (for audio chat), 5100 (for Web cams)	5000–5010 (for audio chat)
Yahoo! Games	11999	

Keep in mind that these may change, so check online for the various port numbers for different instant messaging applications.

Note For more information on how to configure the advanced settings of Windows Internet Connection Sharing, simply click the link "Learn more about Internet Connection Sharing" located next to the Settings button in the Advanced tab, as shown in Figure 15-6.

Note Do not open ports for file-sharing networks, such as Kazaa®, Grokster®, and so forth. The bandwidth you have for a mobile Internet connection is usually very limited, so you don't want to waste it all sharing files with others.

FIGURE 15-6: The Internet Connection Sharing Advanced Settings dialog box.

Once you have selected the services you want to provide, click OK until the Properties dialog box disappears. There will be a slight pause while Windows turns on the Internet Connection Sharing service. When the Internet Connection Sharing service has started, you should be brought back to the Network Connections window, where the connection you selected will now have a hand and be marked as a shared connection, as shown in Figure 15-7.

Note The Internet Connection Sharing tab also lets you choose which network interfaces you want to share the Internet connection on. You can share over wired (e.g., Ethernet), Wi-Fi, and possibly others as new technologies emerge.

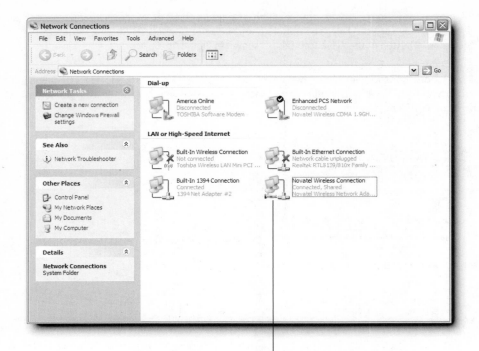

Note hand icon, indicating that the connection is shared

FIGURE 15-7: The Internet connection is now shared.

Step 3: Connect!

Now that your connection is shared, plug the host computer into the Ethernet switch. Then, make sure the firewall is turned on, the antivirus is up-to-date, and the operating systems are up-to-date on all the machines connecting to your network and plug them in to the switch. Each *client* (connected) computer's Ethernet connection should be configured to retrieve IP address and DNS server information automatically (all geeks know how to do this), as shown in Figure 15-8. They should now all be able to get connected to the Internet!

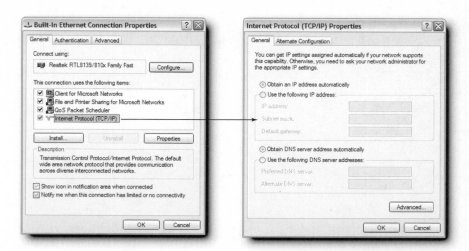

FIGURE 15-8: The Ethernet connection properly configured on a client machine.

Summary

In this chapter you set up a network in your car and shared your Internet connection. Keep in mind the Internet should only be interactively used by passengers. It's usually fine for the driver to receive short traffic alerts and other textual information from the Internet as long as no interaction with the display or input devices is involved.

Adding Television Access

Approximate project cost: $275

Entertainment is one of the key factors for safely enduring, and enjoying, long road trips. It's also a standard judging criteria for competitions—the more gizmos and gadgets you have to entertain yourself and your passengers, the more impressive your setup. One ideal solution for in-car entertainment is robust television reception, letting passengers watch their favorite shows while you pay attention to the road. In this chapter we will go over a number of different approaches to adding television access, including terrestrial (a.k.a. over-the-air), broadcast, and satellite television, and how to add these solutions depending on the setup you want to pursue—either via a computer or a stand-alone television receiver.

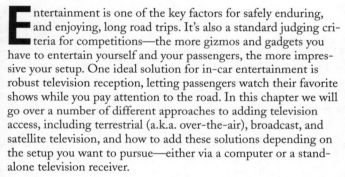

in this chapter

☑ Standard versus high-definition TV

☑ Choosing the TV receiver

☑ Choosing and placing the antenna

☑ Installing the TV

Note Satellite television reception is at best difficult to install and tune, so I can't cover all the aspects of installing it in this chapter. However, I will give you as much information as possible, including resources to help you get satellite television reception in your car. Be forewarned—it is *very* expensive to install and operate satellite in a mobile environment, and even my friends who had the money to do it say it wasn't worth it! Of course, these costs and installation issues may lessen over time.

Standard NTSC versus High-Definition Television

There are two types of free over-the-air television broadcasts you can receive these days. The most prevalent is standard NTSC (National Television Standards Committee) television, which you've been receiving for years (in the United States; international standards also include PAL and SECAM). NTSC television has been broadcast for around 65 years and, other than the additions of color and stereo sound, hasn't changed much. The next big evolution of television is digital television, commonly referred to as DTV, and its counterpart—high-definition digital television, or HDTV. You can receive DTV and HDTV signals in your car using an antenna similar to what you use for standard television—many antenna solutions are actually good for both analog and digital television reception and are labeled so right on the box.

DTV supports DVD resolutions of 480i and 480p, sometimes called SDTV, or *standard definition digital television*, and HDTV sports 720i, 720p, and 1080i resolutions, or about six times the resolution of DVD. While you will likely not be displaying full-resolution HDTV in your car, yet, you actually can if you add a display that can support such high resolutions. The 720p-capable LCD displays are starting to become available in headrest form factors.

Did You Know Many smaller displays and lower-priced plasma sets don't support full HDTV, instead boasting EDTV, or *enhanced digital television*, which is just the marketing department's way of saying the display can't show full HDTV resolution even though they still put an HDTV logo on the set.

Did You Know The digital television standard for over-the-air (i.e., broadcast) television in the United States is managed by the ATSC, or Advanced Television Systems Committee. You can find more information about the ATSC at www.atsc.org.

You Can't Always Get What You Watch (at Home)

Due to natural phenomena interfering with signal reception, such as buildings in cities and interference from any number of other sources, you won't always be able to get a clear signal. Odd as it may seem, fairly clear audio continues from broadcast analog TV even while the picture is fading in and out. Yet, digital TV—and digital satellite—will usually either be all there (a perfect picture), or there will be no picture and sound at all.

Media Dashboard Software

With any emerging technical market there tends to be geeks who write software to showcase the capabilities and potential of the technology. Likewise with the Car PC and telematics markets, there are awesome open source, freeware, shareware, and commercial solutions on the market that are specifically geared towards Car PC users. If you want to use Linux, you'll obviously need an alternative to Microsoft's solution. There are many free, powerful solutions out there, and many of them also sport television-tuning capabilities, full GPS integration, DVD playback, FM radio tuning, Web-browsing capability, and sometimes more—all in an interface designed specifically for displays on a car dashboard and for use by drivers (although that's not to say it's safe to watch TV or a DVD while driving and so forth). Download locations for these products are listed in Table 16-1. There is also an entire section for Car PC–geared software in Appendix C, "Additional Resources."

Table 16-1   Car PC Software Solutions

Package	Download URL
CentraFuse	www.fluxmedia.net
FrodoPlayer	www.frodoplayer.com
MediaCar	www.media-car.fr.st
MediaPortal	http://sourceforge.net/projects/mediaportal/

Choosing the Television Receiver

Your choice of a television receiver will depend on whether you are going to tune your programs in via a Car PC you've already installed in your computer, or you want to forgo the computer and just install a receiver and connect it directly to one or more analog display inputs in your car.

For Cars with a Car PC

If you already have a PC installed in your car, you have a number of options when it comes to adding television access. There are both internal and external tuners for both NTSC television and DTV reception. You can buy many of the following systems at any retailer who sells computers and graphics cards, including Best Buy, Circuit City, and CompUSA:

- ATI TV Wonder (internal, $49)—PCI card that receives standard NTSC television.

- ATI HD Wonder (internal, $199)—PCI card that tunes standard, DTV, and HDTV signals. Comes with antenna.

- ATI All-in-Wonder Series (internal, $149–$499)—A great AGP graphics card upgrade that comes with a television tuner and video-out for connecting to multiple displays. I suggest the Radeon 8500DV or 9600XT products because they don't use a terribly high amount of power and give great performance for everything from television to gaming.

- Hauppauge WinTV (internal, $49)—PCI card that receives standard NTSC television.

- Hauppauge WinTV PVR (external USB, $149)—external device that receives standard NTSC television, receives FM radio signals, and can record television and radio to your computer's hard drive, as shown in Figure 16-1.

FIGURE 16-1: The Haupauge WinTV PVR television receiver and radio tuner.

For Cars without a Car PC

To tune standard NTSC television without a PC, you will need a television tuner (sometimes called a *receiver*) to tune in television. Stand-alone television tuner boxes are hard to find in the United States due to the popularity of cable, although they are very popular in Asian countries. If you can find one, all the better. If not, pick up an old VCR or DVD player with a built-in tuner or a handheld television receiver that has one of the small 3-inch or smaller LCD screens, built-in VHF/UHF tuner, and a video *output* port (many just have video *input*) and use that instead. The portable receivers usually sell for under $150, just a little more than a device that connects to a PC. If you go this path, make sure to mount the handheld display/tuner to the car interior in some manner so that it is not a free-flying object should an accident occur. If you have installed the auxilary A/V (audio/video) input jacks from the project in Chapter 9, "Building a Single-Source A/V System," you easily plug the tuner's A/V output into your auxiliary A/V jacks and feed the television output to your entire car, and then easily take the tuner out of car when it's not in use.

Getting an over-the-air DTV tuner (which tune HDTV as well) is not very difficult, fortunately. However, the stand-alone DTV tuning boxes tend to run around $200–$500 new, so be prepared to spend significant dollars if you are going to implement DTV in your car. PC solutions tend to be much cheaper, running for around $199–$249. A few USB-connectable HDTV tuners are shipping as of this book's writing. Many USB and PC card DTV tuners are expected to arrive in 2005 as well.

Choosing and Placing the Antenna

You can find an antenna at any store that sells TVs, such as Best Buy, Walmart, CompUSA, Radio Shack, and many others. Both NTSC and DTV television signals are broadcast horizontally, so make sure you pick one up that can lie flat in the back of your car near the window and out of the way. This will help maximize reception and let you easily remove the antenna when needed. I suggest you stay away from bunny-ear antennas, because they will flap around in the back of your car, potentially distracting you and fellow drivers. NTSC television antennas tend to run under $20, whereas HDTV antennas tend to run under $100. Radio Shack, as well as many auto and RV centers, sells specialized gull-wing-style antennas that can be mounted on the roof or trunk of the vehicle.

Note Make sure you buy an antenna that is adequate for your use. If you are going to receive HDTV, make sure the antenna you buy can tune both. Most can.

Warning When purchasing an antenna, verify whether it is a powered antenna. If you purchase a powered antenna, you will need a long enough power cable and an AC inverter, so make sure you're prepared to run all those cables and install an inverter if you go the powered-antenna route! If you are installing television in an RV, this may not apply to you because many RVs have antennas already built in that you can use, as well as AC outlets installed in the walls of the vehicle. Some powered antennas simply require 12 volts DC, which can be supplied from your switched car battery connection terminals.

Installing Television Capabilities in Your Car

This section will go over what you need and how to install over-the-air television access in your car. If you are considering satellite television, see the sidebar "Considering Satellite (DirecTV, Hughes, etc.)" later in this chapter.

What You Need

- A television receiver, either for a Car PC or stand-alone (see above for details).

- One or more display devices (see Chapter 7, "Choosing a Display Device," for more details).

- An appropriate antenna for the type of signal you want to receive (NTSC, DTV, or both), as discussed earlier in this chapter. Figure 16-2 is an example of a flat antenna that can tune both broadcast types (~$99).

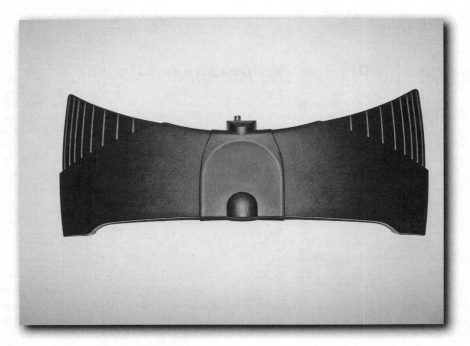

FIGURE 16-2: A flat television antenna.

- Coaxial cable for running to and from the antenna, of the length from the device to where the antenna will be kept and with enough slack as is necessary to run inside car molding, under seats, and so on (shouldn't be more than $40).

Note Some truck and RV stores will sell special small-diameter coaxial antenna cabling, which may make this routing easier.

- AC inverter capable of providing at least 150 watts, for powering the television receiver and possibly the antenna as well (~$50, although you can use the same inverter used in other chapters). Antennas and receivers generally draw under 20 watts total. A few draw only 5 to 10 watts. Battery powered receivers don't require additional power, of course, but it's useful for long trips during which the battery could run out.

- Velcro—enough to run along the perimeter of your antenna and television receiver (~$20).

- Electrical tape (~$5).

Note Spend extra for electrical tape with extended temperature capabilities if you live in an area with extreme temperature swings. It will stay sealed longer and better.

Step 1: Find a Suitable Location for the Receiver

The receiver location you decide upon will depend on what solution you are implementing.

If you are installing a PC-based television tuner, you will do most of your channel selection either through the computer's display (i.e., on-screen), or using an included remote control. With the PC solution, the receiver can be out of sight, either by default if it's internal or tucked away next to the computer if it's external.

In the case of a stand-alone receiver, you will either have to keep the unit out in the open so you can use the tuning buttons on it or use an included remote control. If your unit has an infrared remote control, then your remote must be able to see the receiver, so you have to keep it in the open where passengers can point the remote at it. In this case, either the back window or just under the seat are very handy locations. If your remote uses RF (radio frequency), you can place the unit anywhere you like.

Note To tell whether you have an infrared remote or an RF remote, check the front of the remote for a translucent plastic or a round black bulb. If either is there then you have an infrared remote. If not, you likely have an RF remote. The receiver will also have a dark plastic infrared receiver window on the front as well, usually with the words *remote* or *IR* above it. No visible receiver is needed for RF reception since it uses radio waves that can pass through the outside box to an internal receiver.

Step 2: Find a Suitable Location for the Antenna

The antenna placement can be tricky. I recommend placing it behind the rear seats in full view of the rear window. Place Velcro on the bottom so it doesn't move (as shown later in Figure 16-7). Then run the cable inside the car molding and out of the way so nobody trips on cables or sits on the antenna cable. See Chapter 5, "Working with Cables," for more details on properly running cables. Note that the antenna placement around the rear-window defogger wires can be critical. Moving the antenna a few inches one way or the other can drastically change the quality of reception, because the wires tend to shield the antenna from the TV signals.

If the antenna you are installing requires a power supply, you will likely have to purchase an appropriate extension cord so it reaches your AC inverter. A standard home appliance extension cord, like the one shown in Figure 16-3, can be used.

FIGURE 16-3: A household appliance extension cord.

Make sure you use electrical tape to keep the power supply plug and extension cord socket held together so they won't come loose. Furthermore, make sure you close off any unused sockets with socket plugs and try to keep the outlets off the carpet, as shown in Figure 16-4, so that drink spills, mud, snow, and other elements don't enter the electrical sockets and cause a potentially dangerous situation, such as fire or electrical shock.

Step 3: Install the Receiver and Related Software

If you are installing one of the computer solutions, install all of the necessary software by making sure you have all the software CDs as well as any updates downloaded and saved on a CD-R. Once you have the original software installed, install the updates and test that the software launches correctly. Do these installs with the car running so you don't wear down your battery. Now is also the time to install any third-party software applications for watching television, such as those outlined earlier in this chapter in the "Media Dashboard Software" section earlier in the chapter.

Note Follow the instructions for each hardware and software package carefully. It's usually a good idea to read all the steps through first and *then* do the install, so you know what to expect. It's also a good idea to minimize the amount of time this will take because it is unsafe to sit in a running car for extended periods of time due to exhaust fumes that can make their way into your car.

If you are installing a stand-alone receiver, simply install it where you decided upon in Step 1. Make sure the controls are facing your passengers. If you have an infrared remote, make sure the infrared receiver faces your passengers so they can use the remote.

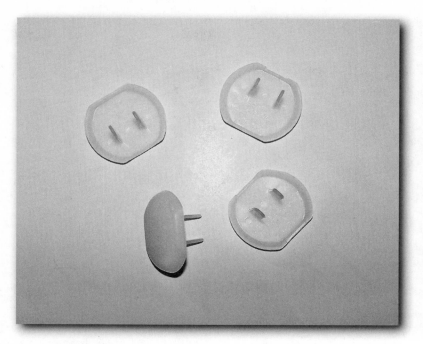

FIGURE 16-4: Socket plugs.

Step 4: Connect the Display(s) and Audio

First, measure the bottom of your receiver and cut the Velcro strips so you can run them along the receiver's bottom perimeter. Attach the fuzzy side on the bottom of the receiver, and the hook side of the same length of Velcro attaches to the fuzzy side. Apply the receiver in the location you decided upon in Step 1.

After you have installed the receiver, connect its audio and video outputs to your display or displays and to your car's head unit. In the case of multiple displays, you will likely need to purchase a video splitter, available for under $20 from any retailer that sells televisions, such as Best Buy, CompUSA, Radio Shack, Circuit City, or Good Guys,.

If you have more than one A/V device in your car (such as a game system) and you need to switch between the television and that other system, you will need to purchase a A/V splitter. These usually run under $50 and look similar to the one in Figure 16-5.

FIGURE **16-5:** An A/V switcher.

You will likely be running composite (a.k.a. RCA) cables to your display. If you decide to install a large widescreen LCD display, it may support S-Video, in which case you should use S-Video cabling. If you are installing something out of the ordinary, such as an HDTV receiver and a plasma display (which, by the way, would require *a lot* of power—plasma displays are entirely impractical for car environments!), you will likely end up using component video cables for the highest-resolution picture.

See Chapter 7 for details on choosing the right video solution for your car.

Step 5: Install the Antenna

First, measure the bottom of your antenna and cut the Velcro strips so you can run them along the antenna's bottom perimeter. Score the antenna casing plastic with a scissor or razor blade so the Velcro sticks well, as shown in Figure 16-6. Then attach the fuzzy side on the bottom of the antenna, and the hook side of the same length attaches to the fuzzy side (see Figure 16-7). Apply the antenna in the location you decided upon in Step 2 and run the cables to the receiver by running through molding and conduit to keep the cables out of your passengers' way. Refer to Chapter 5 for how to properly route cables in your car.

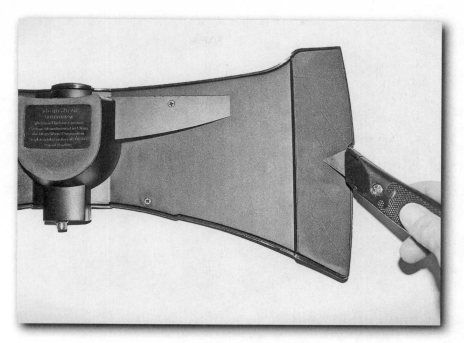

Figure 16-6: Score the antenna casing plastic so the Velcro sticks to it well.

Step 6: Store Local Channels

After you have installed your receiver, you should scan and save your local channels for quick access while on the road. Refer to your receiver's manual on how to do this (PC tuner solutions will ask you to do this the first time you run the manufacturer's television-tuning software). If you travel out of your local area, you will likely have to rescan for channels or just tune them directly with the receiver or remote.

Step 7: Watch TV!

This step is easy—tune in a channel and watch TV! But please, not while you are driving!

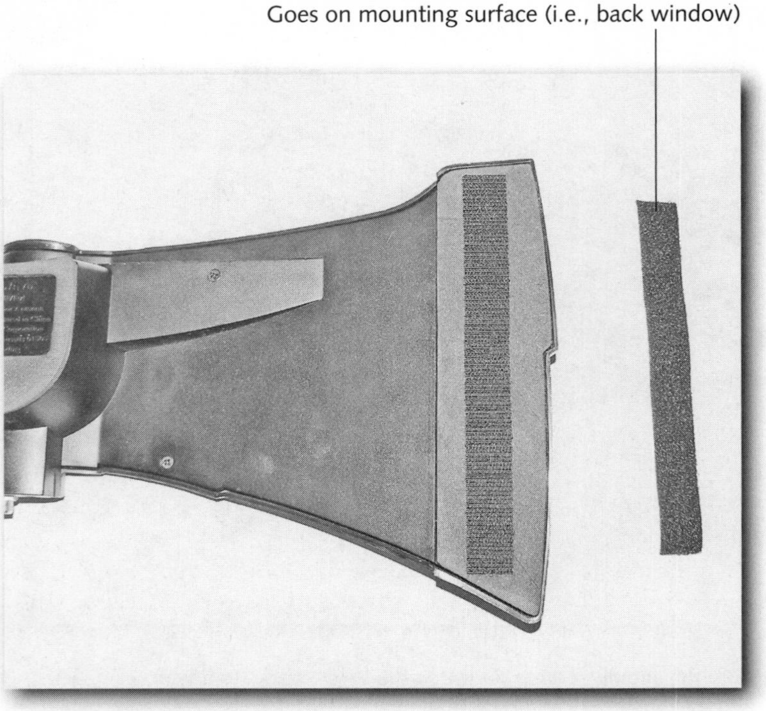

Goes on mounting surface (i.e., back window)

FIGURE 16-7: The fuzzy and hook sides of the Velcro properly applied to
the bottom of the antenna (note that your antenna will likely look different).

Considering Satellite (DirecTV, Hughes, etc.)

Satellite providers DirecTV and Dish Network (EchoStar) have offered DBS mobile reception systems for many years. These systems need to aim their sizable (pizza-dish) antennas at a spot in the sky about as small as your own thumb at arms distance. As a result, very complex (and costly!) motorized antenna aiming systems are needed, usually under a protective radome cover. Systems that track satellites while moving are two to three times costlier than systems that can be quickly aimed while the vehicle is parked.

The Federal Communications Commission (FCC) has mandated that consumer mobile satellites can only receive, not transmit, while in motion. It is a federal crime to transmit data while mobile, so if you get satellite Internet access (this does not apply to cell phone and Wi-Fi Internet service providers), you are only allowed to *receive* data with this solution when mobile. This regulation comes from a snafu in the late 1990s when a mobile satellite transmitted to the wrong satellite and wiped out all of Wal-Mart's data uplink for an entire day. If you are caught transmitting while mobile, it could lead not only to federal fines and jail time but also to litigation and prosecution by companies or entities your transmissions affect.

Satellite television access tends to be impractical because of the fairly expensive equipment and installation expertise necessary to make it work. The satellite must also be mounted on top of your car to receive a clear signal—something many people will not want to do, and only invites thieves to take a closer look.

To install satellite television access you will need a dish, a service plan, a vehicle on which you don't mind bolting a satellite receiver, and a professional installer (let them take the blame if a mistake is made).

Don't forget about the service costs with satellite television: You not only need to buy the equipment, you must also sign up with a service provider, such as Hughes and their Direcway service. Of course, with the self-aligning dish you should be able to receive both satellite television and Internet access, if you opt for such a plan. Most people I have discussed this topic with, however, have told me not to install satellite anything in a vehicle because it's just plain unreliable. People I know have spent small fortunes to install neat-o technologies in their cars, and satellite appears to have been their least favorite.

The largest obstacle for satellite television access is that you must have a clear view to the southeast to communicate with orbiting satellites—while you drive (this of course wouldn't apply when parked)—requiring constant realignment of the dish, which must be mounted on the top of your vehicle. Should you be in a city, the satellite television reception just won't be there, and standard terrestrial broadcast television could be your backup for watching your favorite shows. Remember, most people think of satellite as a residential service, a service provided to and from those huge satellites next to radio stations and on the tops of tall buildings, and a service for military personnel in the middle of the desert.

If you are considering installing satellite, it is fairly easy today to get a self-aligning dish. Searching on the Internet will bring up any number of providers of these satellites. One such provider is DataStorm (www.datastorm.com). There is also a DataStorm users forum online (www.datastormusers.com) so you can chat with other users of the product and see how their experiences have been. More satellite resources are provided in Appendix C, "Additional Resources."

Finding an installer should not be difficult. Any high-end A/V store in your area can probably recommend a custom installer for such services. Whether they are any good could be hard to judge. Check with online forums for individual experiences (again, check out Appendix C for forum sites and other resources).Keep in mind that just because you spend the money on satellite television that doesn't mean it will work everywhere you go. The same goes for terrestrial television broadcasts, but its coverage area and performance is much more predictable, and it's a lot cheaper to experiment with.

Satellite technology is always improving, however. Future satellite transceivers may solve many of the line-of-sight issues experienced with satellites today. For now, unless you have a lot of money, stay away from it.

Summary

This chapter discussed methods of receiving television in your car, from satellite to standard NTSC television to digital television and HDTV. It then gave you instructions for how to install a modular solution into your car and enable your passengers to enjoy television while you keep your eyes on the road. If you are going to install more A/V devices than just television, take a gander at Chapter 9, which covers installing an A/V switch and A/V distribution amplifier for connecting multiple A/V devices.

Syncing Music Library with Your Existing Home Network

in this chapter

☑ Keeping home and car music collections in sync

☑ Windows offline file synchronization

☑ Dialing-in your music

Approximate project cost: $250

Perhaps nothing is a more common experience in a car than listening to music. But today's CDs, even MP3 CDs, don't give us access to our entire music collection. It sure would be nice to build a solution for a car where we could have access to our music collection at home, only in our car instead. Even better would be for our car and home music collections to always be in sync. Well, that's what we are about to build!

Components and Tools Needed

To complete this project, you will need the following:

- A Car PC.

- Windows XP Professional or Windows 2000 Professional (or higher) for the example in this chapter (~$179–$299, but college students can usually get either from their school bookstore for only $5). We will be using Windows XP in the screen shots here, but Windows 2000 will closely reflect what you see (minus the Windows XP theme, of course). Other synchronization programs are available for other operating systems, such as FileSync 1.1 and Laplink File Mover. Links to those other programs are at the end of this chapter. I won't go over installing a Linux solution in detail, but I will list alternative solutions in case you're running Linux.

Note   If you are running Windows XP Professional, you must disable *Fast User Switching* in order to use the Windows Offline File Synchronization feature we use in this chapter. See "Setting Up Windows Offline File Synchronization" for instructions on how to disable Fast User Switching.

- A network connection. Wireless is the most convenient here, and the faster the better. You can also connect to a wired network when you pull into your garage, or other place with wired access, but this can be inconvenient (and far from automatic!). Wireless adapters cost about $40–$50, whereas an Ethernet port is already built into most systems.

- Music files (hopefully legal ones!).

- Plenty of hard drive space to store all of your music files (or at least a subset of your music files) on your Car PC.

- A Media Player application, such as CarTunes™, iTunes®, Windows Media Player®, or MusicMatch®. It can be convenient to have one that also gets Internet radio if you're so daring.

- A full tank of gas! (You'll need it for your initial synchronization, unless you do it indoors instead.)

Preparation

First, let's get ready for the synchronization.

Choosing the Network Connection

You will obviously need a network connection in order to transfer files from your home *network* to your car. Note that I discuss synchronizing portable music players in the next chapter.

Music files tend to be between 2 and 7 megabytes in size, depending on the bitrate (or quality) you encode them at. A few megabytes can take tens of seconds to transfer on a slow network such as an 802.11b at its peak 11-megabit rate (which you will rarely, if ever, achieve), and under ten seconds on a faster one, such as a 54-megabit 802.11a connection or 100-megabit wired ethernet connection. Multiply this by the number of songs in your collection, and you can see you'll be transferring a lot of data initially! However, once you have synchronized the music collection, updating it to include your latest tracks should be a breeze.

I suggest a wireless connection for your vehicle, not only because of the sheer convenience of synchronizing without wires but also because of the great entertainment of being on the road and seeing how many unprotected networks are out there (a.k.a. *war driving*). The faster the connection, the better, and wireless technologies are getting better and faster all the time.

There are a number of different approaches to the network connection. I would suggest doing it in two phases if you can. If your Car PC can be used indoors and outdoors (i.e., you can take it out easily and plug it in at home), I would run through these steps indoors on your local network to perform the initial synchronization and then move the device into your car for subsequent syncs. Since you'd still be connecting to the same network, only wirelessly, your synchronization should still work fine.

You should already know how to set up the network. It's best to keep your car using a dynamically served address via DHCP. Most Windows and Linux solutions are already set up to do this. This chapter will not go over how to set up a network at home. However, I recommend that you refer to your product documentation on securing a wireless network if you are deploying wireless.

Configuring the Software

There are two parts to this configuration step: the server(s) and the Car PC. You may have music in many locations in your home and want to synchronize them all to your Car PC. In this case you will repeat the "Configuring the Server(s)" step, which follows, for each server. Note that I recommend you keep all of your music on a single compter, which I will call a *server computer*, since most people don't have dedicated servers in their homes.

Configuring the Server(s)

In this chapter you will be using Microsoft Windows XP Professional and its built-in synchronization software, also known as *Offline Files*. Microsoft's software, as usual, is tightly integrated into the operating system. This makes it very convenient, and fairly simple to use.

If you will be using a different product to do synchronization, this section doesn't entirely apply to you, but you should read it anyway to set up the network connection properly.

The first thing to do is set up a computer as a server to share music.

Keeping security in mind, set up an account on your server computer specifically for sharing the folder with all of your music files (and the folders related to them). This way, if someone infiltrates your wireless network, the most they should be able to do if they hack the music-sharing account is access the single folder you are sharing. Of course, since I'm *sure* you have a backup of all your music, it's okay if it gets hijacked <evil grin>.

Note I recommend that if you're only using your wireless network for music synchronization, you turn it off when it's not being used. There's no reason to keep it on all the time if you're not using it.

Note Wireless bandwidth is available from a single pool. Each device connecting uses some of the total bandwidth and does not have a separate channel. Unlike Ethernet, where you can have multiple devices all with 100-megabit connections to a shared switch, five computers connected to a 54-megabit hub may only see around 6 megabits each if they all started transferring files at once (this takes into consideration the overhead in the wireless transmissions, which limits the total amount of available bandwidth).

Adding a New User in Windows XP

In this case I created a standard user account named *MusicUser* with a semi-difficult password. Windows makes new users standard users by default, not administrators, so you shouldn't have to change anything. Do not make the user an administrator on the machine (this is due to security concerns). Never use simple passwords—you should know that already. You will be saving the password later anyway, so don't be afraid to use something difficult.

To add the MusicUser account to your server computer, first open Control Panel. Under Pick a Task, click "Create a new account," as shown in Figure 17-1. When Windows asks for the user name, enter **MusicUser** and click Next. Set the user account type to Limited user and click Create Account. Now click the newly created account and click "Create a password." Enter the password and click Create Password. Close the window, and voila—the new account has been created!

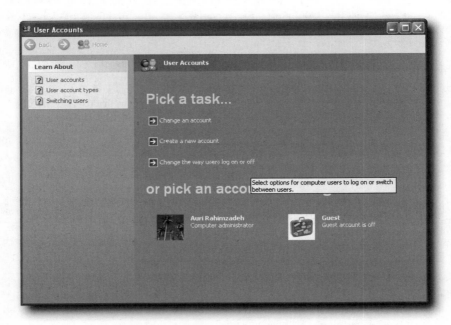

FIGURE 17-1: The User Accounts control panel with the new MusicUser account.

Adding a New User in Windows 2000

To add a new user in Windows 2000, right-click My Computer and select Manage. The Computer Management window will appear. Select Local Users and Groups and expand the folder. Right-click Users and click New User. For User Name enter MusicUser, and also enter a password. A description is optional. Uncheck "User must change password at next logon" and click Close. The account is now created, so go ahead and close the Computer Management window. By default, Windows 2000 makes the user a Standard user, not an administrator, so no access changes should be necessary after you create the account.

Setting Up Network Sharing

Now we need to set up the sharing on the server. You can share with any computer in your home, and it doesn't have to be with a single computer. You can perform this step on any Windows 2000 or greater operating system and synchronize all that music with your Car PC as long as you have enough storage space to hold all the music on your hard drive drive!

Caution

Windows Offline File Synchronization stores all offline files on the boot partition of the computer, so make sure if you use the Windows synchronization capabilities you have enough room on that partition for all your synchronized files.

Pretty easy—find the folder that holds all of your music (the topmost folder), right-click it, and select Sharing and Security.

Click the Sharing tab, if it's not already up, and click Share this folder on the network. For Share name set it to **Music**, as shown in Figure 17-2.

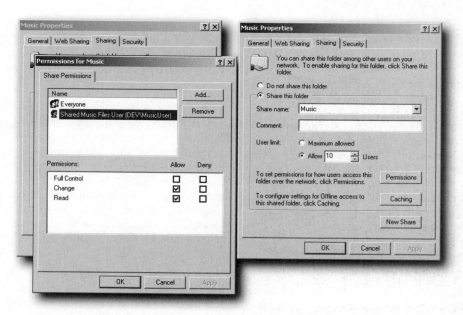

FIGURE 17-2: The properly configured Sharing tab settings in Windows 2000.

In Windows XP, check the box next to "Allow network users to change my files" as you can see in Figure 17-3.

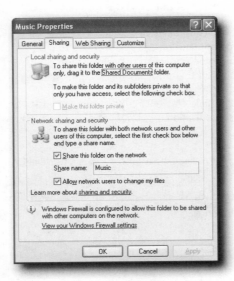

FIGURE 17-3: The properly configured
Sharing tab settings in Windows XP.

Note

If this is the first time you have shared files on the machine, you may not see any the information previously mentioned. Instead, you will see a link that reads, "If you understand the security risks but want to share files without running the wizard, click here." Click it and a dialog box will come up. Click "Just enable file sharing" and click OK.

In Windows 2000 the setup is similar but not exactly the same. Set the maximum number of users to **4**, just in case you leave some open connections and so more than one computer on your network can use the share. Then click Permissions. You will see the list of users available with access to the folder. You can keep "Everyone" because, by default, Guest access is off on both Windows 2000 and Windows XP installations.

Now, click Add. The Select Users or Groups box will come up as shown in Figure 17-4. Type **MusicUser** in the Objects text box (the large white box under the list of all the users and objects) and click OK. You should be taken back to the Share Permissions window, and you should see MusicUser in the list. Click the MusicUser account and allow it Change and Read privileges. Do *not* click Deny on anything, because this should be taken care of by default.

Note

If you are running a domain in your home (wow, you're really a geek), you may want to set up a single user for use across your network that you can just add here so you don't have to set up a user on each machine.

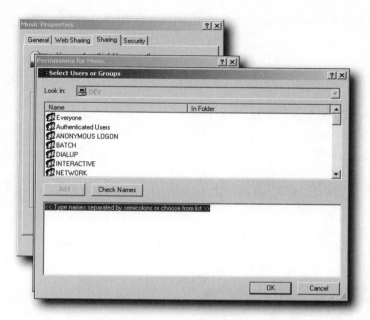

FIGURE 17-4: The Select Users or Groups window in Windows 2000.

Note If you are using Windows XP Professional and you are joined to a domain (you will know if this is true if you are), some of the Windows 2000 screens will apply to you instead of the Windows XP screen shots. The specific windows should be obvious as you work through this chapter.

Note Some security experts may ask why I ask you to allow *Change* on such an accessible account. This is because the synchronization functions in Windows XP need to set a synchronization bit and if Read-Only is all the permissions you have, then synchronization will fail. This limitation may not apply to other synchronization applications, which may utilize their own database for synchronizing files.

Continuing with our Windows 2000 sharing setup, click OK until you are out of the sharing windows and back to your desktop. Some people click Apply first—this doesn't really matter since it is implied by clicking OK after making settings changes.

Whether you are using Windows XP or Windows 2000, the folder should now have a sharing icon of a hand on it (see Figure 17-5), indicating that the folder is now shared. Your "server" computer is now properly configured for sharing. Repeat this step on any other computers for which you will be sharing music with your Car PC. You do *not* need to set up sharing on your Car PC for synchronization to work (but you *are* welcome to).

FIGURE 17-5: The sharing icon indicating that the folder is shared.

Configure the Car PC for Synchronization

Now that the servers are configured, we need to map their shares to drives on the Car PC.

First, open up My Computer. Under the Tools menu, select Map Network Drive as shown in Figure 17-6.

Start with Drive **M:** (for Music, although you can use any unused letter you desire) and set the folder to the name of the computer, a backslash, and **Music**. Also, check "Reconnect at logon" so it automatically connects and checks for new music files when your network is available. In my case, my music server's name is DEV, so I entered:

```
\\DEV\Music
```

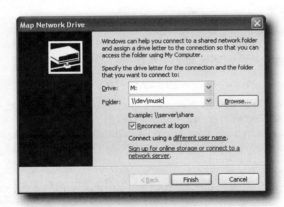

Figure 17-6: The Map Network Drive dialog box
set to connect to \\DEV\Music.

Click Finish. If this is your first time connecting, you will be asked for a username and password. Use MusicUser for the username and the password you entered. Also check the box "Save this Password" so you don't have to enter the password every time you use the shared folder on the server.

After you have entered your logon credentials, the newly mapped drive will appear.

To verify you have done this step properly, open My Computer and see whether your drive is there, as shown in Figure 17-7.

FIGURE 17-7: The newly mapped drive appears in My Computer as the M: drive, along with what it maps to.

Note

If you get an error telling you that Windows cannot connect to the server, make sure your firewall is allowing you to talk to your server. Many firewalls support profiles. Keeping your computer set to an office network or "home network" profile should enable you to connect to your servers. If you block everything, the server can't take certain steps to verify that you are who you say you are, and thus it will refuse to let you talk to it. If you're running Windows XP Service Pack 2 or greater and you use its built-in firewall, it should by default allow you to share files on your local network, both wired and wirelessly in most cases. If you still cannot get the Windows XP Service Pack 2 firewall to work, either make sure Enable Exceptions is turned on (search the Windows Help Center under Start, Help and Support for how to do this) or try a different firewall product.

Repeat this step for each server on your network that you will be synchronizing files with, incrementing the letter for each additional mapped drive.

Note

If you ever want to disconnect, or unmap, a network drive, simply open My Computer, right-click the drive you want to unmap and select Disconnect network drive, and it will be removed. When you unmap a drive, Windows will ask you whether you want to delete the offline files. I suggest clicking Yes, because if you're not going to synchronize the drive again, there's probably no reason to keep the files. Note that this does not delete all the files on your server. Note that it is unwise to delete files on a mapped drive while you are using it offline, since it may cause Windows to delete the file on the server.

Now that we have the drives configured, we need to set up offline storage for each of the drives, so all of their files are stored on the Car PC.

Note Make sure you have enough space on your hard drive to store your entire music collection! If you don't think you have enough room, either synchronize only specific folders (say, a Favorite Music folder you create on your server computer), or buy a larger hard drive.

Performing Synchronization

Now that we have the drives mapped, it's time to set up the Windows Offline Files synchronization feature.

Setting Up Windows Offline File Synchronization Feature

If you are running Windows XP on your Car PC, you have to be in Single User mode first. This doesn't mean you can only have one user account on the computer, you just can't have multiple users logged in at once. Normally you won't have multiple user accounts on a Car PC anyway, so you shouldn't experience any issues (except possibly faster performance due to less overhead!). To set your PC to Single User mode, go to Control Panel, User Accounts, Change the Way Users Log On or Off and uncheck Use Fast User Switching (see Figure 17-8). After you've done this, click Apply Settings and close the window. Note this does not apply if you are running Windows 2000 on your Car PC.

FIGURE 17-8: Disabling the Fast User Switching feature.

Now that you're in Single User mode, open up My Computer and right-click the first of the mapped drives you created earlier in this chapter.

Here's the hard part—click Make Available Offline as shown in Figure 17-9. A Confirm Offline Subfolders dialog box will appear. Make sure you check "Yes, make this folder and all its subfolders available offline," as shown in Figure 17-10, which will make sure all files on the mapped drive are synchronized to your local hard drive. Wow, that was tough, wasn't it?

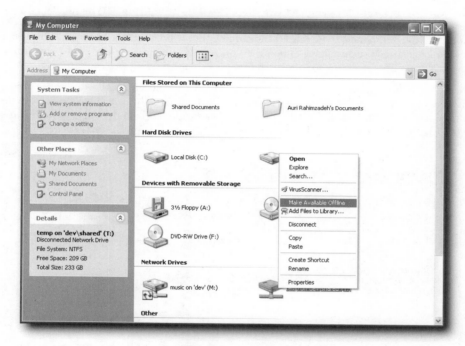

FIGURE 17-9: The Make Available Offline option available in the contextual menu for the mapped drive.

FIGURE 17-10: The Confirm Offline Subfolders dialog box.

After you click OK, the synchronization will begin. Repeat this step for each mapped drive you want to synchronize.

While your Car PC scans the shared drives for files and synchronizes them you *must not turn off the car and you must let it finish*. If you don't let it finish, the offline music collection will be incomplete and may not automatically synchronize itself in the future. This is where that full tank of gas (and hopefully a high-speed connection) comes in. If you're synchronizing your computer in your home and *then* moving it into your car, this is no big deal. Since I didn't have the AC adapter for my car computer (it's connected directly to the battery), I grabbed my spare set of keys, locked my car, and went upstairs to watch a movie. I'm in a fairly good neighborhood, so your willingness to leave your car running (but still locked), is up to you. This is the reason I suggested synchronizing at home. Allow a few hours for your Car PC to synchronize; check it every 30 minutes or so to make sure things are progressing well.

You're not entirely in the clear just yet, though. We need to allocate more space to the offline files because, for whatever reason, Windows defaults to using only 10% of the drive space for offline files. That's no good, since we want all of our shared music in the car while we're on the road. Figure 17-11 shows the files synchronizing.

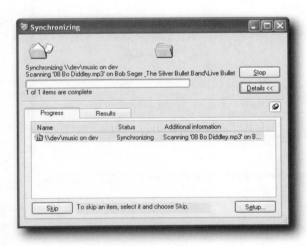

FIGURE 17-11: The files being synchronized.

After a drive has been set for synchronization, it will have a special icon attached to it, as shown in Figure 17-12. This also happens on any individual folders you decide to synchronize. For example, if you decide not to share the entire drive at one point, but rather only certain folders, you can follow the offline files configuration by right-clicking a particular folder and making it available offline just as you did the entire mapped drive.

FIGURE 17-12: The icon
signifying the drive or folder
is available offline.

Some may ask why we are mapping drives when we could just type \\DEV\Music when we
need access to the folder. For one, it's easier to map the drive since we can treat it as a drive letter and not have to remember all the different share names. Second, some applications may not
let you enter a direct network path when browsing for files, but they will let you access any
drive letter under My Computer.

To increase the storage space made available for our music files, open up My Computer and
from the Tools menu select Folder Options.

Select the Offline Files tab, as shown in Figure 17-13. If you have less than 10 gigabytes of
music to synchronize, move the slider all the way over to the right. If you have enough music to
use up all of your drive, then keep the slider at 80% just to keep enough hard drive space available for other tasks.

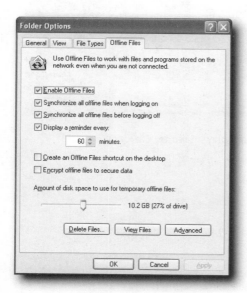

FIGURE 17-13: The Offline Files tab under
Folder Options.

Choosing a Music Player

Obviously you have a lot of choices for music players in your car. The problem is that most of them use small text or are made for an interface with a mouse. Also, many of them won't easily synchronize all of your music. Since a mouse isn't feasible for use while driving, and small text doesn't help me much, and because I have a touch screen in the car, I wrote my own music player: CarTunes™ (see Figure 17-14). You can use any software you want, but I wrote CarTunes for easy synchronization with all of the music in my car and with an easy interface made specifically for touch screens. For example, it has big buttons and big text and some useful features none of the other media players have. CarTunes is available for download from the CarTunes Web site at www.cartunes.ws.

FIGURE 17-14: The touch-screen-oriented music player I wrote, CarTunes.

Adding a Knob to Your Car PC

A cool little gizmo I found for my car was the Griffin PowerMate. This little device looks like a knob from a good-looking stereo and can be programmed to work with any application. It supports clicking by pushing in and rotating. The obvious use for this would be in a music program, where you could select music by scrolling through and then pushing in to select the music. I programmed it to work with my CarTunes music player, but it can also be used in any application, including scrolling Web sites, documents, maps, and so forth. It's very cool and is under $40! I mounted it near my steering wheel so I could dial-in music while driving. The PowerMate, shown in the figure below, is available from many computer stores, including CompUSA, and available from Griffin Technology's Web site at www.griffintechnology.com.

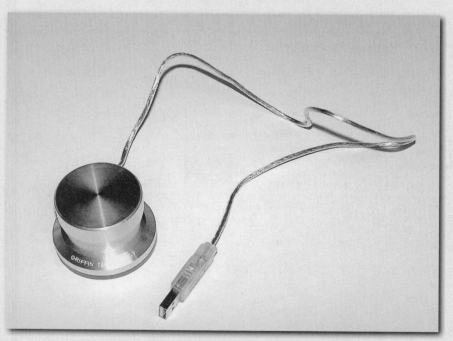

The Griffin Technology PowerMate USB dial.

The Test

Now that we have everything synchronized, the only test is to see whether we can access the music. Fire up your music player and add the music you just synchronized to the player. So where do you find the music? It's easy—go to My Computer and select the files you want from the mapped drives. They should work whether or not you're connected to the network and should work just like regular drives. The folders should also stay in sync by automatically synchronizing every time your home wireless or wired network becomes available.

Additional Resources

Table 17-1 lists software packages you can use for file synchronization.

Table 17-1   Software for File Synchronization

Software Package	Price	Platform	Web Site
FileSync 1.1	Free	Windows	www.genevaonline.com/~scott/
Laplink File Mover	$30	Windows	www.laplink.com/products/filemover/
Windows File Synchronization	Free	Windows 2000, XP	n/a (built into Windows)
Folders Synchronizer X	$40	Mac OS X	www.softobe.com/
RsyncX 2.1	Free	Mac OS X	www.versiontracker.com/dyn/moreinfo/macosx/16814
kBag	Free	Linux	http://kir_smirnov.tripod.com/kBag/

Summary

This chapter discussed how to set up sharing on home computers for gaining access to our music collection at home from the car. Keeping all of your music in one location makes it easy for you to access your music from any computer in your home and enjoy any music you want while on the road.

Syncing Portable Music Players

Approximate project cost: $150

Portable digital music players such as Apple's iPod or the Creative Zen have become the latest craze and true icons of style. Carrying thousands of songs in your pocket, possibly even your entire music collection, has become the norm. With access to all the music you own comes the obvious question of how you would listen to all of that music in your car. In an earlier chapter you explored how to sync your music collection with your home network. But if you already have all the music on your portable music player, why even bother? This chapter will go over how to build a USB port into your car that you can conveniently plug your portable music player into and synchronize, gaining access to all of your music from your Car PC.

in this chapter

☑ Install a USB hub into your dash

☑ Play your music anywhere

☑ Buy music legally in your car

☑ Charge your media player while driving

A Few Notes about Syncing

There are a few items you need to take into consideration before installing a USB hub in your car.

Keep Cable Lengths in Mind

When running the USB cable to your car computer it is important that it not be over 16 feet in length. The USB specification does not permit a cable to be longer than 16 feet, and you may lose data if you use one longer.

Syncing Takes Power

Normally you won't have your portable music player plugged into a power supply while you drive. Unfortunately, while you use your music player you are also draining the battery. On long road trips this may become a problem.

Higher-end modern digital music players are capable of charging themselves by using the power provided over the Firewire or

USB 2.0 port they are connected to. If your car computer does not have a Firewire or USB 2.0 port and your digital music player supports either for charging, I recommend purchasing an expansion card that enables you to take advantage of the charging capability. This will let you enjoy your music *and* have a charged-up music player when you reach your destination!

Note If you want to charge your music player using Firewire, make sure you are using a six-pin Firewire port, as shown in Figures 18-1 and 18-2. The four-pin or "mini" Firewire ports do not provide any power for charging devices.

Note USB 1.1 and USB 2.0 cables and ports look identical. Check with your computer manufacturer to see if you have a USB 2.0 port on your computer. Sometimes there will be a sticker on the front of the computer case that says "Hi-Speed USB," denoting you have USB 2.0 ports built into your computer. Another way to tell is by plugging a USB 2.0 device into a USB port on your computer. If a balloon pops up saying "This device can perform faster," then you have plugged the device into a USB 1.1 port.

Did You Know Firewire is actually a brand name for the *IEEE-1394* standard. Apple Computer, the manufacturer of iPod music players and Macintosh computers, came up with the name. Sony and Philips have their own name for IEEE-1394—it's called *i.Link*.

FIGURE 18-1: Six-pin Firewire port and its connector.

FIGURE 18-2: Four-pin Firewire port and its connector.

Some Devices Require USB 2.0

Some devices you purchase will require USB 2.0, the high-speed version of the popular peripheral connection technology. USB 2.0 supports speeds of up to 480 megabits per second (Mbps), whereas USB 1.1 only supports up to 14 Mbps. USB 2.0 can also provide more power over its bus than USB 1.1, making it capable of charging certain devices, such as Apple's iPod, without a separate power adapter.

What If You Need Firewire?

If you need Firewire for your media player instead of USB, you can install an internal PCI or PCMCIA card to get such functionality. If you are going to have more than one Firewire device, such as a removable hard drive, in addition to your music player, you can find a Firewire hub from many reputable providers, such as Belkin and Orange Micro. If you are looking for a USB-Firewire combo hub, I found a few by searching for *USB 1394 Combo Hub* on Froogle, Google's shopping search site (www.froogle.com). The first that caught my eye was the compact D-Link DFB-H7 for about $60.

Installing a USB Hub in Your Dash

I was getting tired of having to run USB cables to my computer under the seat. Having a USB hub on the floor didn't seem like a good idea either. I decided I could take my ashtray and a micro USB 2.0 hub and add the hub directly to my car's dash. This made it easy for me to connect my iPod, removable storage devices, game controllers, and more to my car without dealing with a lot of messy cables. Here's how I did it.

Note If you don't have a removable ashtray or you don't have one that can fit a hub, you can still add a hub to your car. Mounting the hub inside your center console or in your glovebox, or even cutting into your dash and mounting it there, can be just as effective. If you decide to cut into your car to make a hole for the hub, make sure you know where you're cutting. You don't want to cut through any critical wires or get an electric shock.

What You Will Need

- An ashtray that you don't care about messing up (or similar removable item that you can replace if you sell the car or mess up). Make sure the hub you buy can actually fit into the ashtray! (~Free to $100+ to replace)

- A two- or four-port micro USB hub (~$20–$50, these are the small USB hubs, also called thumb-USB hubs). I chose a four-port for convenience (see Figure 18-3). I also recommend that the hub be USB 2.0 instead of 1.1, because a 2.0 hub supports much faster devices and can also support USB 1.1 devices. Make sure the hub doesn't *require* a power adapter but can utilize an external power supply if needed (some even come with the external power adapter).

FIGURE **18-3: The Belkin Micro USB 2.0 hub.**

- A USB extension cable, of appropriate length to reach your car computer (~$10–$40).

- A Dremel® tool (or similar rotary cutting tool or other tool capable of cutting metal) with a metal cutting bit and a sanding bit (see Figure 18-4), available from most hardware stores (~$40).

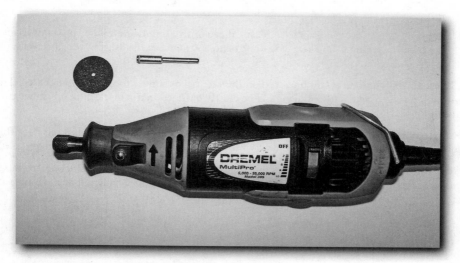

FIGURE 18-4: Dremel® tool with an appropriate cutting bit.

- A hot-glue gun and the super-glue sticks to mount the hub in the ashtray and to make sure it doesn't move (~$20). (Make sure that if you're in a warm climate you check the temperature range for the glue because some glues could melt in the 185-degree (or hotter) car interior temperatures possible in a parked car during summer in the desert southwest).

- Electrical tape (~$3).

- An available USB 1.1 or USB 2.0 port on your car computer.

Step 1: Prepare the Ashtray

The first thing to do is determine where and what you want to drill. Remove the ashtray (or whatever you chose to install this into) from your car. *Do not do this project in your car—it is too dangerous!* Measure the hub's perimeter so you know how big of a hole to make, and outline that in pencil where you are going to drill. I found that my ashtray allowed me to unscrew the plastic piece so I could drill the metal separate from the plastic.

Make sure that before you drill you remove any plastic or rubber pieces, if possible. This will prevent you from making melted areas in the plastic while you cut.

Step 2: Drill the Metal

This is where the Dremel comes in. Make sure you do this in a well-ventilated area and wear hand, eye, and mouth protection. You don't want to breathe in the metal dust, you don't want to get bits in your eye, and you don't want to cut off fingers or cut yourself. If you don't know how to use a Dremel, or you aren't comfortable with using a cutting tool, ask a professional to do it for you.

Mount the ashtray in a vice grip so it doesn't move or fly around and injure you, injure someone else, or break anything. Make sure you don't bend any metal in the ashtray, because you want it to fit cleanly back into the dash when you're done with this project.

Choose the appropriate rotary bit based on the Dremel or similar tool you've purchased. This will vary on the manufacturer but should be clearly outlined in the manual for a bit that cuts metals.

Now, cut a hole in the front of the ashtray so you can slide the hub in. After you've done this, cut a 1-inch by 0.5-inch hole in the back of the ashtray to run the USB cable through.

After cutting the metal, use a sanding bit as shown in Figure 18-5, if you have one, to smooth out the edges of the just-cut metal. The metal shouldn't be exceptionally hot after cutting or sanding, but I still wouldn't touch it for a few minutes.

FIGURE **18-5**: Sanding bit for the Dremel tool.

Step 3: Cut the Plastic

Using the Dremel, or other cutting device, cut out the area in the plastic you will be inserting the hub into. You have to be pretty precise about this, because if you make the gap between the hub and the plastic too wide, it will be more difficult to fill in the gap with the super glue, and thus the hub may come loose. Try to use a lower-RPM setting if using a variable motor speed Dremel, because high RPMs may quickly melt the plastic and make things a tad ugly.

Step 4: Install the Hub

Now that you've cut everything, reattach any plastic you have removed and slide the hub into the hole. Make sure it is easy to access the back of the hub so you can run the extension cable, and make sure the connector on the back of the hub is not touching any metal in the ashtray.

Warm up the hot-glue gun with the super-glue stick. Once you have everything in place, use the hot-glue gun to put super glue on all sides of the hub, and hold the hub and the ashtray together for at least a minute, allowing the glue to cool a bit. Set the hub and ashtray down in a position where there's no tension or force on the hub, allowing it to stay in the desired final position until the glue cools (see Figure 18-6). I would wait about an hour here—go watch a movie or something.

FIGURE 18-6: The hub after being inserted in the ashtray.

Step 5: Run the Cable to Your Car Computer

Now that the hub is in the ashtray, we need to test that it doesn't budge. Do this by plugging in a couple of USB devices or cables and then unplugging them. Don't try too hard or you *will* break the adhesive—just use the force you would normally use for adding and removing a device from a hub. If the hub comes loose, you will need to reglue it, possibly with a stronger glue. If it is stable, run the extension cable through the hole in the back of the ashtray to the back end of the hub and connect the two. Tightly wrap some electrical tape around the two once they are connected so a passenger doesn't accidentally step on a cable to cause it to come loose. Run the other end of the USB cable behind your dash (or under your center console, depending on where your ashtray is located) and to your car computer and plug it in, preferably to a USB 2.0 port, but a USB 1.1 port will do.

Step 6: Test the Hub

This is pretty easy—turn on the computer and plug in a device, as shown in Figure 18-7. If it shows up, it works! Try plugging a digital music player and synchronizing your car computer with its music collection for use on the road. When you leave your car, simply unplug your music player from the dash and take it with you! How cool!

FIGURE 18-7: The finished product.

Using Media Players in Your Car

Obviously, once you have access to your media player on your car's computer, you will want to play the music (and possibly other media) that resides on it. While there are a number of applications that come with your media player, such as Apple's iTunes or MusicMatch Jukebox, among others, not all of these are meant to be used while driving.

Beware of Distracted Driving

When using your music or media in your car, get the music playing and then keep your eyes on the road. If you have to fidgit with the music player, make sure the text is large so you can quickly glance at your computer display, make your selection, and be done with it. In Chapter 7, "Choosing a Display Device," I describe different types of displays you can install in your car. The best is a touch-screen display, where you can just tap what you want on the screen and get back to driving. If it's raining or snowing, or you otherwise have no other choice but to fully concentrate on the road and driving conditions, have a passenger change the mix—don't get into an accident because you didn't like the song that was playing! Many states have "distracted driving" laws, and an accident with a visible screen may get you a much stiffer ticket in addition to the crash damages itself.

Tip You may want to secure your player from sliding around the car while driving by using adhesive Velcro fastener or hook-and-loop fastener strips.

Tip I wrote a music playing application specifically for touchscreen displays called CarTunes. You can download it from the *Geek My Ride* Web site at www.carhacks.net (or go to Wiley's mirror site at www.wiley.com/go/extremetech).

Use the Media Player's Hard Drive

Many music players store their music in a readily accessible format, oftentimes mounting as a removable storage device once you plug them in. This can be very handy because you can use the music player of your choice and just drag the MP3, Windows Media, and other files into your media player and they will automatically be added to your library. My own design of music player, CarTunes, was made specifically for this, so you could have multiple media players and a single playlist and just plug them in and play their music when you have them in your car.

Not All Music Is Portable

Instead of downloading music illegally from the Internet, you may have downloaded music from one of the popular online music stores, such as Apple's iTunes Music Store, Real's Rhapsody service, Sony's Connect, MP3.com, or the former-pirate-network-turned-legit Napster. Unfortunately, the music you purchase through these services is copy-protected and will not play in any media player other than the one for which it is authorized. For example, Apple's iTunes music uses Protected MPEG-4 audio files with a file extension of *.mp4*. Apple's copy protection system is called *FairPlay*, Microsoft has a competing solution named *Janus* and Real uses a system called Helix DRM.

**Did You
Know**

Many music players play different media formats (MP3, WMA, MP4, AAC, and so on), and some music formats aren't compatible with each other. This poses a problem when you rip your music in one format and then your media player won't play it. In order to combat this problem, Microsoft has an initiative called *PlaysForSure*. If your media player has the Plays For Sure logo on it then it is supposed to play any music from any Internet music store or media format supported by Microsoft's own Windows Media Player software—for sure. Apple has tried to combat this to some extent with iTunes automatically converting Windows Media files to Apple's MPEG-4 AAC (iPods can't play Windows Media files), but this can cause a loss of audio fidelity and isn't an ideal solution. MP3 files you own can be directly placed on an iPod using the iTunes music manager software for your PC or Mac.

I am a firm believer, however, that if I paid for music and I don't plan on sharing it with anybody, I should be able to use it wherever I want. Although it may violate some user agreements, there are a number of ways around the copy protection in these systems. There are many programs on the Internet that will strip Apple's copy protection as well as many other content providers' protection.

Many copy-protection schemes are also rendered useless once you burn the music to an audio CD. Once the music is on an audio CD, you can rip the music right back to your computer using any ripper (a program that takes the music on a CD and turns it into a digital file on your computer) and bring the music into any music program you wish.

Of course, all of this is assuming you will only be eliminating copy protection so you can use your music on your own devices. I don't want anyone illegally posting music on the Internet or sharing it with their friends—you should buy all of the music you want.

Accessing Apple's iPod via My Computer

In order to use some media players as a hard drive, or make them appear under My Computer in Windows, you may need to enable that feature on the device. Apple's iPod, the most popular media player as of the writing of this book, requires such an action to be taken.

To access your iPod as a hard drive:

1. Open Apple's iTunes application.

2. From the Edit menu, select Preferences.

3. Click the iPod tab.

4. Click the General tab.

5. Check the box next to "Enable disk use" as shown in Figure 18-8.

FIGURE 18-8:"Enable disk use" option for your iPod in iTunes.

Buying Music While Driving

If you would like to buy music over the Internet for playback in your car, on your portable media player, and on your home computer, you can do so from the comfort of your car. Follow the instructions in Chapter 14, "Adding Internet Access," to add Internet access to your car, and then use your favorite media player and Internet music store to buy the music you want. Most music stores allow you to play your purchased music on multiple computers, usually up to five of them, so you can play your music on your media player, your car computer, a couple home computers and your laptop without having to buy the music more than once. Windows Media 10, which includes Windows Media Player 10 (see Figure 18-9), is a free download that you can get via Windows Update at http://windowsupdate.microsoft.com (which must be visited with Internet Explorer), or from Microsoft's main Web site at www.microsoft.com/windowsmedia.

Tip Whenever you buy music from an online store—back it up! If you lose your purchased music files and have no backup, you may have to buy those tracks again!

FIGURE **18-9: The shopping interface in Microsoft's Windows Media Player 10.**

Microsoft's latest media player included with Windows Media 10 supports multiple Internet music stores from the same interface. This means you can shop for music from multiple Internet music stores and play all of that music in the same media player. This is all part of Microsoft's Plays for Sure initiative, which I described earlier.

Summary

In this chapter you learned how to connect and use your portable digital music player in your car. You also learned how to legally buy music online and make sure it plays everywhere you go. Rock on!

Videoconferencing

Approximate project cost: $160

Sometimes you need to communicate with other drivers. Whether you do it by some sort of hand gesture or by calling each other on cell phones, there's probably nothing cooler than keeping a video-feed open between your two cars. In this chapter you'll learn how to do just that, using a couple 802.11 wireless transmitters and a nearby vehicle.

Note For this project, a Car PC is required, so make sure you've built one into your car so you can do this project!

Choosing a Videoconferencing Camera

There are a couple types of cameras that will work fairly well in your car. The first is a USB Web cam with a built-in microphone, often found in retail stores, and the second is just a stand-alone minitature video camera with just a video output coming from it. In this chapter I will concentrate on the USB solution, one of which is shown in Figure 19-1. You can still use a stand-alone video camera, but your computer will need an A/V (audio/video) input card that can accept its input.

FIGURE 19-1: A Sony laptop-mount Web cam.

Note Many stand-alone video cameras are just that—video. Getting audio feed often requires a separate microphone to be purchased.

You may already have a Web cam at home you'd like to use. The key here is that the Web cam should be small enough to be easily mounted in your car on the dashboard, pointing at the driver. The flat ones built for mounting on laptop screens are often the best choice, because they are both portable and easily mountable, and they include a built-in microphone and wider-angle lens. They can also be easily Velcroed to the dashboard.

Warning Do *not* mount the Web cam on your steering wheel—the wires from the Web cam can interfere with your driving and cause an accident! Also, do *not* mount the camera where direct or reflected sunlight will strike the lens. At best, the sunlight will cause a permanent streak in the image. At worst, the camera will be destroyed! Look for cameras with either slide-covers to protect the lens and internal imager or cameras that offer a snap-on lens cover.

Warning Keep your eyes on the road! The video portion of videoconferencing should be used by passengers—not by the driver. You should be able to participate in the conversation without looking at the screen. Keep in mind that your job is to pay attention to the road. Your passengers, of course, can look at the screen, at maps being shown on the camera, and so forth, so ask them to tell you what's on the display. (Make them work for the ride!)

Watch Your Distance

Because this solution uses 802.11, you are somewhat limited as to how far away the car you are conferencing with can be. Of course, if you are communicating over the Internet, distance should no longer be an issue (although upload and download latency [delay] speeds will be). For the most part, the other car you are communicating with shouldn't be more than 100 feet away; otherwise, you will likely lose your connection.

Connecting with and without the Internet

There are a couple of ways to connect to the other vehicle. One is where you don't have an Internet connection, and instead you have to use an ad hoc wireless network to communicate from your computer to theirs using a program such as Microsoft's free NetMeeting. The second is where you have an Internet connection and use an application like MSN Messenger or AOL Instant Messenger and videoconference between those instant-messaging applications.

Both solutions require different network and software setups. For the non-Internet-connected car, any network videoconferencing software will do. These include Microsoft's free NetMeeting package (www.microsoft.com/netmeeting), Intermedia's (also free) ThruCam 3.0 (www.im.co.kr/English/), and many others. Both software solutions also work over the Internet.

For Internet-connected cars, you can still use the solutions mentioned earlier or, especially when distance requires it, you can use instant-messaging applications that support video, such as AOL Instant Messenger (AIM) or MSN Messenger. Another great application that supports video chat for all the major service providers is Cerulean Studios' Trillian product (www.trillian.cc), which lets you do video chat with any service that supports it, and also lets you instant message between AIM, MSN Messenger, Yahoo! Instant Messenger, ICQ, and IRC.

Many other videoconferencing solutions (free, shareware, and commercial) can be found on popular Internet download search sites, such as CNet's Download.com (www.download.com) and VersionTracker (www.versiontracker.com).

Choosing a Wi-Fi Adapter for Your Car

The type of Wi-Fi adapter you decide to install will depend on the type of computer you are installing and how gung-ho you are about installing Wi-Fi in your car. There are a few different types—USB, PCI (i.e., *internal*), PCMCIA, Compact Flash, and Secure Digital Input/Output (SDIO).

If you are installing a slimline computer in your car, and you don't have many PCI slots (i.e., one or none), you should go the USB route. If your computer only supports USB 1.1, you will be limited to the 11 megabits per second (Mbps) speed supported by 802.11a, b, and g (see Figure 19-2). If you have USB 2.0, however, you can utilize the maximum 54 megabits that 802.11a and 802.11g provide (and possibly more with proprietary wireless solutions from some manufacturers).

When selecting a USB solution, I decided on a slimline solution from Belkin® that was all-in-one and very portable. After installing a USB hub into my dashboard (see "Adding a USB Hub to Your Dash" in Chapter 14, "Adding Internet Access"), I simply plug it in when I need it, and unplug it when I don't. Since USB draws power from the computer's bus, I don't keep the wireless adapter plugged in when I'm not using it. I also remove it when I'm not in the car because thieves may notice the device and decide to smash 'n grab.

FIGURE 19-2: The Belkin slim 802.11g wireless adapter.

Another available USB solution is one of the less portable products that sport a removable antenna. These units have the advantage of supporting more capable antennas, such as the range extenders readily available at CompUSA, Best Buy, and many other computer stores. You can run these antennas to the platform near your rear window (possibly less enticing to thieves) to improve reception. Range extenders run anywhere from $20 to well over $100 and usually provide at least a 6-milliwatt (mW) receiver (most router and card antennas are 2 mW or less).

Warning

Do not splice your Wi-Fi antenna feed into your car's antenna feed! Many car antennas have very balanced input stages—sharing 802.11 can swamp the radio or cause damage of any attached satellite radio, interfere with antitheft systems that use cellular transmitters or LoJack® antitheft frequencies, possibly blowing not only the warranty but also voiding insurance coverage. Some German cars have a GPS antenna going through that antenna also, and those systems are *not* expecting 600 mW of transmitter power appearing at many points in the spectrum!

If you're unsure as to whether you have USB 1.0, 1.1, or 2.0 slots in your computer, check your user's guide. Some computers have USB 2.0 slots (which are backwards compatible with USB 1.1 and 1.0), and then some have USB 1.1-only slots as well. I know it's confusing, but hey, I don't design motherboards. Also, the USB 1.1 and USB 2.0 cables look identical, so slots usually won't be tell-tale signs of what type they are. You can, however, look for the "USB High Speed" logo, which computers sporting USB 2.0 tend to have featured on stickers plastered to the front of their case.

If your computer has available PCI slots, your options are more plentiful, because there are numerous PCI (i.e., internal) wireless adapters that are pretty cheap (under $50), and very effective (see Figure 19-3). Speed is also not an issue as it would sometimes be with USB, as I discussed earlier. The problem with the PCI solution is that the card is always drawing power and you can't easily share the card with multiple computers (such as a laptop). Since you're likely not going to be able to use the wireless while driving, there's no reason to have the continuous drain, so I recommend against the internal wireless solution.

FIGURE 19-3: A PCMCIA (i.e., PC Card) wireless adapter.

Note Do not use Bluetooth Wi-Fi adapters. In my experience, they're just not worth it for the car application because they're just too slow (Bluetooth tends to be limited to 1 Mbps data transfers).

The PCMCIA, Compact Flash, and SDIO solutions can all support the high-speed wireless solutions, and just like USB they are removable. The problem with these solutions is that they are very specialized. PCMCIA drives usually come only with laptops, so there's no reason to buy a PCMCIA drive just for a wireless card (although it would enable you to use many of the cellular connection cards). Compact Flash and SDIO solutions are usually only featured on PDAs. If your computer has a drive capable of using SDIO or Compact Flash cards, then you may have a slight power advantage over the USB solutions, so long as the card adapter isn't itself powered by USB.

Warning Not all Compact Flash and SDIO adapters will work with PCs for Internet Access. Be wary of buying a media card *reader*, because most of these will not allow you to use the cards for Internet access!

What You Need

- Car PC
- USB Web cam with built-in Microphone (~$79)
- USB extension cable (if the supplied cable isn't long enough to reach your computer or USB hub, ~$39)

- Wireless 802.11a, 802.11b, or 802.11g Interface (either USB-based, PC-card based, or internal, depending on your configuration; see Chapter 14 for more details on these card types; ~$40)

Note Each network interface card must support the other card's protocols. For example, if you have an 802.11a wireless interface, you must talk to another unit over 802.11a wireless, and so it much support 802.11a as well. The same goes for any protocol.

- Videoconferencing software (many free and commercial solutions, see "Connecting with and without the Internet" earlier in this chapter)

Install Videoconferencing

The following sections cover the steps required to install videoconferencing in your car.

Step 1: Install Wireless Adapters in Each Car

Each car communicating must obviously have a wireless network adapter. Install these in your car per the instructions provided with the device (see "Choosing a Wi-Fi Adapter for Your Car," in the preceding section, for more information on how to choose the right wireless network interface). These may already be in the car if you've already installed a wireless system as outlined in Chapter 14.

Note There is a project in Chapter 14 that shows you how to install a USB hub in your ashtray so you could just plug a USB wireless adapter into that hub and remove it when it's not in use.

Step 2: Mount the Web Cam or Video Camera

Now that you have the wireless adapters installed, you need to mount the Web cam and video camera. A good suggestion is to the right of the driver, on the dashboard, so you can swivel the camera between the driver and the passengers. Most Web cams come with a mount for this. If not, you can often buy a swivel at a local hardware store that you can mount the camera on and screw into or Velcro onto your dash. Again, try to make sure that direct or reflected sunlight cannot enter the camera lens.

Make sure the USB cable or video cable is not in the way of any devices. Running the cable down toward the floor and under the center console and finally to your PC is a good route to take with the cable. Depending on the Web cam or video camera, you may need the USB extension cable or a video cable extender. See Chapter 5, "Working with Cables," for more information on properly routing and hiding cables.

Step 3: Install the Web Cam or A/V Input Device Software

If you are installing a Web cam, start up your PC and install the Web cam software per the instructions that came with it.

If you are instead installing a video camera, make sure you have installed an appropriate A/V capture card, such as a Hauppauge WinTV, ATI TV Wonder, or other similar device as well as the software for it. Your video camera will then plug into that A/V capture board, and your Web cam software should work with that device to retrieve your audio and video feeds in the stead of a Web cam.

Alternatively, many consumer camcorders now come with either USB ports (allowing Web cam streaming) or Bluetooth connectivity. Many Sony camcorders have enjoyed these features since 2002, and most Sony camcorders have the added benefit of NightShot® infrared imaging, which allows the cameras to capture a very good image in near total darkness.

 Note For a fun project, you could have multiple video cameras mounted in your car and connected to a video switch. Connecting the video switch's output to an A/V receiver in your computer could give you the ability to give multiple camera angles to the person you are chatting with or to monitor the actions of people in your car just by pressing a button. I won't go into how to install that here, but it should be pretty self-explanatory if you're successfully installing the other projects in this book, such as the "Building a Single-Source A/V System" (Chapter 9) or "Integrating a Game Console" (Chapter 10).

Step 4: Configure Your Wireless Adapter in Each Car

I will assume that because you are a geek you know how to find a wireless network and connect to it. If you already have a wireless access point or router, you should be able to see and connect to your wireless network. If each car has an access point, they should both have the same service station ID, or *SSID*. If only one car has an access point, the other car should be able to see your car if it's within 100 feet of the access point.

If you do not already have an access point in either car, you can configure an ad hoc network, which means the two wireless network interfaces will speak directly to each other without an access point in between. Refer to your wireless adapter's manual on how to configure an ad hoc network.

Windows XP will show you all wireless networks, both infrastructure and ad hoc, by default. If you choose a different operating system, you may need to configure it accordingly. See Figure 19-4 for a screen shot of Windows XP's wireless network selector—the network we ended up connecting to here was MLAN. Although the figure shows many wireless networks, you will often only see yours. Keep in mind, however, that because you are building a wireless network, other geeks reading this book may be able to see your network and attach to it, so make sure your firewall and antivirus software are properly configured and that your operating system is up to date.

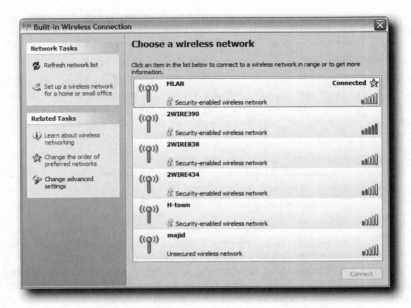

FIGURE 19-4: Windows XP Service Pack 2's wireless network connection
dialog box.

Step 5: Assign a Unique IP Address to Both Wireless
Adapters

In order for your two computers to talk to each other, you must both have PCs with wireless
interface cards. Each wireless card needs a unique IP address in order to address the other card
in the conversation. This will differ depending on whether you already have an 802.11a, b, or g
access point or router installed in your car or whether you just have the wireless interface
installed.

Note Two wireless interfaces talking directly to each other without a wireless router is called an *ad hoc*
network. Wireless interfaces talking to each other via a wireless base station or router are set up
in an *infrastructure* network, because all packets have to go from one card to the router and then
to the destination.

If You Are Using a Router

If you have a router or base station installed in your car, find out what IP-addressing scheme it
is using. Assuming you are a geek, you should know what this means. However, even if you're
not, it's easy to tell. In Windows 2000 and XP, simply press Start, then Run, then type **cmd**. In
Windows 98 or earlier, you will do the same, but type **command** instead. A black command
prompt will come up. Type **ipconfig** and look for your wireless network interface. You should
see something like Figure 19-5.

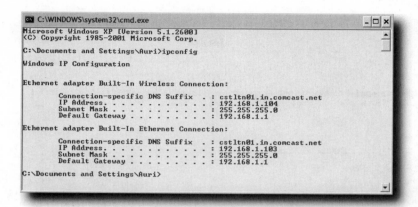

FIGURE 19-5: The Windows XP command prompt running the ipconfig command.

What you want is the *IP Address* of your card, the *Subnet Mask*, and the *Default Gateway* for your *Built-In Wireless Connection*. In this case you will see that my wireless IP address is 192.168.1.103, my subnet mask is 255.255.255.0, and my Default Gateway is 192.168.1.1. The other car needs to be handing out LAN IP addresses that are 192.168.1.x, and a subnet mask that is 255.255.255.0. The other car's network identification, called the SSID also needs to be the same as your router's.

Once you have the above information, set the other car's IP address to an unused 192.168.1.x address, with the same subnet mask and gateway address. You should then be able to verify the other machine is reachable by using the same command prompt and typing **ping 192.168.1.x,** where the *x* is the number assigned to the other PC. You should get responses from the other PC. If not, make sure all your settings are correct and that there is no firewall turned in use on the other PC.

Refer to your wireless router's manual on how to set the SSID and LAN IP-addressing schemes. The screens should be similar to Figures 19-6 and 19-7.

Tip

You don't need two wireless routers if your cars are close to each other. In fact, only one car needs a router, and then you can share your network between the two cars, enabling not only videoconferencing but sharing of files, Internet access, and more!

If You Don't Have an Internet connection

If you don't have an internet connection, you will need to configure an ad hoc network as mentioned in Step 4. Your wireless network adapter's manual should explain how to do this.

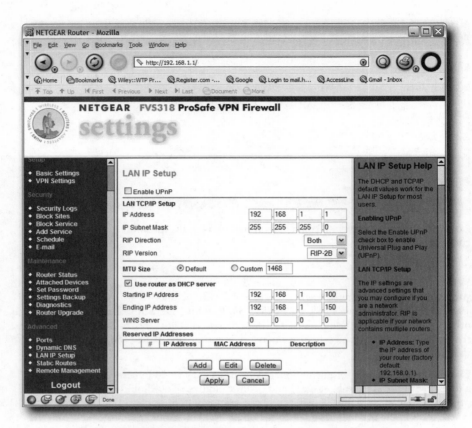

FIGURE 19-6: The LAN IP-addressing configuration screen from a Netgear router.

Step 6: Connect!

Now that everything is connected, bring up the appropriate software package and connect! How you connect will vary depending on the software you use. If you are using a network-conferencing client, such as Net Meeting, each machine will have to enter the other's IP address (entered in Step 5). If you are using an instant-messaging application, such as AIM, you will need to connect to the Internet, instant-message your friend, and then start the video conversation by clicking the appropriate button in your instant-messaging window.

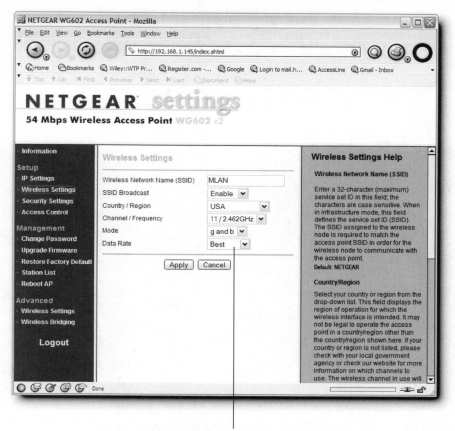

Note: Using lower data transmission rates, such as
1-2 magabits/sec, will increase your maximum broadcast range

FIGURE 19-7: The SSID configuration screen from a Netgear wireless access point.

Summary

In this chapter you installed a Web cam and configured a wireless Internet connection so that two or more vehicles can communicate with each other. Keep in mind—as cool as this project is, you need to keep your eyes on the road, not on the screen!

Being Big Brother: Adding Video Surveillance

Approximate project cost: $650

Sometimes you want to know what's going on when you're not in your car. Did that car next to you hit your door because it was parked too close? Are certain neighbors hanging around your car too often? Did your ex really key your car? Maybe you just want to watch what's going on in the back seat. Adding video surveillance to your car can help you find these things out, and in this chapter we will install just such a video surveillance system.

There are two key components to video surveillance in your car: the camera and the recorder. Because your car isn't always powered on, and you likely don't want to run off your car's battery for a long period of time, I will focus on self-powered solutions in this chapter. Of course, I encourage you to try other approaches, especially if you are trying to record more than four to eight hours of video or overnight video if you suspect vandalism or worse happening while you sleep.

Know the Laws

Some states don't allow you to record video of other people without their permission. Video recordings may also be disallowed as evidence in courts of law. If you're installing video surveillance in your car for legal reasons, I suggest you check with your local law enforcement agency or library as to how you can use your recordings to pursue prosecution. Note that Appendix A, "Legal Concerns," has some tips on how to get legal information from practically any state for free.

Choosing the Camera

As mentioned earlier, the camera is one of two key components in this project. In the car, you ideally want a wireless video camera so you can place the unit anywhere without a lot of hassle. Second, you want it to be battery-powered so you don't have to worry about running any power cables all around the car (which goes hand in hand with the desire for a wireless solution). I found a couple solutions that are both affordable and worthwhile:

- The New Way Technology wireless video camera (~$35, shown in Figure 20-1). This camera is practically impossible to find for sale in stores, but you can find it easily on eBay by searching for "wireless video camera." Make sure that when you buy it on eBay you get one that comes with the 9-volt adapter so you can use a battery pack to power both the camera and the video receiver.

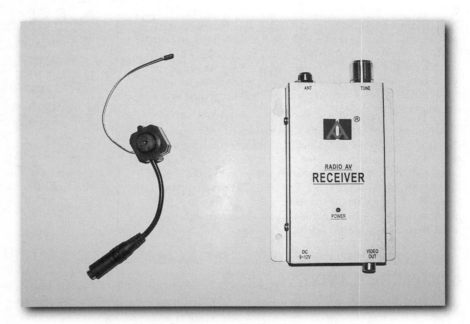

FIGURE **20-1: The New Way Technology wireless video camera and receiver.**

- The X-10 systems XCam 2 wireless video solution (~$79, www.x10.com, shown in Figure 20-2). For under $100 it comes with a wireless camera, wireless video receiver, VCR commander (for telling a VCR when to record), motion detector, remote control, and tripod—not bad at all!

FIGURE 20-2: The X-10 XCam 2 wireless video camera and receiver.

Did You Know You may recall X-10 as the folks who brought you those pop-ups on every Web site for almost a year featuring their little video camera.

Determine Where to Place the Camera

Determing where to place the camera depends on what you want to monitor. I suggest putting it on the roof of the passenger compartment, near the front of the car facing back, or on the dash of the car facing back. This should give you enough of an angle to watch for cars bumping into you, doors hitting your sides, and others walking around your car. Of course, having the camera in plain sight may not be the best idea, so having it Velcroed to the roof of the passenger compartment is likely the best place. Since the unit is wireless, you can always remove it when it is not in use, keeping it in the glove compartment, center console, or trunk for when you need it (see Figure 20-3).

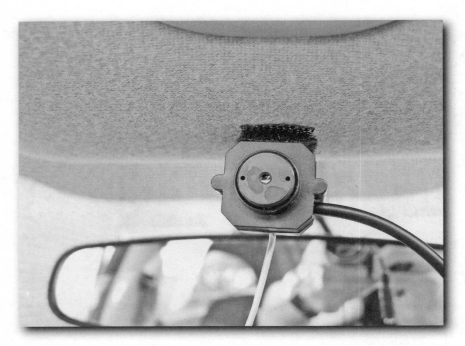

FIGURE 20-3: The New Way Technology camera Velcroed to the roof of the passenger compartment.

Powering the Camera and Receiver

Whether you decide to go with a wireless or wired video solution, both the camera and the video receiver will require some sort of power. Preferably, you want as few wires as possible so you can have more flexibility in camera placement locations. Instead of running power from the AC adapter usually accompanying wireless video solutions, batteries can be used to power both devices.

Wireless cameras and receivers may be powered up for extended times by using 9-volt battery packs with more power than the traditional small rectangular 9-volt battery sold in most stores. Radio Shack and other stores sell *battery holders* (or *battery sleeves*), which accept either 6 AA or 6 C cells and feature the same 9-volt battery snap connector as smaller batteries. The battery pack's snap connector attaches to an adapter that plugs into the device, as shown in Figure 20-4. These offer from 5 to 50 times more battery operating time than standard 9-volt batteries. Also, for shorter operating times, rechargeable 9-volt batteries or special long-life Lithium 9-volt batteries (designed for smoke detectors) can be used.

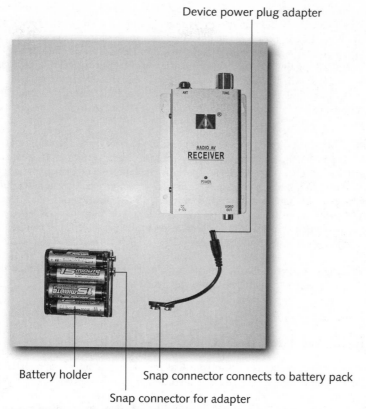

Device power plug adapter

Battery holder   Snap connector connects to battery pack

Snap connector for adapter

FIGURE 20-4: Battery pack with adapter.

Furthermore, by using rechargeable batteries in your battery packs, you can save money and get more battery life in the case of Nickel-Metal Hydride (NiMH) and Lithium Ion (LiIon) recharageables. Rayovac, Duracell, and other battery manufacturers sell rechargeable batteries that charge in 15 minutes or less.

Regarding Portable Digital Video Recorders

You used to have to record video to tape, unless you had an expensive digital camera that could record short clips of video to digital film, such as a SDIO (Secure Digital Input/Output) or CompactFlash card. These days, compact hard drives are inexpensive, and video compression technology has come so far that we can record 80 hours of high-quality video on a single 20-gigabyte hard drive, and hundreds of hours at a lower quality. Many video surveillance systems used in parking garages and other scenarios are starting to move to the disk-based solutions because tapes wear out, have much more limited recording time (the length of the tape, basically), and take forever to review. You can bring this same advantage to your car.

Many consumer electronics companies are releasing personal video recorders, which use a compression technology known as MPEG-4 to compress high-quality video and then record it to a hard drive or memory card. These recorders run anywhere from $249 for the memory-card based ones to $549 for a good 20-gigabyte hard-drive-based solution. In this chapter I will be using the Archos AV400 20-gigabyte pocket video recorder, which runs for over eight hours of recording video and can store over 100 hours of video on its built-in 20-gigabyte hard drive. It can also store music, such as MP3s, Windows Media (WMA), and many others, as well as provide additional storage capacity to any PC you have in your car, all provided through the USB port.

So what about good ol' battery-powered VCRs? Can't you use those? Well, it's not that good of an idea, to be honest. If you try to record to tape in the middle of a hot summer, that tape could warp, melt, jam, and so forth. Hard drives, especially the laptop-type drives that are built into this new generation of personal video recorders, as well as memory cards, can take quite a bit more heat than thin, flexible tape can withstand in its home-use plastic housing. This is especially true with MiniDV tape-based cameras—the last thing you want to do is leave your $1,000 DV camera recording in your car, and DV tape can usually get at most 90 minutes of recording time (and still doesn't hold up well to heat).

 Tip   The MPEG-4 video recorder can also double as a music and video jukebox for having your music collection in your car as well as streaming video to the various screens in your car!

Determine Where to Place the Recorder

The ideal place to mount the recorder is next to your Car PC. The goal here is that, after you have captured video, you can review it on either the recorder, or simply via your Car PC, since the Archos video recorder connects to any PC over USB. By using Velcro to keep the recorder from moving, you can keep it safely hidden under your seat; and when you want to take it with you, just unplug the power and video and take it to the gym, home, or wherever.

What You Need

The following is a list of items you need for this project:

- Wireless video camera and receiver or similar wired or wireless video camera and video receiver (~$79, see the "Choosing the Camera" section earlier in the chapter)
- Archos MPEG-4 AV400 20-gigabyte Pocket Video Recorder (~$549, see Figure 20-5)
- Velcro strips ($7, see Figure 20-6)
- AC inverter to keep the Archos charged when your car is running ($49–$149, depending on whether you will be adding a computer later on—so, 120 watts with no computer or 350 watts with one, unless you already have one installed)

FIGURE 20-5: The Archos AV400 Pocket Video Recorder.

Regular Velcro for
mounting items on floor

Industrial-strength Velcro for
all other mounting locations

FIGURE 20-6: Velcro strips.

Step 1: Measure and Apply Velcro to Video Recorder and Video Receiver

Measure the bottom of the Archos video recorder and wireless video receiver and cut two hook-side Velcro strips to cover two parallel sides of the recorder, and the same for the wireless video receiver, as shown in Figures 20-7, 20-8, and 20-9. You want to have the hook side facing the carpet. The reason you use the hook side is that it usually hooks very well into carpet on cars. If your car does not have carpet, or the hook side of the Velcro doesn't stick well to your carpet, you will want also to apply a same-size strip of Velcro to the floor of your car where you will be placing the recorder.

FIGURE 20-7: The wireless video receiver.

Don't cut Velcro wider than the battery

FIGURE 20-8: The Velcro applied to the video recorder.

FIGURE 20-9: The Velcro applied to the wireless video receiver.

Once the Velcro is applied, mount the recorder and video receiver next to the Car PC, as shown in Figure 20-10. If you don't have a Car PC, make sure the recorder and video receiver are mounted under the seat.

FIGURE 20-10: The video recorder and wireless video receiver placed under the seat next to the Car PC.

Keep the video recorder easily accessible so you can remove it at any time. For example, when you are away on long trips, you may want to take the video recorder with you, especially if it doubles as a media player.

Note I am using the term *video recorder* here in place of *the Archos*, since you may choose a different video recorder.

Caution In hot weather, I suggest that any video recorder with a built-in LCD screeen be kept in as cool an area as possible. These screens are not as resistant to heat extremes as larger LCD entertainment screens and might be damaged (usually darkened) by high heat.

Step 2: Mount the Video Camera

Mount the video camera as discussed under "Determine Where to Place the Camera." Full instructions usually come with wireless video cameras on how to mount them, so follow those instructions, including how to properly insert the battery. Keep in mind that you should keep the battery compartment easily accessible so you can replace it without any fuss. Be mindful that internal batteries tend to supply power for recording for just a few hours at most.

Step 3: Configure the Video Camera and Wireless Video Receiver

Configure the wireless video camera and wireless video receiver per the instructions that came with the devices. You will want to make sure the devices talk on the same channels and that they are not receiving video feeds or interference from nearby sources. The XCam 2 mentioned earlier in "Choosing the Camera" (and some other wireless video cameras) uses the unlicensed 2.4-gigahertz frequency (which means device manufacturers don't have to pay to broadcast over that frequency). Many other devices (such as wireless access points and Bluetooth devices) may be using the same frequencies near you, so make sure you configure and test accordingly.

Step 4: Connect Video Connections from Wireless Video Receiver to Video Recorder

Connect the video output from the wireless video receiver to the video recorder by using the supplied A/V (audio/video) cables, as shown in Figure 20-11.

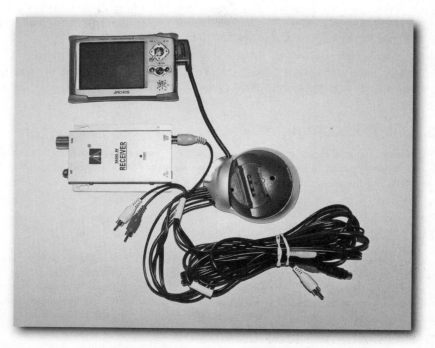

FIGURE 20-11: The video connections to the video recorder from the New Way Technology camera's wireless video receiver.

Step 5: Connect USB from Video Recorder to Computer

Connect the USB from the video recorder to your Car PC, if you have one. This will be useful for reviewing your video without messing around with the video recorder. A USB cable usually comes packed in the box with pocket video recorders. If you didn't get one, just run to your local CompUSA or Best Buy or any other retailer that sells computer equipment and pick one up—they're pretty standard.

Step 6: Run Power from Video Recorder to AC Inverter (Keep It Charged between Rides)

Since you will be running the video recorder unattended and in battery mode, you will want to keep its battery charged between recording sessions. Plug the AC adapter that came with the video recorder into the AC inverter so you can charge the battery while you drive. Another option is to take the video recorder out of your car temporarily and charge it indoors. Because it's just Velcroed in, you should be able to just unplug the video, USB, and power cables; detach it from the carpet and take it out of the car.

Note You may not have enough sockets left on your AC inverter to plug the video recorder in. In this case, buying a small power strip will work just fine—you can find them at any local hardware store, usually with only three plugs. The household appliance extension cords are only about $2 and are also very useful because they are very compact and can take a few transformers without taking up a lot of space. If you do purchase a power strip, though, make sure you buy outlet plugs to cover the unused sockets to keep spilled drinks and other elements out of the power sockets (they run about a buck for a small box).

Warning When placing a power strip in your car, you should mount it upside down (from the seat, for example) or sideways, to minimize water pooling, electrocution, or shock.

Step 7: Start Recording!

Now that everything is plugged in and configured, you can just park your car, turn on the video camera and video recorder, and start recording! Don't forget to turn all the devices off when you are done using them—if their battery is dead, they're no use to you!

Summary

This chapter discussed video surveillance and how to install it in your car using wireless technologies and advanced video recorders that can record many hours of video. Using video surveillance can help you see if people are eyeing your car, hoping to break into it, or determine blame if someone slams their door into your car. It's also fun to use this setup to record road-trips and share them with your friends without keeping the camcorder out. Have fun!

Talking to Your Car's Computer

Approximate project cost: $150

For too many years we geeks have had to bring our cars into the dealership to find out what's wrong. We were somewhat befuddled by our computers being practically incapable of figuring out the problem. Fear no longer! Due to standards across the automotive industry, not only can we diagnose many of our own problems for less than the cost of a few oil changes, but we can also modify many of our engine and other car system settings from the comfort of our graphical user interfaces!

OBD-II and ECU

In the early 1990s there was an industry-wide movement to standardize the method of reporting errors in a car's computer, getting away from proprietary systems that cost dealerships too much money and were too hard to maintain. An industry standard named OBD-II was formed, which stands for On-Board Diagnostics Version 2. All cars made since 1996 have this feature, and an entire market has sprung up to let auto enthusiasts read the "codes" from their car's diagnostics system and figure problems out for themselves. It also gave them proof that the modifications they made to their car were actually *doing* something (other than draining their pocketbooks, of course). With the advent of affordable wireless chipsets and transceivers, OBD Version 3 is in the works, with the ability to read the car's data wirelessly.

Another benefit of OBD-II is that it constantly monitors engine performance and vehicle emissions and ultimately informs drivers when they need to take their car in for repair or emissions tuning. Unfortunately, with OBD-II working in conjunction with your engine control unit (ECU), your car will read the diagnostic information and retune itself appropriately, changing timing, air intake, and so forth to stay within proper thresholds. This has been a problem for auto enthusiasts and their modifications, because over time the system adapts to their performance modifications and tries to bring the car back to its idea of normal. Hence, older ECUs that aren't OBD-II-compliant are in much demand, as are "mod chips" that prevent such automatic adjustments from occurring. You can usually find these solutions discussed in online enthusiast forums for your vehicle and sold on eBay and performance car-tuning stores.

With OBD-II you can:

- Determine engine and car system issues (knocking, bad turbo, and more).
- Clear the Check Engine light.
- Analyze your engine statistics in real-time. ELM v2.0 chips sample at about 10 times per second, whereas earlier versions only sampled at 1 to 3 times per second (rated as hertz in some ODB-II applications).

Elm Electronics (`www.elmelectronics.com`) makes many of the chipsets used in OBD-II scanning solutions.

- Tune your performance when racing (commercial package Digimoto does this in real-time).
- See analog guages and watch your vehicle speed (miles per hour and kilometers per hour) and RPMs.
- Download great diagnostic utilities for free—such as the software from ScanTool.net (knows the definitions of many codes) and ScanMaster (very nice interface and allows you to record multiple car sessions). Many more software packages are listed in Table 21-2 and in Appendix C, "Additional Resources."
- Determine fuel efficiency (GameCube increased load by 3%, AC 2% to 3%).
- Clear your engine's trouble codes (a boon for performance enthusiasts testing their modifications).
- And do much, much more!

Be forewarned! Tampering with some "locked" connectors may affect or nullify your car lease or warranty. Unfortunately, some auto manufacturers don't want you tweaking your car's settings or doing your own diagnostics. Manufacturers such as Ford and Mercedes are either already installing or contemplating placing hardware-locking devices over the OBD ports in their vehicles. Of course, this has nothing to do with money for service centers—they say it's to preserve quality (yeah, right).

Controller Area Network (CAN)

Just when you thought it was going to be easy, I've gotta give you the bad news—there's a competitor to OBD-II (and the eventual OBD-III). CAN, or *Controller Area Network*, solutions run through the existing OBD-II interface ports and offer much more access to the workings of your car's various system modules. This technology is appearing in modern vehicles as their computing capabilities become more powerful. CAN systems have started appearing in 2003 model years and later and are a possible replacement for OBD-II. CAN was originally developed by Bosch and has become another car diagnostic standard. The latest version as of the writing of this book was CAN 2.0.

The following car makes are starting to require CAN-compatible interfaces:

- Ford
- General Motors (GM)
- Jaguar
- Mazda
- Mercedes
- Nissan
- Porsche
- Toyota

CAN software interfaces exist for PCs, as well as for Palm and PocketPC devices. One of popular CAN-compatible tool is *AutoEnginuity*, which also works with OBD-II systems. AutoEnginuity is a commercial product, unlike many of the free OBD-II tools out there, running for about $229 from www.autoenginuity.com, plus another $60 for their CAN Expansion interface.

In this chapter I will focus on OBD-II because of its widespread hardware and software availability and the fact that the tools are both free and very capable. If you would like to research the CAN specification, you can find information at www.can.bosch.com. The Equipment and Tool Institute's Web site also has a listing of vehicles implementing CAN interfaces, available at http://etools.org.

No Car PC Required

You don't have to have a computer in your car to diagnose problems. Although it's very cool to have the OBD-II interface built-into your car, a laptop is just as usable. So in this chapter you will build an OBD-II interface that you can keep in or out of your car, letting you score points with your friends as you diagnose problems with their cars while wowing them with the cool software showing your car doing all sorts of stuff while you drive.

Also, since OBD-II is so prevalent, you don't even have to have a computer to read any diagnostic codes. Many automotive supply stores have portable (internal embedded computer) OBD-II readers that read your codes and present them on a small screen. Often you will have to look up the code descriptions on the Internet, but I don't want you to be turned off from diagnosing your car just because you don't have a laptop or Car PC. Appendix C, "Additional Resources," has a complete listing of auto manufacturers' Web sites you can research your car's codes on.

 Just because you've read the diagnostic codes from your car's computer, that doesn't mean you should try fixing your car yourself. If you aren't a mechanic and don't want to void your warranty, be very careful taking action based on your car's output. It's the same as assuming you can cure yourself without a doctor's help just because you used a thermometer.

Finding the Right OBD-II Interface for Your Car

Not all cars take the same OBD-II interface. There are three primary types: ISO (the most common), VPW, and PWM. Fortunately, there are OBD-II interfaces for all three types of interfaces, and they are all relatively inexpensive. In this project you will find an appropriate interface board and enclosure and put it together.

Appendix D, "Vehicle OBD-II Interface Types," contains a list of cars and their appropriate interfaces. If yours is not listed, you should look online, ask a car enthusiast group, or check with your dealer. If you don't see your car in the list, oftentimes a car from the same manufacturer and model year will use the same interface. You should still double-check, of course.

Building and Using an OBD-II Reader

The OBD-II interface, once connected to a computer, provides real-time diagnostics covering many aspects of your car. You do not need a computer in your car in order to use OBD-II, but you will need a computer available to use the software I will mention later in this chapter. Basically this means you will be able to use the interface inside or outside of your car. In this section you will build the interface (see the preceding section to determine which one you need) and use it to measure codes in your computer.

What You Will Need

- An OBD-II interface board with appropriate cables (~$79 + shipping and handling from ScanTool.net, www.scantool.net). See "Finding the Right OBD-II Interface for Your Car" earlier in this chapter.

- An OBD-II interface board enclosure (~$40 + shipping and handling from ScanTool.net). You can also build your own enclosure if you are so inclined. I originally made one out of a wooden box from a local crafts shop that I Dremeled to fit the interface board. The ScanTool.net enclosure, however, is much better looking, more rigid, and fits the interface board perfectly.

- An available RS-232 serial port on your computer. If you don't have a serial port, you can use a USB adapter, such as the Belkin USB PDA Adapter or the KeySpan USB PDA Adapter for about $20–$30. Note that some USB-to-serial adapters have issues communicating with OBD-II due to power fluctuations over the serial interface.

- If you are going to use your PDA with the OBD-II interface, make sure you buy the appropriate connector from the OBD-II interface board provider for connecting to your PDA.

 Note You can buy multiple interface boards for the three different OBD-II interface types and swap them out of the enclosure so you can work on different types of cars. You could also buy a couple more enclosures and just have the different OBD readers available for use on the different interface types when you need them. This really helps you score points with your friends!

 Note The ScanTool.net systems use the ELMscan chipsets. You can buy the chipsets and build the interface board(s) yourself by visiting ELM on the Web at www.elmelectronics.com. ScanTool.net also has an excellent resource page for building your own interfaces and even writing your own software to talk to those interfaces at www.scantool.net/resources.htm.

Building the Interface

Once you have the individual components, all you need to do is put the interface board into the enclosure. If you did not buy the enclosure from ScanTool.net, you can build your own interface board as I described above by Dremeling a wooden box from a local crafts store or screwing the interface board to a piece of wood (although the enclosure from ScanTool is just plain awesome). See Figure 21-1 for my original reader that I placed into my own enclosure and Figure 21-2 that shows the ScanTool product.

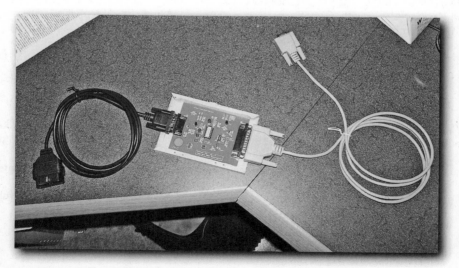

FIGURE 21-1: My jerry-rigged reader mounted inside a wooden craft box.

FIGURE 21-2: My jerry-rigged reader moved to the ScanTool enclosure.

Connecting the Interface

The location of the OBD-II interface varies by vehicle make and model. If you check online with your dealer or with an auto enthusiast group, you will find out where the interface is. Many resources are available to help you find this information in Appendix C, "Additional Resources."

Does My Car Need to Be Turned On or Started to Use the OBD-II Interface?

Many cars do not need to be started to use their OBD-II diagnostics interface. You will likely be able to just plug the OBD-II cable into your car's OBD-II port and the other end into your laptop, launch your OBD-II scanning software, and be able to start looking at codes. Of course, if you car isn't turned on or the engine isn't running, you won't be able to get certain diagnostic information, such as engine RPMs, speedometer readings, and so forth. Furthermore, if you have the interface plugged into your Car PC, you will need your car running anyway to use the computer with the OBD-II interface.

What If My OBD-II Interface Is Locked?

As I mentioned earlier, some manufacturers put physical locks on the OBD-II interface to prevent you from jacking in. Unfortunately, you may be out of luck if this is the case. However, you may be able to find a solution online or from an enthusiast group to get around the locking mechanism on the port. Once you're in, though, you shouldn't have to worry about anything else, such as passwords or the like, because OBD-II software often isn't locked down (although it's possible some auto manufacturers may change this at any time in the future).

Finding OBD-II Software to Work on Your Car and Measure Diagnostics

You have a number of options when it comes to using your OBD-II interface. Whether it's the nitty-gritty of using a direct connection and HyperTerminal, a free program from the Internet, or a commercial package, there's an entire industry out there to support you and your OBD-II endeavors.

Communicating with the OBD-II Interface with a Terminal Program

You don't even need an OBD-II program to talk to your car's computer with the reader you just built. Using the HyperTerminal program that comes with all versions of Windows, you can connect directly to your interface and start issuing commands, just as if you were at a DOS command prompt. Although the full graphical applications out there are much more robust, and you don't have to remember any commands, it's a lot of fun issuing commands and having your car respond to your every whim (*oh the power, the absolute power!*)

Configuring HyperTerminal

Before you talk to your car's computer via HyperTerminal, connect your OBD-II reader to your car's OBD-II port and to your computer's serial port. After you have done this, you are ready to connect to your car's computer with HyperTerminal. HyperTerminal can be found by clicking on the Start menu and then going to System, Accessories, Communications, HyperTerminal.

1. When you open HyperTerminal, you will be prompted to make a new connection and to give it a description, as shown in Figure 21-3. Click OK.

FIGURE 21-3: The new connection description in
HyperTerminal.

2. Name the description **OBD-II Interface** since that's what you are building a connection to. Click OK.

3. You will then be presented the Connect To window, as shown in Figure 21-4. You don't need to enter the country/region, area code, or phone number information. However, for "Connect using:" select the port your serial cable is plugged into, which is usually COM1. Click OK.

FIGURE 21-4: Selecting COM1 as the
interface.

4. You will next be presented with the serial port properties window, usually called COM1 Properties (this will be named differently if you selected a port other than COM1). Change the settings to:

- Bits per second: **9600**

- Data bits: **8**

- Parity: **N**

- Stop bits: **1**

- Flow control: **None**

The screen will look like Figure 21-5. Click OK.

FIGURE 21-5: COM1 properly configured.

5. Your computer will now attempt to connect to your OBD-II reader. After a quick moment you should be presented with the ELM command prompt, which acts as the intermediary between you and your car's computer.

Sending Commands via the ELM Command Prompt

Now that you are connected you can start issuing commands via the ELM interface to your car's computer. There are nine standard OBD-II commands, named 01 through 09, that you can issue, not all of which are necessarily implemented by your car's manufacturer. Your car's manufacturer may also have custom commands that have a number greater than 09. The standard commands are shown in Table 21-1.

Table 21-1   ELM Commands

Code	Description
01	Show current data. This is real-time data coming from your engine, such as tachometer readings and intake temperatures. All OBD-II software packages translate this information into human-readable formats so you don't have to decipher all of your engine's codes.
02	Show freeze-frame data. This information has been in the press quite a bit since it contains information an insurance company could use to deny a claim, such as the speed your vehicle was traveling at before the air bag deployed.
03	Show stored trouble codes. These are the codes defining issues with your car's engine and other systems. Many OBD-II applications, both freeware and commercial, have databases that translate many of these codes into English. However, you may need to look online to find or verify codes presented to you.
04	Clear trouble codes and stored values. If you clear these, your engine may run fairly rough while your car recalibrates itself.
05	Test results, oxygen sensors.
06	Test results, noncontinuously monitored. These are results from system tests that aren't constantly being run.
07	Show pending trouble codes.
08	Special control mode.
09	Request vehicle information.

Downloading Free Software for Your OBD-II Interface

You don't need to spend any money getting software that lets you do almost anything with OBD-II. There are many free software packages out there that tell you what the codes mean, provide real-time statistics of your car's engine and systems, and much more. You will find many uses for the information, too many to be covered in a single chapter.

The two best free programs for Car PCs and Windows laptops I've found are ScanTool from ScanTool.net (www.scantool.net) and ScanMaster from Wladmir Gurskij (www.wgsoft.de/).

ScanTool's strengths include a detailed database of error codes and a very small footprint. ScanTool's source code is also available on their Web site so you can write your own OBD-II software based on their code. ScanTool is available for DOS (!!!), Windows, and Linux and has been translated into many languages. You can see the ScanTool interface in action in Figure 21-6.

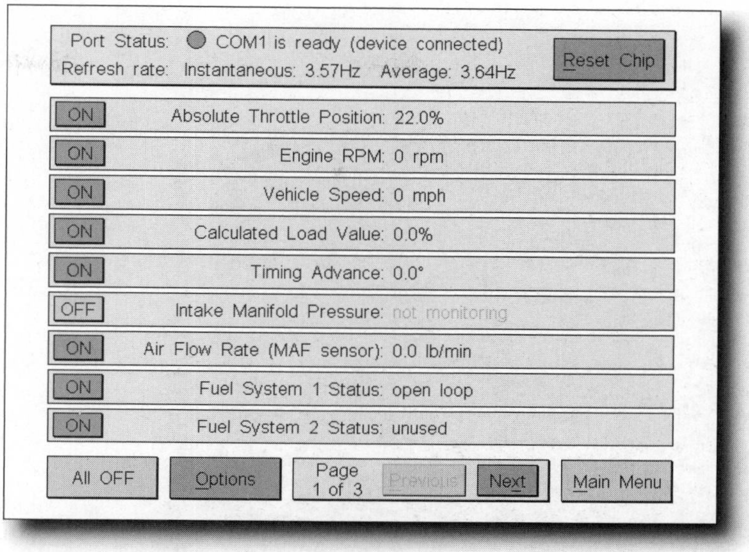

Port Status: ● COM1 is ready (device connected)		
Refresh rate: Instantaneous: 3.57Hz Average: 3.64Hz		Reset Chip

ON	Absolute Throttle Position: 22.0%
ON	Engine RPM: 0 rpm
ON	Vehicle Speed: 0 mph
ON	Calculated Load Value: 0.0%
ON	Timing Advance: 0.0°
OFF	Intake Manifold Pressure: not monitoring
ON	Air Flow Rate (MAF sensor): 0.0 lb/min
ON	Fuel System 1 Status: open loop
ON	Fuel System 2 Status: unused

All OFF	Options	Page 1 of 3	Previous	Next	Main Menu

FIGURE 21-6: ScanTool.net's ScanTool software.

ScanMaster is available only for Windows 95 and above and features a more modern interface than ScanTool. ScanMaster provides an analog guage mode where you can see a speedometer and tachometer updating themselves while you drive based on what the engine is saying. This is useful for seeing how accurate your speedometer is, and is also just way cool to look at, as you can see in Figure 21-7. ScanMaster also lets you set up and save profiles for multiple cars, so you can track information from various cars you use the product on, a real boon for auto enthusiasts and aspiring mechanics.

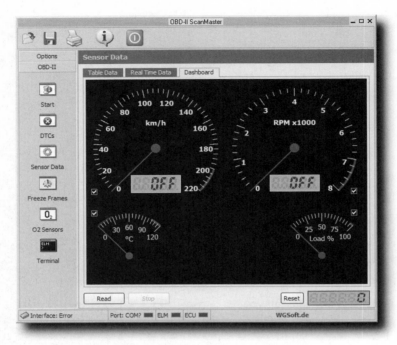

FIGURE 21-7: ScanMaster's analog gauge interface.

There are many other free software packages available for many different computing platforms. Table 21-2 shows a list of are some of them, sorted by computing platform, and with the URL for where the software can downloaded.

Table 21-2   ODB-II Software Packages

Platform	Package	URL
Apple Macintosh	pyOBD for Mac OS X, by Donour Sizemore	http://kentuck.spc. uchicago.edu/cars/pyobd/
DOS	Diagnose	www.obddiagnostics.com/ program.html
ScanTool	ScanTool.net	www.scantool.net/software/ scantool.net/index.shtml
Linux	FreeDiag	http://sourceforge.net/ projects/freediag

Platform	Package	URL
Palm OS	OBD Gauge by Dana Peters	`www.qcontinuum.org/obdgauge/`
Perl	OBD Logger by Jonathan Senkerik	`http://pages.infinit.net/jsenk/obd_Perl.htm`
Pocket PC	OBD Gauge by Dana Peters	`www.qcontinuum.org/obdgauge/`
ScanTest	by Ivan Ganev	`www.geocities.com/a_ser_files/`
Windows	Diagnose for Windows	`www.obddiagnostics.com/ProgWin.html`
GM	Mode 22	`http://ca.geocities.com/t_kolody/Scantool_V0.1.zip`
OBD-II	ScanMaster	`www.wgsoft.de/`
OBD Logger	by Jonathan Senkerik	`http://pages.infinit.net/jsenk/obd_Win.htm`
OBD-II	For ELM322 by David Huffman	`www.geocities.com/huffyfire/obd2/index.html`
RDDTC	by Pete Calinski	`http://home.adelphia.net/%7Epjcalinski/RDDTCd.htm`
wOBD 1.4	by OBD2Crazy	`www.obd2crazy.com/software.html`

Commercial Software Solutions

Although the free packages are good for most consumers, commercial software packages offer a number of well-tested, necessary features for auto enthusiasts. OBD-II can be used for tracking engine torque, timing quarter miles and 0-to-60 times, dyno statistics, data logging, on-board test information, sensor readings, diagnosing engine misfires, and so forth—all critical information for enthusiasts modifying their cars and wanting to make sure they're getting what they want out of often-expensive modifications.

Commercial software packages also offer you the benefit of upgrades and a support team that keeps the database of vehicle diagnostic codes up-to-date. Commercial software also may have fewer bugs than personal projects offered for free by enthusiasts who happen to know how to code, but there is no guarantee that a commercial package will be any more reliable than a free package or one that you write yourself.

There are many packages to choose from. Your needs will vary, so searching the Internet for commercial packages and their reviews, or checking with a local auto enthusiast group and possibly even your car dealer will help you make the right decision.

Vehicle manufacturers are also getting into the OBD-II craze by offering subscriptions to specialized Web sites that provide diagnostic codes and even software you can download for interfacing with your car. Check with your car dealer for information on whether you can get a subscription for your car.

Here is a sampling of popular commercial packages, some of which include the OBD-II scanner. Most of these can be purchased online or via an authorized auto parts dealer.

- AutoEnginuity for Windows, $229, www.autoenginuity.com
- DigiMoto for Windows, $120 with OBD-II Scanner, $49 without www.digimoto.com
- AutoTap for Palm OS and Windows, $200 www.autotap.com
- Auto X-Ray EZ-PC (comes with their EZ-Scan 6000 OBD-II scanner), $700 www.autoxray.com

Additional Resources

There are a number of places on the Internet where you can find more information on OBD-II and discuss your experiences with others. You will find a forum on the official *Geek My Ride* Web site, of course. Other resources include:

- ScanTool.net Forum (covers OBD-II use, software, hardware, specific manufacturers) http://scantool.net/forum/index.php
- OBD-II.com (forums, shopping tips, reference books) www.obdii.com/
- ECI Multi Forum (covers ECU ROM modifications and engine computer hacks) www.ecimulti.org/phorum/

Most auto manufacturers provide Web sites for finding vehicle service information, such as wiring diagrams and diagnostic codes. A complete list of auto manufacturers' Web sites is located in Appendix C, "Additional Resources." There you will also find links to more OBD-II software, online forums, and more.

Summary

In this chapter you learned how to talk to your car's computer, diagnose trouble codes, and find information to become your own service technician. Oftentimes if you find the problem yourself, you can go to your dealer with a better idea of what to expect for extensive repairs, or you can be better prepared to challenge a bill should some false need for service be listed. If you decide to modify your car, many of the tips in this chapter should help you test your modifications and make sure you are getting the performance you were expecting.

LED Message Displays

chapter

22

in this chapter

- ☑ Choosing an LED display
- ☑ Properly mounting an LED display
- ☑ Determining when and where an LED display is appropriate

Approximate project cost: $250

A popular trick for a vehicle is the ability to flash or scroll a message for passerby's to see. In this chapter you will learn how to install a scrolling LED message display in a vehicle, including the caveats.

Not Ideal for All Cars

LED message displays are cool, and they can serve practical purposes located in trucks, buses, vans, and other numerous passenger transit vehicles. However, not all vehicles were made to have scrolling displays mounted in them. For example, my Dodge SRT-4's wing gets in the way of the display being visible and for all intents and purposes would serve to distract other drivers rather than providing any real entertainment value. This chapter's project is intended for use in show cars that aren't driven on roads, or vehicles where a flashing, scrolling display is allowed, which will vary from state to state and from purpose to purpose.

Know the Laws!

Should you install the LED display in your car, beware of the laws in your area, town, city, county, or state (possibly even regional or federal laws). An LED display is very distracting. If you were to flash "Do you have any Grey Poupon?" from your car and another driver was watching and barreled into another vehicle, you may be at fault. Your state may also disallow use of any such message display without a special permit, or forbid them altogether on public roads. Although a computer display is not very visible, and it is unlikely that many officers are looking to pull over people with compuer displays in their vehicles unless they're driving unsafely, a flashing LED display will quickly attract attention, possibly a ticket, and your display could potentially be confiscated (or your entire car, if the officer cannot remove it)!

Determine Where to Mount the Display

The most popular positions for LED displays tend to be near the back or side windows of a vehicle. In some instances they are located in the front, but the mounting for the front is similar to a rear-mounted solution. Figure 22-1 shows suggested mounting locations for vehicles. In the next section I will discuss how to properly secure the LED display.

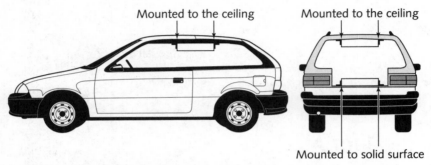

FIGURE 22-1: Suggested mounting locations in a vehicle.

Secure the Display Well

Since these displays tend to be mounted to windows or in the back of the car, and because they tend to be large (although usually not too heavy), a sudden heavy application of your brakes could send the display hurling through the car, injuring or even killing passengers (including the driver, causing an even more dangerous situation). It is imperative that when you add an LED display, or any other large object, to your car, you securely bolt it down to prevent movement—do not Velcro it in place or apply suction cups.

You can find appropriate equipment, such as the L-bracket mounting brackets and groove mounts shown in Figure 22-2, at your local hardware store. The L-brackets screw into the sides of the display and then into the surface below or above the display's mounting surface. The groove mounts are screwed into the same surface, but not into the display—they are used for extra support to prevent the display from moving back and forth, while the L-brackets prevent it from moving from side-to-side and keep it mounted. Many displays also include mounts that you can use to securely screw the display into place. Figure 22-3 shows suggested areas for making mounting screwholes in your display in case it does not already have them.

L-bracket mounting brackets go on
either side of the display

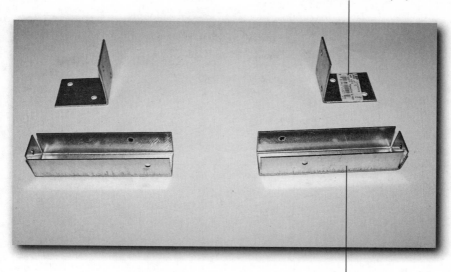

Groove brackets go on the left and right of the display to keep
it from moving. The end pieces may need to be flattened, since
otherwise they will interfere with the L-brackets.

FIGURE 22-2: L-bracket mounting brackets and groove mounts for securing the display.

Warning

If you're traveling 70 miles per hour and you slam the brakes on, which causes the display to fly toward the front of the car—the display is also going to be traveling close to 70 miles per hour ! Ouch!

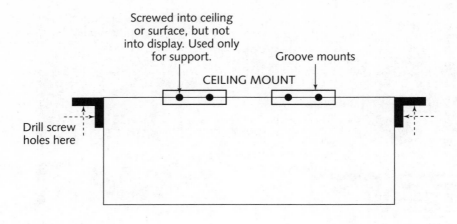

Screwed into ceiling or surface, but not into display. Used only for support.

Groove mounts

CEILING MOUNT

Drill screw holes here

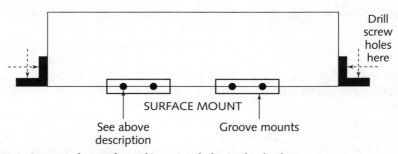

Drill screw holes here

SURFACE MOUNT

See above description

Groove mounts

FIGURE 22-3: Suggested areas for making screwholes in the display.

Choosing a Display

Many LED displays are the same. There are few made specifically for cars, but you can pick one up at practically any office store or wholesaler, such as Sam's Club or Costco, for under $200. The Beta Brite product (see Figure 22-4) I chose is very capable, lightweight, and comes with a keyboard and PC software for programming the display with and without a PC.

FIGURE 22-4: The Beta Brite Electronic Message Display.

What You Need

Here is a list of items you need for this project:

- An LED display, such as the Beta Brite Electronic Message Display ($159)

- Optionally, a Car PC to run the display configuration software (although a keyboard comes with the Beta Brite and with many other display products)

- An AC inverter of at least 120 watts, if you don't already have one, to power the display ($49)

- A household power extension cable as shown in Figure 22-5, in case the power cable from the display doesn't reach ($2)

- Outlet plugs for unused power sockets, as shown in Figure 22-6 ($1 for a small box of them)

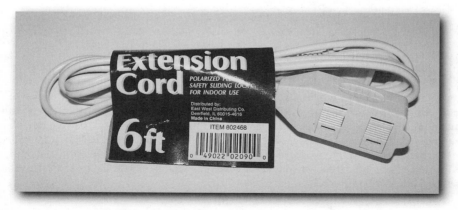

FIGURE 22-5: A household power extension cable.

FIGURE 22-6: Outlet plugs for the household power extension cable.

- An appropriate screwdriver for the mounts that come with the display (prices will vary depending on the included mounts, and you should already have screwdrivers if you're reading this book!)
- Optionally, mounting brackets, to secure the display into the back of your vehicle ($7–$20, depending on how many you need—look at your display to determine this)

Step 1: Install the Display

Install the display into your car, taking care to mount the display solidly onto whatever surface it will sit on top of or hang from. If your display doesn't have mounting holes or come with mounting brackets, you will need to Dremel or drill the holes into the display (be careful not to go to deep because you can damage the circuitry) and attach the L-brackets (mounting brackets) to the display and to the surface in the car. Do *not* Velcro the display or use suction cups. Also, do *not* attach the display to any surface that can flip up, such as the back of a hatchback vehicle with the flip-up cover for the trunk.

Step 2: Run Power from the Display

Run the power cable from the display to an available AC power socket, such as one on your AC inverter, one built into your car, or one on a household extension plug similar to the one in Figure 22-5.

 Don't run the LED display for long periods of time while the car is not running. This will only drain your battery, and you don't want to come back to a car that won't start!

Step 3: Install the PC Software (Optional)

Some LED message displays come with PC software that lets you program the display from a computer in addition to the included configuration keyboard. If you have a Car PC, you should install this software so you can easily set up the display from your Car PC. Any laptop can be used for convenient programming of the display as well.

Step 4: Set the Message

This step is pretty straightforward—read the manual on how to configure the display and set the message. Each display has different capabilities, but most are easy to configure and support many colors and animations.

Step 5: Test!

Now that your display is configured, test it!

Summary

This chapter discussed how to install and mount an LED message display in a vehicle. I do not suggest that you place one of these in a car for use while you drive—it will distract other drivers and may cause a serious accident, injuring or killing passengers in both vehicles. LED message displays are meant for show cars on show floors, or where permitted in specific scenarios, such as tour vehicles, commuter buses, and so forth.

Installing Wireless Headphones

Approximate project cost: $600

There are times where you want peace and quiet while your passengers want to listen to music. Whether it's thumping sound or some hot new DVD release, wireless headphones let those in the car enjoy audio while you concentrate on the road. This chapter will cover how to choose and install a wireless headphones solution. Keep in mind that headphones should *be worn only by passengers*, because drivers need to hear oncoming cars, ambulances, and so forth (oh yeah, it's illegal in many states to wear headphones while driving).

Buying from an Auto Performance Store

Multiple-source wireless solutions are usually available only from higher-end audio stores and automotive supply dealers. Look in your yellow pages for companies that specialize in in-car audio. Retail chains such as Best Buy and Circuit City may have a limited selection you can choose from, but for the full gamut you'll want a car-audio specialty store.

Will You Have Single or Multiple Audio Sources?

Depending on how you want to set it up, you can have wireless headphones that support a single audio feed, or *channel*, where every passenger using the headphones listens to the same feed; or you can have multiple audio channels, where each passenger can choose which audio feed they want to listen to (say, a DVD, MP3, or a CD). All of this depends on how much you really want to spend. Both solutions are easy to implement—the multiple-source solution just requires more cables and a more advanced audio switcher, and possibly a distribution amplifier. Both solutions will usually be available at the store you decide to purchase your solution from.

Infrared and Radio Frequency Solutions

There are two types of wireless headphones you can buy: IR, or *infrared*; and RF, or *radio frequency* (which includes new Bluetooth-compatible headphones). Infrared solutions use beams of light to transmit the audio feed from a *transmitter* to a *receiver* on the headphones. Because infrared uses light, the receiver must be in view of the transmitter in order for the signals to reach it. You've seen this before with infrared remote controls in your home—if someone walks in front of the remote while you change the channel, it doesn't work. The same goes for IR headphones—they won't work if the transmitter is covered. Infrared solutions have the highest audio quality due to their high bandwidth and the sheer amount of investment in the industry in IR solutions. Although they are the solution of choice for automotive wireless audio installs, there are a few drawbacks:

■ The IR transmitter needs to be installed on the roof of the car (on the inside of course), as shown in Figure 23-1.

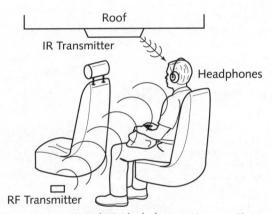

FIGURE **23-1: IR and RF ideal placement suggestions.**

■ Infrared is light, so if it's very bright outside and you don't have tinted windows, your headphones may not work. In this case, you may have to shell out for tinted windows.

■ Infrared light won't work in a convertible (well, maybe at night, and if you put the transmitter in the seats, and . . . well, it's not worth it).

Did You Know

Infrared keeps your music *private*. If you commute to work in heavy traffic or travel on vacation on congested roadways, your music will be loud and clear, whereas RF solutions can be affected by other vehicles' RF systems as they pass or cruise along with you.

The alternative technology to use is an RF solution, which doesn't have to be line-of-sight and is easy to place—you can hide the transmitter anywhere in your car. Although you may ask yourself "What about Bluetooth?," it's really just another RF technology, so you can decide whether you want to pay the extra money for a Bluetooth logo (personally, I don't think it's worth it unless you're going to use it with a PC).

The majority of professionals I've spoken with say to go with an IR solution because of the better audio quality, even though it's line of sight. Whichever one you decide to install, it won't affect the installation instructions that follow, because the actual installation of the wireless audio transmitter will be different depending on which manufacturer's product you purchase. Figure 23-1 shows the difference between IR and RF in a wireless transmission scenario and ideal places to install the two setups.

Note that regardless of whether you buy an IR or RF solution, you can purchase entire packages that have everything you need to do an install. One of the leading providers of wireless headphones is UnWired Technology, and their entire lineup can be found at www.unwiredtechnology.com. In addition to wireless headphones, UnWired sells a complete line of wireless audio solutions for cars.

Caution Make sure you purchase a *stereo* audio transmitter; some are only monaural! Pay very close attention to the product description before you buy!

Choose Whether to Install This Yourself

Installing the wireless audio transmitter for the headphones usually involves mounting the IR or RF transmitter into the roof of your vehicle, either via glue or screws. In all other chapters we were able to cut and pry in places passengers didn't see, but here you may have a solution where if you make a mistake it may be very visible indeed! It may be worth the extra couple hundred dollars to have a professional at the retailer install the solution—not because of your skill level but because they have to fix and pay for any mistakes out of *their* pockets. (And fixing car upholstery can be expensive!)

Note Some IR transmitters can be hidden inside of existing dome and courtesy lights. When shopping for solutions, see if you can find this type of solution to keep your transmitter as invisible as possible.

Don't Forget the Power!

Wireless audio solutions obviously require power. If the solution you choose doesn't use your cigarette lighter port (sometimes called the AC plug port), it will likely want to connect directly to the battery. Refer to Chapter 3, "Giving Your Creation Life: Power Considerations" for a project that brings a barrier terminal switch into your car where you can connect these types of devices to your battery from the inside of your car!

What You Need

The following is a list of items you need for this project:

- A wireless audio transmitter and headphone solution (varies, $200–$1000+), such as the Unwired Technology F3T-M05 three-source stereo RF audio transmitter (see Figure 23-2) and F0H-11099 three-source headphones (see Figure 23-3).

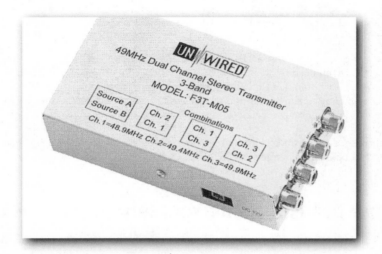

FIGURE **23-2: The F3T-M05 stereo three-source wireless audio transmitter.**

Note Many IR headphones are compatible with other IR audio transmitters, so you can usually mix and match your transmitter with multiple headphone brands and save money!

- An audio switcher (if it doesn't come with the tranmitter; $29, just use an audio/video switch).

- A power solution (see Chapter 3).

- An audio source (such as a DVD player or a Game Cube).

- Monster cable (or similar zero-loss noise-resistant audio cables) for each audio source you want to run to the transmitter ($30–$50 each).

- Batteries (for the headphones, $10) Note that batteries left in a hot car interior may have a very short lifetime or be totally dead the next time you plan to enjoy them.

FIGURE 23-3: The F0H-11099 three-source RF
headphones.

Install the Wireless Headphone System

The next sections walk you through the installation of a wireless headphone system.

Step 1: Install the Transmitter per Instructions

This step should be fairly straightforward. For optimal placement, follow the instructions that came with the solution you purchased. This will vary depending on whether you purchased an IR solution (which must be line-of-sight with the headphones to work) or an RF solution (which can be Velcroed under the seat). IR solutions, which are usually roof-mounted, will come with mounting screws (preferred) or Velcro for mounting the device on the roof of the passenger compartment.

Step 2: Run Power Cables per Transmitter Instructions

Your transmitter's instructions should also include how to power the device. If it requires a direct connection to your battery, follow the instructions in Chapter 3. If it requires an AC adapter, you will need an inverter solution, which is also described in Chapter 3. If the system is battery-powered (the headphones will be, of course, but we're talking about the transmitter here), make sure you have batteries!

Step 3: Install an A/V Switch (Optional)

If you are installing more than one A/V (audio/video) device, such as a computer and a Game Cube, you will likely need an A/V switch so you can switch the different audio sources with your stereo's auxilliary audio input. So why use an A/V switch when you're only switching audio? The A/V switch will allow you to use your display with multiple gaming systems if you decide to add them, as well as switch between your audio from your computer and your games. The A/V switch can also let you listen to music from your computer while your video is fed to video displays in the back seat, which usually will have their own A/V switch built in.

If you are going to have multiple audio and video sources, the audio splitter that comes with wireless audio transmitters won't be worthwhile. One excellent and portable A/V switch is the MadCatz solution shown in Figure 23-4, which you can buy at practically any retail store, such as Best Buy, CompUSA, and GameStop. After you have installed the A/V switch (one idea is having the switch under the emergency brake and then running the breakout box under the seat near all the other A/V device wires, as shown in Figure 23-4), you will need your A/V switch's audio output to go to a separate stereo audio one-way to two-way splitter (about $20) or, if you are using multiple video displays, a *distribution amplifier* (about $50), as shown in Figure 23-5. One output from the splitter or distribution amplifier should be run to your car's head unit (stereo) or audio transmitter for your stereo, and the other to your wireless headphones audio transmitter's audio input.

Note This step requires an additional purchase of a distribution amplifier and one additional set of Monster (or similar) stereo audio cables, as well as another set of Monster (or similar) audio cables for each additional A/V device you are connecting. Figure 23-5 is an example of a distribution amplifier available from Radio Shack.

Step 3: Run Audio Source(s) to the Transmitter

Run the audio sources to the transmitter. Some IR transmitters support another RF audio breakout box that can be hidden under the seat where all the audio sources connect and then wirelessly transmits to the IR transmitter for transmitting to passengers. RF-only solutions skip the IR transmitter, of course, and transmit directly from one box.

FIGURE 23-4: The installed A/V switch.

Step 4: Configure Headphones (Don't Forget the Batteries!)

Configure the headphones per the instructions that came with your solution. This includes setting the appropriate channel if you are going with an RF solution.

Step 5: Play!

Not too hard—test to make sure your audio works. Try switching sources (if you have more than one) and make sure it works. If it doesn't, first check to make sure power is running—usually pretty obvious (is the power light on the transmitter on or off, and are there batteries in the receiving headphones). Second, make sure all of your wiring and cables are tight—see Chapter 5, "Working with Cables," for more information on cabling and making sure everying is well-connected.

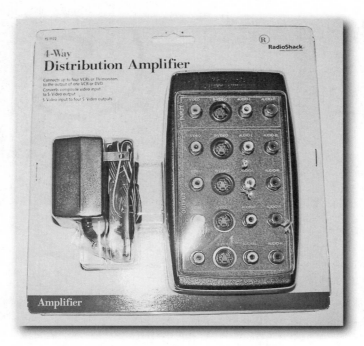

FIGURE 23-5: A distribution amplifier from Radio Shack.

Tip If you are using an IR source, make sure to do your testing while exposed to bright sunlight. When an IR transmitter competes with too strong a sun beam or reflected light, the result can be an annoying "rush" or noise—or outright silence.

Summary

In this chapter you installed a wireless audio transmitter and the associated headphones for it. Keep in mind that the headphones should be worn only by passengers, *not by the driver!*

Legal Concerns

Although the projects in this book are fun and cool, legal concerns abound as the legal system starts trying to catch up with technology. For example, GPS systems constantly updating in front of the driver and in-dash DVD players readily available can all lead to what the legal system calls *distracted driving*. It used to be a generic term that meant you weren't paying attention to the road and was a ticketable offense. Some cities and counties and, rarely, the entire state, have graduated to covering the use of cell phones, PDAs, and handheld computers (including Game Boy and other similar devices) while driving a car (at least, Chicago and Washington, D.C., passed these laws in 2003 and 2004).

Now legislators are eyeing video-capable devices. These tickets have generally been written after traffic accidents have occurred rather than as the result of drivers being pulled over just for having a video display in their cars. Nonetheless, although it's likely that police officers have better things to do than watch for screens in cars, it is best to know which states have which laws governing the use of video-capable devices in vehicles. Some manufacturers, such as Alpine, are actually disabling their in-dash video display screens while a car is in motion (buyer beware)!

In this appendix I will go over many representative states based on my research. Given that this is a book, I obviously can't update it as quickly as a Web site. I will try to keep everything up-to-date on the *Geek My Ride* Web site at www.carhacks.net (or www.wiley.com/go/extremetech), but I would also suggest verifying with your state legislature if you want the most current info. Keep in mind that every state legislature has a research department. If you're looking for information, call your state legislature and ask for that department—they usually even have a library and people who will look up legal information for you at no charge!

The Four Types of Laws

In my research I discovered that since most states are just starting to catch up with car technology, there are four general types of legislation covering computers and video devices in cars.

- **Type 1**—States with actual laws banning use of video and computer displays. These laws specifically cover real-time video displays, where displays can be placed in a vehicle, and so forth.

- **Type 2**—States with laws banning television reception and viewing. These laws usually cover any device that receives television signals and displays them in a moving vehicle. Some of these laws were enacted as far back as 1949!

- **Type 3**—States with laws only covering distracted driving. These laws are the generics of the bunch, with lots of room for interpretation, and often grouped together with driving while intoxicated.

- **Type 4**—States with no apparent law applying to displays in vehicles.

For the states without Type 1 legislation, many of those states are considering enacting such legislation based on the number of accidents in the last few years where a video device and distraction contributed to a fatal accident. Watch out, the political wheels are turning! Just as cell phone usage and accidents caused similar legislation, you'll see the same, or similar, arguments in these new bills coming to the senate and house floors. Keep in mind that not all of these come to fruition, and that still few U.S. states ban cell phone use while driving (although states and cell phone manufacturers do appear to be trying to educate drivers about making phone calls while on the road). For instance, Georgia failed to pass some related bills in 2004.

 My research shows that most distracted driving legislation proponents appear to be Democratic legislators, whereas the proponents of limiting cellular phone usage in moving vehicles tended to be Republican. Visit the National Council of State Legislators Web site to look up current bills and their status.

Useful Reports

There has been a lot of research on the effects of distracted driving, with many free reports available on the Internet and for sale. Table A-1 provides some excellent resources for your use.

Table A-1   Resources on Distracted Driving Research

Source	Web Site
National Conference of State Legislatures (NCSL)	www.ncsl.org Web site features an extensive legislation search for finding activate, inactive, and suggested laws for all 50 states. Many reports exist as well that cover distracted driving, including an excellent book called *Along for the Ride* (2002).

Source	Web Site
National Highway and Traffic Safety Administration	www.nhtsa.gov Many reports on distracted driving and highway safety procedures.
AAA Foundation for Traffic Safety	www.aaafoundation.org Many reports and information on driving safety. Excellent report on distracted driving titled "Distractions in Everyday Driving" (2003).

State Legislation

The following are laws from many states for reference. The bill number and year each law was enacted are listed in parentheses if available. As you look through these, you will see that many states are still enacting laws only related to motor vehicle cell phone usage and not video device usage. You may also notice that these laws could be retracted some day because many of them have clauses requiring statistical data be collected, making some of these laws potentially temporary (as the political tides change, of course). Some states are even fighting their own inner jurisdictions to make sure there is a single state-wide law for cellular phone, video, and so forth use in motor vehicles. Thanks go to the National Conference of State Legislatures for helping me with this section! Their Web site is very useful for finding many kinds of pending and current legislation.

The U.S. Department of Transportation has not passed any legislation covering video and computer displays in vehicles and their relationship to distracted driving.

For states not listed, no information was readily available. You should contact your state's Department of Motor Vehicles or state legislature to get the facts on laws regulating the use of the devices described in this book. Furthermore, before you drive through other states in your car, it's a good idea to understand the traffic laws prior to your trip.

Alabama

The current law applies only to television displays, which cannot be forward of the driver's seat. This bill was apparently enacted in 1949!

Alaska

There has been no statewide legislation; safety has been left up to common sense. They are expecting legislation sometime in 2005 due to related accidents.

Arkansas

- The law prohibits the use of a cellular telephone while operating a school bus. (HB 1042, 2003)
- There cannot be anything interfering with the driver's view of the road or his or her rearview mirror, but nothing is specifically stated about television or video players or displays.

California

- The law prohibits any person from driving a motor vehicle if a video monitor or a video screen or any other similar device that displays a video signal is operating and is located forward of the driver's seat or is visible to the driver. Laws provide exceptions for emergency equipment, mapping displays (i.e., GPS systems), vehicle information displays, or displays enhancing the driver's view of the front, side, or rear of the vehicle for the purposes of maneuvering the vehicle. (AB 301, 2003)
- California Highway Patrol is required by law to study driver distraction. (AB 770, 2001)

Colorado

There are no laws regarding distracted driving, although a bill attempting to ban cell phone use while driving was introduced and defeated.

Connecticut

No video displays are allowed unless they are being used for instrumentation or for a view assisting backing up the vehicle when used in reverse gear. This law also was apparently enacted in 1949.

Delaware

- A task force was established by law to study and make findings and recommendations regarding driver distractions, including mobile telephone use. (HCR 30, 2002)
- There is nothing specific in law about distracted driving, but it could be prosecuted under *Wreckless Driving and Careless Driving* in Title 21 of criminal code.

District of Columbia (D.C.)

- The law prohibits the use of hand-held phones while driving, although it provides exceptions for emergency situations. Violators may be punished with fines of $100. Police are legally required to collect information on crash reports about cell phone use, and the Department of Motor Vehicles is legally required to publish crash statistics regarding the relationship between cell phones and motor vehicle crashes. (B15-0035, 2004)

- *Distracted Driving Safety Act* prohibits the use of cell phones and handheld digital devices, such as PDAs and mobile game players, without hands-free accessories while operating a motor vehicle. (2004)

Florida

- The law requires distracted driver annual accident reports. Local jurisdictions are pre-empted from enacting restrictive ordinances. (SB 358, 2002)
- There cannot be "television or television-type receiving equipment" in view of the driver. This law "does not prohibit the use of an electronic display in conjunction with a vehicle navigation system" (i.e., GPS)

Idaho

There are no laws pertaining to video devices, television, or similar devices in vehicles.

Illinois

- The law prohibits school bus drivers from using a cell phone while operating the school bus; however, there are exceptions for emergency situations. (SB 1795, Public Act 92-730, 2002)
- The use of headsets while driving is prohibited except for single-sided headsets used for cellular phones. (HB 10, 2001)

Indiana

There is distracted driving legislation, but nothing pertaining specifically to the devices in this book.

Kentucky

- The law prohibits local governments from restricting mobile telephone use while driving. (HB 154, 2003)
- Local jurisdictions cannot regulate against people who use cell phones while driving. (HB 1207)
- The law prohibits driving a motor vehicle with a television capable of receiving any pre-recorded visual presentation unless the TV is behind the driver's seat or not visible to the driver while he or she is operating the vehicle. However, the law provides for certain exceptions. (SB 70)

Louisiana

A task force has been created through legislation to study and make recommendations concerning driver distractions. (HCR 35)

Maine

The law requires those under age 21 to obtain an instruction permit and complete training prior to obtaining a drivers license. A person with an instruction permit is prohibited from using a mobile telephone while driving. (SP 477/LD1439, 2003)

Mississippi

The law prohibits local jurisdictions from restricting people from using cell phones while driving. (HB 1551, 2002)

Nevada

Local jurisdictions are prohibited from regulating against people who use cell phones while driving. (SB 10, 2003)

New Jersey

- The law prohibits the use of a cell phone while operating a motor vehicle but allows hands-free devices. The law makes such use a secondary offense. The Department of Motor Vehicles is legally required to collect data on crash report forms. (SB 338, 2004)

- The law prohibits holders of driver examination permits (a.k.a., learner's permits) from using any interactive wireless device while operating a motor vehicle. However, it creates exceptions for emergency situations. (AB 3241, 2002)

- School bus drivers are prohibited from using a cell phone while driving. (AB 445)

- Legislation established the Driver Distraction and Highway Safety Task Force to study driver distractions and make recommendations. (SJR 21, 2002)

- The law also requires the Task Force on Driver Distraction and Highway Safety to study and make recommendations on driver distractions, including communication technology such as wireless telephones, pagers, faxes, locator devices, and AM/FM radios, and non-technical distractions. (SJR 21, 2001)

- The law requires the Commissioner of Transportation to annually compile information on cellular phone in vehicles during an accident and whether the operator was using the phone. It also requires accident report forms to contain that information. (SB 1867, 2001)

New York

The law requires that no person operate a motor vehicle while using a handheld mobile phone but provides emergency exceptions. (SB 5400, 2001)

Oklahoma

The law provides for state preemption of legislation relating to inattentive driving and cellular telephone usage in automobiles. It also provides that certain orders, ordinances, or regulations be null and void or not be more stringent than those state. (HB 1081, 2001)

Oregon

Local governments are prohibited from passing or enforcing any provision regulating the use of cellular telephones in motor vehicles. (HB 2987, 2001)

Rhode Island

School bus drivers are prohibited from using a cell phone while operating a school bus. However, the law provides emergency exceptions. (HB 6924 and SB 2164, Public Laws 146 and 251, 2002)

Tennessee

- Legislation prohibits the use of a cell phone while operating a school bus. (HB 564, 2003)

- When a driver is using a mobile phone when driving, the driver must have both hands on the steering wheel at all times. No criminal sanction is imposed for violations, but if a driver is in violation and is involved in a crash, there is created a rebuttable presumption of negligence. Substituted by HB 564, in the first point. (SB 208, 2003)

- The law permits computer or other electronic displays in utility motor vehicles to be used by a utility employee only while the vehicle is stopped, standing, or parked. (SB 3, 2001)

Virginia

Legislation requests the Department of Motor Vehicles to study the dangers imposed by distracted drivers and to specifically examine the use of telecommunications devices by motor vehicle operators. (SJ 336, 2001)

Washington, D.C.

See District of Columbia (D.C.)

Project Gallery

In this appendix you will find images and details on other Car PC projects I have seen and researched, built by other geeks like yourself. From custom mounts and dashboards to Linux-based systems and custom software, the projects listed here are sure to give you some ideas on how to take what you learn from this book to the next level.

The Dakota Project

Built by Brian Shoemake, www.dakotaproject.com.

The Dakota Project was initially created to provide a database for storing and accessing thousands of MP3 files for playback while on the road. That objective was accomplished, and Brian added even more features than originally planned. It is also used to play CDs, DVDs, MP3s, and movies stored on the hard drive and even to run a navigation system. In the future Brian plans to integrate his security system into the Car PC using small digital video cameras and the "Wake on LAN" feature with motion detectors and intrusion detectors tied to a paging system. Brian's had many requests for some examples of our latest Car PC project so what follows are some images and tips to help give you some insight into what he did and how he did it.

The Dakota Project was installed in, go figure, a Dodge Dakota. The system uses Brian's own PW120 and PW120A DC-DC converter products and his "Car Power Package."

Brian's project makes use of the compact, low-power VIA EPIA M10000 Nehemiah motherboard and VIA C3 1 GHz processor and the complete Audioforge Car Power Package with his PW120A DC-DC converter.

The main design consideration was a clean professional-looking installation. Brian wanted the inside of the Dakota to appear clean and as close to stock as possible, while staying within budget.

Each image will show you another step in the design and construction process. Although it doesn't go deeply in-depth, the photos and some of the descriptions should give you a good idea of what was accomplished in this project. If you like what you see and would like to construct your own Car PC like Brian's, his Web site at www.dakotaproject.com will help. Brian can also be e-mailed at audioforge@hotmail.com.

What's Inside

Here's what's inside the Dakota Car PC, including estimated costs for purchasing the components yourself:

- VIA EPIA M10000 Mini-ITX motherboard (~$160)
- 1 GHz Via C3 Nehemiah processor (~$40 purchased separately, often comes with the M10000 motherboard)
- Maxtor 7200 RPM 3.5-inch 40 GB hard drive (~$50)
- Mushkin 512MB PC2700 DDR SDRAM (~$115)
- Kenwood LZ701W 7-inch-wide TFT color LCD flat-panel monitor (~$399)
- Slimline CD/DVD ROM converted from PCMCIA to USB power (~$99)
- IOGear Bluetooth Wireless USB LAN (~$45)
- Audioforge Car Power Package with Audioforge PW120A 120-watt DC-DC converter (~$80)
- Gyration wireless RF mouse and keyboard suite (~$129)
- LEDs, cables, connectors, plugs, and so on (varies, likely up to $100)
- Windows XP Professional (~$179–$299)
- Windows Media Player 9 (free, latest as of this book's publication is Windows Media 10, which is also free and backwards compatible with Windows Media 9)
- Power DVD (DVD playback software, ~$50)
- X-10 remote (~$40)

The Custom Glovebox

In order to preserve the original glovebox in the Dakota, Brian decided to find a second stunt-double glovebox that he could cut into without feelings of guilt. He found a perfect match at a wrecking yard in Portland, Oregon, and paid $35 for it. This way he was able to preserve the original glovebox with all the factory numbers and labels inside. Brian says that, when he decides to trade in the Dakota someday, he'll be able to swap the original glovebox back into place.

Figure B-1 shows evidence of an impending paint scheme along with a cutout at the bottom where the hard drive will eventually reside.

FIGURE **B-1: The initial cutting into the glovebox for hard drive placement.**

After a couple hours of taping, the paint was done. In Figure B-2 you can begin to see where the PC will live. The chassis is sitting in place but is not bolted in yet.

Figure B-3 shows the hard drive in place with shock-absorbing foam under it. You can also see the Plexiglas platform where the VIA EPIA M mainboard will be mounted. The hole in the back of the glovebox is for routing cables and wiring out of the box. There is about a 1/8th-inch clearance between the hard drive and the Plexiglas platform. This should be plenty since the hard drive will be anchored securely with nylon straps.

Note the holes drilled at the corners of the Plexiglas that match-up with the mount holes in the motherboard. Corresponding holes are also drilled in the aluminum chassis, as well as in the glovebox.

Nylon spacers were then used between the mainboard and the platform to prevent the mainboard from actually contacting the bare Plexiglas. Rubber grommets were placed under the Plexiglas to act as spacers and additional cushioning between the mainboard and the glovebox. This helps with vibration protection in a high-vibration environment such as that experienced in a car.

FIGURE B-2: After taping and painting.

Even though the ideal hard drive for a mobile environment is a laptop-type drive because of its vibration and G-shock handling characteristics, Brian's project is running a full-size hard drive in the Dakota, and it hasn't missed a beat. Brian has spoken with many others who are doing the same with no ill effects as of yet, although it's still safest to use a laptop drive.

Figure B-4 shows the glovebox with the EPIA M mainboard installed. You can clearly see the PW120A compact 120-watt DC-DC power supply neatly snapped into the ATX connector of the motherboard. There is no other power source needed in this installation.

There are four stainless-steel bolts installed through each of the four corner mounting holes that run all the way through the mainboard, nylon spacers, Plexiglas platform, rubber grommets, and finally through the glovebox itself, secured with flat washers and nylon-lined lock nuts. That way the entire structure is snugged up together as one solid unit, with the rubber grommets allowing for vibration protection.

Hard Drive

Shock-absorbing Foam

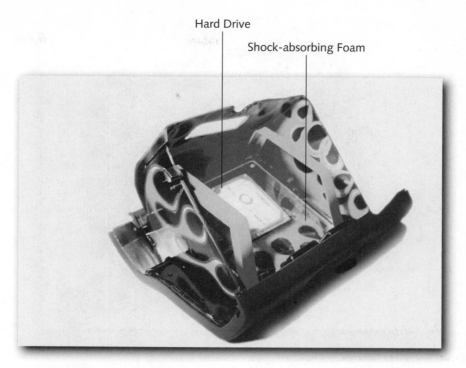

FIGURE B-3: The glovebox and the hard drive with shock absorbing foam underneath it.

One mounting hole in the motherboard is offset from the other mounting holes. Brian says he was unable to route that bolt through the actual frame, so he used spacers and a rubber grommet and bolted through the Plexiglas and glovebox.

Next there will be another Plexiglas platform installed on top of the chassis to hold the slimline CD/DVD ROM.

The angle of the top rail of the frame had to be just perfect to allow clearance for the DVD tray to open without obstruction when the glovebox is in the opened position.

Figure B-4 also shows where Brian installed the additional USB and firewire ports. They are mounted using Plexiglas above the other connectors off to the right side of the frame.

FIGURE B-4: The motherboard installed in the modified glovebox.

Figure B-5 shows the PC fully assembled with the DVD removed. A USB Bluetooth wireless LAN module is off to the right.

Figure B-5 also shows the Plexiglas mount with heavy-duty Velcro on it for mounting the DVD-ROM drive, which is also mounted on Plexiglas for added stability.

FIGURE B-5: Top view of the mounted PC.

Figure B-6 shows the PW120A and the ITPS low-dropout (LDO) power sequencer (inside the white box.) that make up the Audioforge Car Power Package Brian used to power his Car PC (he also sells them on his Web site at www.audioforge.com). No fans or secondary power supplies were needed.

PW120A Power Supply

ITPS Power Sequencer

FIGURE B-6: The PW120A and ITPS LDO power sequencer.

Figure B-7 shows the final Car PC completely installed in Brian's Dodge Dakota glovebox. You can also see the CD/DVD drive mounted securely on the top rail of the aluminum chassis. Figure B-8 shows the glovebox "wide open" for easy Car PC maintenance.

FIGURE B-7: The Car PC fully installed into the glovebox.

FIGURE B-8: The "wide open" position for easy maintenance.

To check the status of his Car PC, Brian added LEDs to the glovebox—one for hard drive activity and one for power, as shown in Figure B-9.

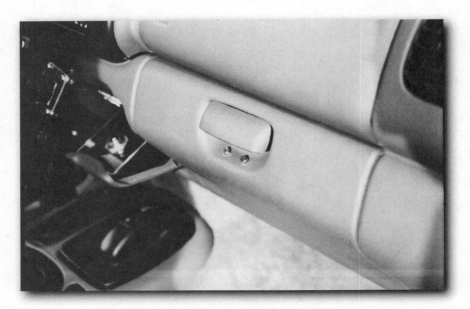

FIGURE B-9: Power status and activity LEDs built into the glovebox.

More Information

More information on the Dakota Project and the Audioforge products used in Brian's project can be found at www.dakotaproject.com. Brian's e-mail address is audioforge@hotmail.com.

The Dashwerks Linux-Based Car PC

Built by Christopher Bergeron, www.dashpc.com.

Using a custom Linux distribution and custom software, Christopher built a fully Linux-based technical wizard's dream car. Keep reading to learn what he used and for photos of his accomplishment.

What's Inside

Here's what's inside the Dashwerks Car PC, including estimated costs for purchasing the components yourself:

- Via EPIA-M9000 motherboard (now replaced by the M10000, ~$160)
- Via C3 Processor (~$40)
- 256 Megs PC133 RAM (~$60)
- 512 MB Memorex CF card (used as boot device, ~$99)
- 40 GB IBM 2.5-inch hard drive (used for general storage, ~$140)
- 6.4-inch TFT touch-screen LCD (~$450)
- Dashwerks startup/shutdown controller (DSSC, ~$49)
- 5-inch Clarion VMA5091 LCD (behind driver's headrest, ~$350)
- Belkin Bluetooth Dongle (~$35)
- Holux USB GPS receiver (~$85)
- Linksys WUSB11 wireless Ethernet card (and Linksys BEFW11S4 Access Point, ~$50)
- Maxim temperature sensor(s) and adapter (~$10)
- Hauppauge WinTV (model 401 w/radio) card (~$70)
- Boston Acoustics Rally RC620 Component 6.5 speakers (2 pairs: front and rear, ~$200 each)
- Alpine MRV-F407 four-channel amplifier (~$360)
- IRman (infrared remote control, ~$55)
- OBDII serial interface (~$100)
- SurfBoard wireless keyboard/Intellipoint™ mouse (~$300)
- CrystalFontz text LCD (~$40)
- Eight-port relay interface board (for interfacing the DashPC to the vehicle door locks, windows, sunroof, and trunk controls, ~$149)
- Creative Labs Web cam (using the ov511 Linux driver, ~$50–$99)

The Software

Following is all the software Dashwerks used to get their Car PC working properly under Linux and to enable support for speech recognition, car systems monitoring, and so forth:

- Linux from Scratch v5.0—Custom-made Linux operating system (`www.linux fromscratch.org`)

- Dashboard Linux/DashPC—The modular interface (`http://sourceforge.net/projects/dashpc`)

- Kismet—The war driving and Wi-Fi network discovery software (`www.kismet wireless.net`)

- Festival—The text-to-speech software (`www.cstr.ed.ac.uk/projects/festival/download.html`)

- FreeDiag—The ODB-II interface application (`http://freediag.sourceforge.net`)

- LIRC—Linux Infrared Remote Control—The infrared control software (`www.lirc.org`)

- LCDproc—A great modular interface for displaying text from various applications to a serial text display (`http://lcdproc.omnipotent.net`)

Visor-Mounted Diagnostics Display

Using the Parallax BASIC Stamp 2 (`www.parallax.com`) programmable microcontroller (shown in Figure B-10) and a programmable LCD display, Christopher was able to provide OBD-II diagnostic information in the visor of his car, as shown in Figures B-11.

FIGURE B-10: The BASIC Stamp 2 programmable microcontroller.

FIGURE B-11: The real-time diagnostics screen built into the visor.

The Custom Dashboard

Figure B-12 shows the custom dashboard Christopher built to house the display in his Volkswagon, as well as the custom keyboard mount.

FIGURE B-12: Custom dashboard used to house the display.

The Custom DashPC Software

Christopher wrote his own software interface and has started his own company to sell the software. Figures B-13 and B-14 show screenshots of the custom software.

More Information

More information on Christopher's DashPC project can be found on www.dashpc.com. Christopher can be reached at CBergeron@Dashwerks.com.

FIGURE B-13: Screenshot of the Dashwerks DashPC software.

FIGURE B-14: Another screenshot of the Dashwerks DashPC software.

Additional Resources

In this appendix you will find many Web sites to help you in your quest to find Car PC discussion forums, hardware, software, service providers, vehicle modification and enthusiast groups, satellite television and wireless Internet service providers, as well as related books.

Car PC Enthusiast Sites

The following sites are places where other car hackers exchange ideas and tips. URLs are usually not case-sensitive, but sometimes you may run into trouble, so always double-check what you entered if a site won't come up. I will try to keep this list up-to-date on the *Geek My Ride* Web site—sometimes site addresses will change and there's little I can do about that, but I'll do my best!

Dashboard Monkey, www.dashboardmonkey.com. Car PC news site and forums.

Geek My Ride **Web Site,** www.carhacks.net. The official Web site for the *Geek My Ride* book.

HP Tuners, www.hptuners.com/forum/YaBB.pl. A high-performance car-tuning forum.

Mini-ITX Web Site, www.mini-itx.com. A popular site for Car PC discussions. Includes news, forums, project ideas, hardware reviews, FAQs, and an online store.

MP3Car, www.mp3car.com. A popular site for Car PC discussions. Includes forums and an online store.

OBD Codes, www.odb-codes.com. A great site for finding definitions for OBD codes reported by your car's diagnostics system. Also, many how-to articles and links, as well as discussion forums.

OpenDiag Yahoo Group, http://groups.yahoo.com/group/opendiag. One of the first online groups for discussing self-diagnostics using personal computers and cars.

PricePC Car PC Projects, www.pricepc.com/html/carpc.php. A number of different Car PC projects to get ideas from, including photos and how-to info.

This Strife Car Computer, www.thisstrife.com/carproject. Lots of information and Car PC–centric software downloads.

Via Arena, www.viaarena.com. Via manufactures the C3 x86-compatible media processor used in many Car PC solutions because of its low power consumption and built-in media processor capabilities.

Via Mini-ITX Car PC Projects Site, www.viatech.com/en/initiatives/spearhead/mini-itx/car-pc.jsp. Via's gallery of Car PC projects with lots of neat ideas.

Via Telematics, www.viaembedded.com/designwin/productDetail.jsp?categorys=14. Via's Telematics resource Web site.

Enthusiast Clubs and Government Agencies

AAA Foundation for Traffic Safety, www.aaafoundation.org. Many reports and other information regarding driving safety.

Car Stuff, www.car-stuff.com/carlinks/enthus.htm. A good Web site for finding enthusiast groups for many different makes and models of cars.

Intelligent Transportation Society of America, www.itsa.org. Industry group for safe mobile technology solutions.

National Conference of State Legislatures (NCSL), www.ncsl.org. Features an extensive legislation search that locates active, inactive, and suggested laws for all 50 states. Many reports exist covering driver distraction. NCSL also publishes the book *Along for the Ride* (2002), an in-depth study on driver distraction.

National Highway Traffic Safety Administration, www.nhtsa.gov. The official government site for traffic safety in the United States.

Society of Automotive Engineers (SAE), www.sae.org. Excellent resource for mobility engineering in many transportation industries.

Society for Information Display, www.sid.org. Find the latest on mobile display technology and safety information.

Sports Car Club of America, www.scca.com. The largest sports-car enthusiast group in the United States.

Car PC Hardware and Software Manufacturers and Resellers

This list contains various hardware, software, and service providers for implementing Car PCs, OBD-II diagnostics systems, video surveillance, and more in your car.

Car PCs (Parts and Complete Systems)

CarTFT, www.cartft.com

Icon TV, www.icon-tv.net

iTuner, www.ituner.com

Mini-Box, www.mini-box.com

PDC, www.pdcstyle.com

Xenarc, www.xenarc.com

Displays

Audiovox, www.audiovox.com

Digital Worldwide, www.digitalww.com

Lilliput, www.lilliputweb.net

Myron & Davis (Johnson Safety, Inc.), www.myronanddavis.com

SAVV, www.savv.com

StarVision, www.starvision.us

Xenarc, www.xenarc.com

iPod® Control Docks

Monster iCruze, www.ipodicruze.com

Precision Interface Electronics iPod Interface, www.pie.net

GPS

Destinator, www.destinator1.com

Magellan, www.magellangps.com

Microsoft Streets & Trips, www.microsoft.com/streets

Pharos, www.pharos.com

Mobile Satellite Equipment & Installation

Audiovox SkyBox, www.audiovox.com

KVH Satellite, www.kvh.com

RaySat, www.raysat.com

Winegard/DataTech, www.dtiwinegard.com

OBD-II Solutions (Car Diagnostics)

AutoEnginuity, www.autoenginuity.com

Digimoto, www.digimoto.com

Elm Electronics, www.elmelectronics.com

ScanTool.net, www.scantool.net

Power Solutions

AudioForge, www.audioforge.com

CarNetix, www.carnetix.com

Dashwerks DashPC, www.dashpc.com

iTuner, www.ituner.com

Mini-Box, www.mini-box.com

White Bream, www.whitebream.com

Processors and Motherboards

Advanced Micro Devices (AMD), www.amd.com

Intel, www.intel.com

Via Technology, www.viatech.com

Software

CarBox, www.stuffandting.com/carbox

CarTunes, www.cartunes.ws

CentraFuse, www.fluxmedia.net

CNS Maestro, www.cns.bg

Dashwerks DashPC, www.dashpc.com

Digimoto, www.digimoto.com

FrodoPlayer, www.frodoplayer.com

GeexBox, www.geexbox.org

MediaCar, www.media-car.fr.st

Media Engine, www.mediaengine.org

MediaPortal, www.sourceforge.net/projects/mediaportal

Microsoft, www.microsoft.com

Video Surveillance

X-10, www.x10.com

Wireless Audio and Headphones

Myron & Davis (Johnson Safety, Inc.), www.myronanddavis.com

StarVision, www.starvision.us

UnWired Technology, www.unwiredtechnology.com

Fix-It-Yourself Sites from Auto Manufacturers and Third Parties

The following Web sites are from auto manufacturers and third parties that provide information on how to fix their cars for the do-it-yourselfer. Many auto manufacturers are starting to provide technical information to auto-savvy consumers so they can get wiring schematics, OBD-II codes, and even downloadable software to help diagnose and fix automobile problems. More manufacturers are jumping on the boat all the time, so I will try to keep this list as up to date on the official *Geek My Ride* Web site.

Chapter 21, "Talking to Your Car's Computer," discusses how to interface a computer, such as your Car PC, to your car's internal computer using an interface called OBD-II.

Auto Manufacturers' Sites

Table C-1 provides a list of the official auto manufacturer Web sites for getting service and support for your vehicle. Just look up your make in the table to find the appropriate Web site.

Note   Many auto manufacturer Web sites require a subscription or charge a fee to access content. Although it is often free to browse, be prepared to pay for the information you need.

Table C-1   Auto Manufacturer's Web Sites

Manufacturer	Web Site
Acura	www.serviceexpress.honda.com
Audi	https://erwin.audi.com
BMW	www.bmwtechinfo.com
Chevrolet	www.acdelcotechconnect.com
Chrysler	www.techauthority.com
Daewoo	www.daewoous.com/SUindex.asp
Ford	www.motorcraftservice.com
General Motors (GM)	www.acdelcotechconnect.com
Honda	www.serviceexpress.honda.com
Hyundai	www.hmaservice.com
Infiniti	www.infinititechinfo.com
Jaguar	www.jaguartechinfo.com
Kia	www.hmaservice.com
Lexus	http://techinfo.lexus.com
Lincoln	www.motorcraftservice.com
Mazda	www.mazdatechinfo.com
Mercury	www.motorcraftservice.com
Mercedes Benz	www.startekinfo.com
Nissan	www.nissan-techinfo.com
Peugeot	http://public.infotec.peugeot.com
Porsche	http://techinfo.porsche.com
Subaru	http://techinfo.subaru.com
Toyota	http://techinfo.toyota.com
Volkswagen	https://erwin.vw.com
Volvo	www.volvotechinfo.com

Third-Party Sites

Autozone's AllData DIY, www.alldatadiy.com. Autozone's do-it-yourselfer resource Web site.

Bentley Publishers, www.bentleypublishers.com. Order many user and service manuals for almost any vehicle.

Equipment and Tool Institute (ETI), www.etools.org. Industry group covering the entire automotive service industry.

Helm Publications, www.helminc.com. Order many user and service manuals for almost any vehicle. Recommended by Hummer.

Satellite Television and Internet Providers

Warning

The Federal Communications Commission (FCC) has mandated that consumer mobile satellites can only receive, not transmit, while in motion. It is a federal crime to transmit data while mobile, so if you get satellite Internet access (this does not apply to cell phone and Wi-Fi Internet service providers), you are only allowed to *receive* data when mobile. This regulation comes from a snafu in the late 1990s when a mobile satellite transmitted to the wrong satellite and wiped out all of Walmart's data uplink for an entire day. If you are caught transmitting while mobile, it could lead not only to federal fines and jail time but also to litigation and prosecution by companies or entities your transmissions affect.

Audiovox SkyBox, www.audiovox.com

DataStorm/MotoSat, www.datastorm.com

DirecWay (also DirectPC, DirecTV), www.direcway.com

KVH, www.kvh.com

Mobile Cellular Internet Service Providers

Many cellular phone companies support wireless Internet access via communications cards they sell separately or directly via cell phones. See Chapter 14, "Adding Internet Access," for more information on adding Internet access to your Car PC (or a laptop or cell phone you bring on the road).

Cingular (includes AT&T Wireless), www.cingular.com

Sprint PCS, www.sprintpcs.com

T-Mobile, www.tmobile.com

Verizon, www.verizon.com

Nationwide Wi-Fi Internet Service Providers

The following are nationwide Wi-Fi wireless access service providers or service provider locators, supporting at least 802.11b. See Chapter 14 for more information on adding Internet access to your Car PC (or a laptop or cell phone you bring on the road).

AT&T Wireless™ Wi-Fi Service, www.attwireless.com/wifi

JiWire Wireless HotSpot Finder, www.jiwire.com

Sprint PCS™ Wi-Fi Access, www.sprint.com/wifi

T-Mobile HotSpot, www.tmobile.com/hotspot

Related Books

Car Hacks and Mods For Dummies, David Vespremi, Wiley Publishing, ISBN 0-7645-7142-7. How to get faster acceleration, shorter stopping, better handling, and more.

Wi-Fi Toys, Mike Outmesguine, Wiley Publishing, ISBN 0-7645-5894-3. Covers wireless and war driving technology and techniques.

Along for The Ride: Reducing Driver Distractions, Matt Sundeen, ISBN 1-5802-4207-3. Covers driver distraction, including technology related to it, legislation, prevention, safety of cell phones in cars, emergency response issues, and more.

Vehicle Interface Types

This appendix will help you determine the OBD-II interface in your car. For more information on actually interfacing with your car with OBD-II, refer to Chapter 21, "Talking to Your Car's Computer."

What Is OBD-II?

In the early 1990s, there was an industry-wide movement to standardize the method of reporting errors in a car's computer, getting away from proprietary systems that cost dealerships too much money and were too hard to maintain. An industry standard named OBD-II was formed, which stands for On-Board Diagnostics Version 2. All cars made since 1996 have this feature, and an entire market has sprung up to let auto enthusiasts read the codes from their car's diagnostics system and figure problems out for themselves. It also gave them proof that the modifications they made to their car were actually *doing* something (other than draining their pocketbooks, of course). With the advent of affordable wireless chipsets and transceivers, OBD Version 3 is in the works, with the ability to read the car's data wirelessly. There was an OBD Version 1 (amazingly, called OBD-I) that is available on some pre-1996 cars, although it was much more limited in capability.

Did You Know

Another benefit of OBD-II is that it constantly monitors engine performance and vehicle emissions and ultimately informs drivers when they need to take their car in for repair or emissions tuning. Unfortunately, with OBD-II working in conjunction with your engine control unit (ECU), your car will read the diagnostic information and retune itself appropriately, changing timing, air intake, and so forth to stay within proper thresholds. This has been a problem for auto enthusiasts and their modifications, because over time the system adapts to their performance modifications and tries to bring the car back to its idea of "normal." Hence, older ECUs that aren't OBD-II-compliant are in much demand, as are "mod chips" that prevent such automatic adjustments from occurring.

With OBD-II you can:

- Determine engine and car system issues (knocking, bad turbo, and more)

- Clear the Check Engine light

- Analyze your engine statistics in real-time. ELM v2.0 chips sample at about 10 times per second, whereas earlier versions only sampled at 1 to 3 times per second (rated as hertz in some ODB-II applications).

- Tune your performance when racing (commercial package Digimoto does this in real-time)

- See analog gauges and watch your vehicle speed (miles per hour and kilometers per hour) and RPMs

- Get great utilities for free

- Use favorites such as ScanTool.net (knows the definitions of many codes) and ScanMaster (very nice interface and allows you to record multiple car sessions)

- Determine fuel efficiency (for example, GameCube increased load by 3%, AC by 2% to 3%)

- Clear your engine's trouble codes (a boon for performance enthusiasts testing their modifications)

- And do much, much more!

Determining the OBD-II Interface in Your Car

There are three OBI-II interface types: ISO, VPW, and PWM. All three do the same thing and generally have the same cable connector (as shown in Figure D-1), but they have different interface boards. To determine which interface you need, match your car type to Table D-1. Interfaces, such as the one in Figure D-2, are readily available online from sources such as ScanTool.net or the official *Geek My Ride* Web site at www.carhacks.net (or at www.wiley.com/go/extremetech). Your OBD-II cable requirement may be one of two different types—type B or C—so check Figures D-3 and D-4 and make sure you order the appropriate cable.

Table D-1 shows a detailed list of vehicle types—sorted by manufacturer, model, and model year—and the OBD-II interface they take. If your vehicle is not listed, you should look online, ask a car enthusiast group, or check with your dealer. Oftentimes if you can find a vehicle from the same manufacturer and model year you have, it will likely use the same interface. Sometimes you will see a manufacturer move from, say, ISO to VPW. It is a good idea to select the interface from the model year closest to yours if yours isn't available and you can't find out from anywhere else. I will try to keep a running list on my *Geek My Ride* Web site at www.carhacks.net (or at www.wiley.com/go/extremetech). You should still double-check with the sources mentioned earlier, of course.

FIGURE D-1: The OBD-II interface in my car and the OBD-II interface cable going to my OBD-II computer interface box.

FIGURE D-2: The OBD-II computer interface box from ScanTool.net.

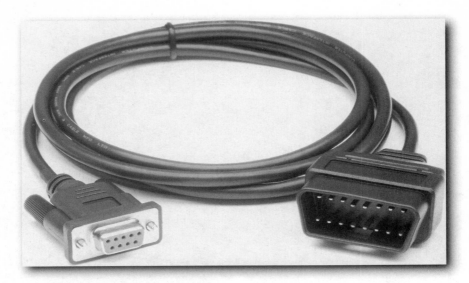

FIGURE D-3: Type B OBD-II connector.

FIGURE D-4: Type C OBD-II connector.

Finding the OBD-II connector in your car shouldn't be too difficult. On many cars, it's just below or to the left or right of the steering column.

Table D-1　OBD-II Interfaces by Vehicle Type

Make	Model	Year	Protocol
Acura	MDX	2003	ISO
Acura	RSX Type-S	2002	ISO
Audi	A4	1998	ISO
Audi	A4	2001	ISO
Audi	A6	1998	ISO
Audi	Cabriolet	1997	ISO
BMW	316i	2003	ISO
BMW	318ti	1998	ISO
BMW	320	2002	ISO
BMW	323 Ci	2000	ISO
BMW	528i	1997	ISO
BMW	528i	1998	ISO
BMW	528iA (E39)	2000	ISO
Buick	Century	2002	VPW
Buick	Riviera	1998	VPW
Buick	Skylark	1996	VPW
Cadillac	Deville	2000	VPW
Cadillac	Eldorado	1998	VPW
Chevrolet	Blazer	1995	VPW
Chevrolet	Camaro	1999	VPW
Chevrolet	Camaro SS	2000	VPW
Chevrolet	Camaro Z28	1997	ISO
Chevrolet	Camaro Z28	1997	VPW
Chevrolet	Camaro Z28	1998	VPW
Chevrolet	Caprice	1996	VPW

Continued

Table D-1 (continued)

Make	Model	Year	Protocol
Chevrolet	Cavalier	1996	VPW
Chevrolet	Cavalier	1998	VPW
Chevrolet	Cavalier Z24	1999	VPW
Chevrolet	Corvette	2000	VPW
Chevrolet	Impala	2000	VPW
Chevrolet	Impala	2002	VPW
Chevrolet	Lumina	1996	VPW
Chevrolet	Malibu	1998	VPW
Chevrolet	S10	2000	VPW
Chevrolet	Silverado	1997	VPW
Chevrolet	Silverado	1998	VPW
Chevrolet	Silverado	1999	VPW
Chevrolet	Silverado	2002	VPW
Chevrolet	Tahoe	1996	VPW
Chevrolet	Venture	1998	VPW
Chrysler	PT Cruiser	2003	VPW
Chrysler	Town & Country Van	1996	ISO
Chrysler	Voyager	1995	ISO
Citroen	Hdi	2000	ISO
Citroen	Xantia Turbo CT	1997	ISO
Citroen	Xsara	1999	ISO
Citroen	Xsara Picasso	2000	ISO
Citroen	Xsara SX 1.6i	2002	ISO
Citroen	Xsara VRT	2000	ISO
Dodge	3500	1996	ISO
Dodge	Caravan	1997	ISO
Dodge	Dakota	2001	ISO
Dodge	Neon	1995	ISO
Dodge	Neon	2002–2005	VPW

Make	Model	Year	Protocol
Dodge	RAM 1500	1999	ISO
Dodge	RAM 1500	2003	VPW
Dodge	RAM 2500	1999	ISO
Dodge	SRT-4 (a.k.a. Neon SRT-4)	2005	VPW
Dodge	Stratus	1996	ISO
Dodge	Stratus	1997	ISO
Dodge	Stratus R/T	2001	ISO
Fiat	Punto	2000	ISO
Fiat	Punto	2002	ISO
Fiat	Stilo	2002	ISO
Ford	Aerostar	1997	PWM
Ford	Contour	1999	PWM
Ford	E150	2000	PWM
Ford	E350	2000	PWM
Ford	Escort	1998	PWM
Ford	Expedition	1998	PWM
Ford	Explorer	1998	PWM
Ford	Explorer	2000	PWM
Ford	F150	1997	PWM
Ford	F150	2003	PWM
Ford	F150 (truck)	1999	PWM
Ford	F150 (van)	1999	PWM
Ford	F250	2000	PWM
Ford	F250 (Australian)	2002	PWM
Ford	Fiesta	1997	PWM
Ford	Focus	1999	PWM
Ford	Focus	2002	PWM
Ford	Focus (UK)	2001	PWM
Ford	Focus SVT	2002	PWM
Ford	Mustang	1998	PWM

Continued

Table D-1 (continued)

Make	Model	Year	Protocol
Ford	Mustang	2001	PWM
Ford	Probe	1997	ISO
Ford	Ranger	1995	PWM
Ford	Ranger	1996	PWM
Ford	Ranger	1997	PWM
Ford	Ranger	1998	PWM
Ford	Ranger	2002	PWM
Ford	Ranger 4x4 Pickup	2000	PWM
Ford	Taurus	1996	PWM
Ford	Taurus	2001	PWM
Ford	Thunderbird LX	1997	PWM
Ford	Windstar	1995	PWM
Ford	Windstar	1996	PWM
Ford	Windstar	1997	PWM
Ford	Windstar	1999	PWM
Geo	Metro	1996	ISO
GMC	Jimmy	1999	VPW
GMC	K2500	1997	VPW
GMC	Lumina	2001	VPW
GMC	Yukon	1998	VPW
Honda	Accord	1998	ISO
Honda	Accord	2000	ISO
Honda	Accord	2002	ISO
Honda	Civic	1996	ISO
Honda	Civic	1997	ISO
Honda	Civic	2000	ISO
Honda	Civic	2001	ISO
Honda	Civic	2002	ISO
Honda	Civic Del Sol	1997	ISO

Make	Model	Year	Protocol
Honda	Civic Type R	2003	ISO
Honda	Odyssey	2002	ISO
Honda	S2000	2000	ISO
Hyundai	Accent	1998	ISO
Hyundai	Accent	2000	ISO
Hyundai	Elantra	1996	ISO
Hyundai	Elantra	2001	ISO
Hyundai	Matrix	2002	ISO
Hyundai	Tiburon	1997	ISO
Infiniti	Q45	1999	ISO
Isuzu	Trooper	1998	VPW
Jaguar	XJ6 (X300)*	1997	ISO
Jeep	Grand Cherokee	1996	ISO
Jeep	Grand Cherokee	1997	ISO
Jeep	Grand Cherokee	1998	ISO
Jeep	Grand Cherokee	1999	ISO
Jeep	Liberty	2002	ISO
Jeep	Liberty	2003	VPW
Kia	Sephia	1999	ISO
Kia	Spectra	2001	ISO
Land Rover	Range Rover	1997	ISO
Mazda	B2300	2002	PWM
Mazda	B2500SE Pickup	2001	PWM
Mazda	B3000	2002	PWM
Mazda	MX-5 (Australian)	2003	ISO
Mazda	MX-5 (Miata)	2003	ISO
Mazda	Protege	2001	ISO
Mazda	Protege 5	2002	ISO
Mazda	Tribute	2002	PWM
Mercedes-Benz	C (W203)	2002	ISO

Continued

Table D-1 (continued)

Make	Model	Year	Protocol
Mercedes-Benz	C200 Kompressor	2003	ISO
Mercedes-Benz	C230	1998	ISO
Mercedes-Benz	C230	2000	ISO
Mercedes-Benz	Class A	2000	ISO
Mercury	Cougar	2000	PWM
Mercury	Grand Marquis	1998	PWM
Mercury	Sable	1996	PWM
Mini	Cooper	2002	ISO
Mitsubishi	Eclipse	1997	ISO
Mitsubishi	Eclipse Spyder	2002	ISO
Mitsubishi	Galant	2003	ISO
Mitsubishi	Lancer	1999	ISO
Mitsubishi	Lancer Evolution	2003	ISO
Mitsubishi	Mirage	1999	ISO
Mitsubishi	Montero	1995	ISO
Nissan	240SX	1996	ISO
Nissan	Altima	1997	ISO
Nissan	Altima	1999	ISO
Nissan	Altima GXE	1997	ISO
Nissan	Frontier	1999	ISO
Nissan	Maxima	1996	ISO
Nissan	Maxima GLE	1999	ISO
Nissan	Micra	2003	ISO
Nissan	Pathfinder	2002	ISO
Nissan	Primera	1999	ISO
Nissan	Sentra	2001	ISO
Nissan	Sentra SE	2000	ISO
Nissan	Sentra SE-R	2002	ISO
Nissan	Sentra SpecV	2003	ISO

Make	Model	Year	Protocol
Nissan	Terrano	1997	ISO
Oldsmobile	Cutlass Supreme	1996	VPW
Oldsmobile	Intrigue	1999	VPW
Oldsmobile	Silhouette	1998	VPW
Opel	Astra	2001	ISO
Opel	Frontera	1999	ISO
Opel	Omega	2001	ISO
Opel	Vectra	1998	ISO
Opel	Vectra	2001	ISO
Opel	Zafira (diesel)	2002	ISO
Peugeot	106	1998	ISO
Peugeot	106	2003	ISO
Peugeot	206	2003	ISO
Peugeot	206 GTi	2002	ISO
Peugeot	406	2001	ISO
Peugeot	406	2002	ISO
Peugeot	406 HDi	1999	ISO
Pontiac	Aztec	2001	VPW
Pontiac	Bonneville	1997	VPW
Pontiac	Grand Am	1996	VPW
Pontiac	Grand Am	2000	VPW
Pontiac	Grand Prix	2000	VPW
Pontiac	Grand Prix	2001	VPW
Pontiac	Sunfire	1997	VPW
Pontiac	Transport	1998	VPW
Renault	Clio	2001	ISO
Renault	Kangoo	2003	ISO
Renault	Megane	2000	ISO
SAAB	9-3	1999	ISO
SAAB	9000	1998	ISO

Continued

Table D-1 (continued)

Make	Model	Year	Protocol
SAAB	9000CDE	1996	ISO
Saturn	SL	1996	VPW
Saturn	SL1	1996	VPW
Saturn	SL1	1997	VPW
Seat	Cordoba 1.4 SX	2000	ISO
Skoda	Octavia	2002	ISO
Subaru	Impreza WRX	2002	ISO
Subaru	Impreza WRX	2003	ISO
Subaru	Outback Wagon	2002	ISO
Suzuki	Grand Vitara	2000	ISO
Suzuki	Sidekick	1997	ISO
Suzuki	Vitara	1997	ISO
Toyota	Camry	2002	ISO
Toyota	Celica GT-S	2000	ISO
Toyota	Corolla	1997	VPW
Toyota	Corolla	1998	ISO
Toyota	Corolla	2002	ISO
Toyota	Corolla (European)	2002	ISO
Toyota	RAV4	2001	ISO
Toyota	Sienna LE	1999	ISO
Toyota	Solara	1999	ISO
Toyota	Solara LE	2000	ISO
Toyota	Tacoma	1995	VPW
Toyota	Tacoma	2000	ISO
Toyota	Tacoma	2002	ISO
Toyota	Tundra	2000	ISO
Toyota	Tundra	2001	ISO
Toyota	Tundra	2003	ISO
Toyota	Yaris	2000	ISO

Make	Model	Year	Protocol
Volkswagen	Beetle	2000	ISO
Volkswagen	Bora	1999	ISO
Volkswagen	Eurovan Camper	1997	ISO
Volkswagen	Golf	1997	ISO
Volkswagen	Golf	1998	ISO
Volkswagen	Golf	2001	ISO
Volkswagen	Golf GL	1996	ISO
Volkswagen	Jetta	1997	ISO
Volkswagen	Jetta	2002	ISO
Volkswagen	Jetta Wagon	2003	ISO
Volkswagen	Passat	1996	ISO
Volkswagen	Passat	1997	ISO
Volkswagen	Passat	1999	ISO
Volkswagen	Passat	2003	ISO
Volkswagen	Sharan	1998	ISO
Volvo	850 T5	1997	ISO
Volvo	850 Turbo	1996	ISO
Volvo	S40	2000	ISO
Volvo	S60	2001	ISO
Volvo	S70	1999	ISO
Volvo	S80 T6	1999	ISO
Volvo	V70	1998	ISO
Volvo	V70 (Sweden)	2000	ISO
Volvo	V70 BiFuel	2002	ISO

Source: ScanTool.net, used with permission.

Index